T0183911

Lecture Notes in Computer Science 11618

Founding Editors

Gerhard Goos
Karlsruhe Institute of Technology, Karlsruhe, Germany
Juris Hartmanis
Cornell University, Ithaca, NY, USA

Editorial Board Members

Elisa Bertino
Purdue University, West Lafayette, IN, USA
Wen Gao
Peking University, Beijing, China
Bernhard Steffen
TU Dortmund University, Dortmund, Germany
Gerhard Woeginger
RWTH Aachen, Aachen, Germany
Moti Yung
Columbia University, New York, NY, USA

More information about this series at http://www.springer.com/series/7411

Marco Di Felice · Enrico Natalizio ·
Raffaele Bruno · Andreas Kassler (Eds.)

Wired/Wireless Internet Communications

17th IFIP WG 6.2 International Conference, WWIC 2019
Bologna, Italy, June 17–18, 2019
Proceedings

 Springer

Editors
Marco Di Felice
University of Bologna
Bologna, Italy

Raffaele Bruno
National Research Council of Italy
Pisa, Italy

Enrico Natalizio
University of Lorraine
Vandœuvre-lès-Nancy, France

Andreas Kassler
Karlstad University
Karlstad, Sweden

ISSN 0302-9743   ISSN 1611-3349 (electronic)
Lecture Notes in Computer Science
ISBN 978-3-030-30522-2   ISBN 978-3-030-30523-9 (eBook)
https://doi.org/10.1007/978-3-030-30523-9

LNCS Sublibrary: SL5 – Computer Communication Networks and Telecommunications

© IFIP International Federation for Information Processing 2019
This work is subject to copyright. All rights are reserved by the Publisher, whether the whole or part of the material is concerned, specifically the rights of translation, reprinting, reuse of illustrations, recitation, broadcasting, reproduction on microfilms or in any other physical way, and transmission or information storage and retrieval, electronic adaptation, computer software, or by similar or dissimilar methodology now known or hereafter developed.
The use of general descriptive names, registered names, trademarks, service marks, etc. in this publication does not imply, even in the absence of a specific statement, that such names are exempt from the relevant protective laws and regulations and therefore free for general use.
The publisher, the authors and the editors are safe to assume that the advice and information in this book are believed to be true and accurate at the date of publication. Neither the publisher nor the authors or the editors give a warranty, expressed or implied, with respect to the material contained herein or for any errors or omissions that may have been made. The publisher remains neutral with regard to jurisdictional claims in published maps and institutional affiliations.

This Springer imprint is published by the registered company Springer Nature Switzerland AG
The registered company address is: Gewerbestrasse 11, 6330 Cham, Switzerland

Preface

We welcome you to the proceedings of the 17th International Conference on Wired/Wireless Internet Communications (IFIP WWIC). The conference constitutes a forum for the presentation and discussion of the latest results in the field of wired/wireless networks and aims at providing research directions and fostering collaborations among the participants. In this context, the Program Committee accepts a limited number of papers that meet the criteria of originality, presentation quality, and topic relevance. IFIP WWIC is a single-track conference that has reached, over the past 17 years, a high-quality level, which is reflected by the paper acceptance rate as well as the level of attendance.

The 17th IFIP WWIC technical program addressed various aspects of next-generation data networks, such as the design and evaluation of protocols, the dynamics of the integration, the performance trade-offs, the need for new performance metrics, and the cross-layer interactions. A highly selective review process allowed us to include 20 accepted papers, and to realize a high-quality technical program. The 30+ members of the Technical Program Committee rigorously checked the scientific quality and technical soundness of all the papers, as well as their degree of innovation and the adequacy of the presentation, and produced at least three single-blind reviews for each submission.

The current edition of the conference was organized by the University of Bologna, at the magnificent Complex of San Giovanni in Monte; we thank the institution for the great support. Finally, we would like to express our gratitude to all our colleagues for submitting papers to the WWIC scientific sessions, as well as to the members of the WWIC Technical Program Committee and the reviewers, for their excellent work and dedication.

July 2019

Marco Di Felice
Enrico Natalizio
Raffaele Bruno
Andreas Kassler

Organization

General Chairs

Marco Di Felice   University of Bologna, Italy
Enrico Natalizio   University of Lorraine, France

Program Chairs

Raffaele Bruno   IIT-CNR, Italy
Andreas Kassler   Karlstad University, Sweden

Publication Chair

Angelo Trotta   University of Bologna, Italy

Web and Publicity Chairs

Deval Bhamare   Karlstad University, Sweden
Simone Bolettieri   IIT-CNR, Italy

Steering Committee

Torsten Braun   University of Bern, Switzerland
Georg Carle   Technical University of Munich, Germany
Geert Heijenk   University of Twente, The Netherlands
Peter Langendorfer   IHP Microelectronics, Germany
Ibrahim Matta   Boston University, USA
Vassilis Tsaoussidis   Democritus University of Thrace, Greece

Technical Program Committee

Stefano Basagni   Northeastern University, USA
Boris Bellalta   Universitat Pompeu Fabra, Spain
Paolo Bellavista   University of Bologna, Italy
Fernando Boavida   University of Coimbra, Portugal
Torsten Braun   University of Bern, Switzerland
Marcos Caetano   University of Brasilia, Brazil
Georg Carle   Technische Universität München, Germany
Fabio Cavaliere   Ericsson, Italy
Gianni Cerro   University of Cassino and Southern Lazio, Italy
Marilia Curado   University of Coimbra, Portugal
Fabio D'Andreagiovanni   CNRS, Sorbonne University, France

Robson De Grande	Brock University, Canada
Svetlana Girs	Mälardalen University, Sweden
Fabrizio Granelli	University of Trento, Italy
Sonia Heemstra de Groot	Eindhoven Technical University, The Netherlands
Geert Heijenk	University of Twente, The Netherlands
Salil Kanhere	UNSW, Australia
Ibrahim Korpeoglu	Bilkent University, Turkey
Bjorn Landfeldt	Lund University, Sweden
Peter Langendoerfer	IHP Microelectronics, Germany
Xavier Masip-Bruin	UPC, Spain
Agapi Mesodiakaki	Aristotle University of Thessaloniki, Greece
Edmundo Monteiro	University of Coimbra, Portugal
Liam Murphy	University College Dublin, Ireland
Panagiotis Papadimitriou	University of Macedonia, Greece
Paul Patras	University of Edinburgh, UK
Danda Rawat	Howard University, USA
Miguel Sepulcre	Universidad Miguel Hernandez de Elche, Spain
Burkhard Stiller	University of Zürich, Switzerland
Violet Syrotiuk	Arizona State University, USA
Fabrice Théoleyre	CNRS, France
Vassilis Tsaoussidis	Democritus University of Thrace, Greece
Carlo Vallati	University of Pisa, Italy

Contents

The Internet of Things and WLANs

Deploying W3C Web of Things-Based Interoperable Mash-up Applications for Industry 4.0: A Testbed

Luca Sciullo[✉], Angelo Trotta, Lorenzo Gigli, and Marco Di Felice

Department of Computer Science and Engineering, University of Bologna,
Bologna, Italy
{luca.sciullo,angelo.trotta5,marco.difelice3}@unibo.it,
lorenzo.gigli@studio.unibo.it

Abstract. In Industry 4.0 scenarios, novel applications are enabled by the capability to gather large amount of data from pervasive sensors and to process them in order to devise the "digital twin" of a physical equipment. The heterogeneity of hardware sensors, communication protocols and data formats constitutes one of the main challenge toward the large-scale adoption of the Internet of Things (IoT) paradigm on industrial environments. To this purpose, the W3C Web of Things (WoT) group is working on the definition of some reference standards intended to describe in a uniform way the software interfaces of IoT devices and services, and hence to achieve the full interoperability among different IoT components regardless of their implementation. At the same time, due also to the recent appearance of the WoT W3C draft, few testbed and real-world deployments of the W3C WoT architecture has been proposed so far in the literature. In this paper, we attempt to fill such gap by describing the realization of a WoT monitoring application of a generic indoor production site: the system is able to orchestrate the sensing operations from three heterogeneous Wireless Sensor Networks (WSNs). We describe how the components of the W3C WoT architecture have been instantiated in our scenario. Moreover, we demonstrate the possibility to decouple the mash-up policies from the network functionalities, and we evaluate the overhead introduced by the WoT approach.

1 Introduction

Recently, the Industry 4.0 has emerged as a new paradigm able to radically transform the organizations' production and business in a myriad of sectors beside the smart manufacturing one [1,2]. The core of the paradigm that justifies also its generality and viability on different markets is the concept of Cyber-physical Systems (CBSs), i.e. the strict integration between physical elements and computational data enabled by the recent advances on the Internet of Things (IoT) [1]. Hence, the ability to collect, aggregate and analyze sensor data is crucial for the growth of the Industry 4.0 model. At the same time, today's IoT is a chaotic environment characterized by heterogeneous hardware devices, network protocol stacks and data formats. The current fragmentation can significantly increase

© IFIP International Federation for Information Processing 2019
Published by Springer Nature Switzerland AG 2019
M. Di Felice et al. (Eds.): WWIC 2019, LNCS 11618, pp. 3–14, 2019.
https://doi.org/10.1007/978-3-030-30523-9_1

the deployment costs, since collected data can remain largely inaccessible in an integrated way unless investing significant manual effort [2]. At the same time, interoperability can represent an opportunity for next-generation IoT applications: the McKinsey report in [3] quantifies in 40% the additional market value that might be provided by achieving full interoperability among IoT ecosystems. Among the several approaches proposed so far in order to address IoT interoperability problems, the Web of Things (WoT) has gained considerable attention, thanks to the popularity and well-known unifying nature of the Web [4,5]. Differently from other stack-oriented solutions (e.g. 6LoWPAN), WoT-based approaches propose to achieve system interoperability at the application layer, abstracting from the sensing and communication technologies: in a first approximation, Things are represented as Web resources, and all the interactions toward and between Things are mapped over Representational State Transfer (REST) services [5]. At the same time, given the lack of a reference architecture, several different WoT frameworks have been proposed in the literature (e.g. [6–9]), introducing further fragmentation and the consequential need of devising ad-hoc solutions for the system integration. Breaking the deadlock, the World Wide Web Consortium (W3C) has recently proposed a reference architecture of the WoT [10] that formally describes the interfaces allowing IoT devices and services to communicate with each other, regardless of their underlying implementation. In the W3C WoT vision, everything can be considered a Thing and to this purpose, each Thing is associated to a Thing Descriptor (TD) providing general metadata as well as the interactions, data model, and security mechanisms of a Thing [10]. In addition, a TD can be serialized and semantically annotated via the JSON-LD language, hence representing a uniform model to enable Machine-to-Machine (M2M) communication toward a Thing and enabling several semantic features, like for instance the Thing Discovery (TD). The generality of the WoT architecture makes it suitable for all those scenarios characterized by the need of aggregating data from multiple, heterogeneous sources, like the Industry 4.0. However, due also to its recent appearance, few implementations and test-bed of the W3C WoT have been described so far in the literature [11,12].

In this paper, we attempt to fill such gap, by describing the design and implementation of a WoT testbed, consisting of a monitoring system of a generic production site that must retrieve and process sensor data from heterogeneous devices using different wireless access technologies (i.e. Wi-Fi, 802.15.4/Zigbee, BLE). The overall goal is to devise mash-up applications able to orchestrate the sensing operations over the target scenario regardless of the network protocols and hardware, hence decoupling the rationale of the monitoring process (e.g. minimal scenario coverage) from its implementation (i.e. the technology used to query the sensor). More specifically, we introduce three main contributions in this study:

– First, we describe how the scenario can be modeled within the WoT W3C framework. We associate one Thing to each sensing device, and one Thing to the sensor network, by defining the metadata of each. Moreover, we discuss how the components of the WoT W3C architecture have been made concrete in our application.

- Second, we describe the design and implementation of mash-up applications aimed to orchestrate the sensing operations on the target scenario. We considered four different sensing policies, aimed to balance the coverage of the scenario with the network performance (e.g. delay, packet delivery ratio and energy). All the policies are in charge of dynamically selecting the sensors to query at each instant in order to maximize the policy-specific metric: to this purpose, given the dinamicity of the environment, we employ the Reinforcement Learning (RL) framework [17] to optimally balance the exploration-exploitation tasks.
- Third, we report a subset of the experimental results from the WoT testbed. We investigate the performance of the sensing mash-up applications with respect to the policy goal (e.g. delay), and the convergence over time. Moreover, we show the benefit introduced by the WoT architecture in terms of adaptive design, i.e. the possibility to dynamically switch the sensing policies over time without re-configuring the communication infrastructure, and the overhead introduced by the WoT components.

The rest of the paper is structured as follows. Section 2 reviews the WoT W3C architecture, and its recent applications. Section 3 introduces the test-bed, and the modeling of the network components within the WoT W3C architecture. Section 4 introduces the mash-up policies. Section 5 presents a subset of the experimental results. Conclusions and future works follow in Sect. 6.

2 Related Works

Since 2007, when the concept of WoT appeared in the literature, several research studies have explored how to interconnect IoT devices through standard Web technologies. This has also lead to a proliferation of WoT frameworks and architectures, which are quite different in terms of WoT-based interaction patterns supported and functional goals addressed. For instance, the authors of [6] review more than twenty WoT frameworks on the basis of twelve elements which are taken as key components of the WoT. Although the REST paradigm is considered the reference solution to implement WoT-oriented services (e.g. [7]), alternatives to the HTTP protocol have been considered: for instance, CoAP-based architectures are proposed, among others, in [8] and [9]. A generic model supporting interoperability and mash-up operations from different hubs is proposed in [4]: here, the authors warn about the proliferation of WoT tools, and advocate for the need of standard solutions.

To this purpose, the W3C WoT group started its activities on 2015 with the goal of defining a reference WoT set of standards, enabling interoperability among different IoT systems. In this paper, we refer to the W3C WoT draft presented in [10]. In brief, the W3C WoT architecture is composed of four main blocks:

- *Thing*: this is an entity that can be semantically represented. Using the W3C words: "A Thing is the abstraction of a physical or virtual entity... This entity

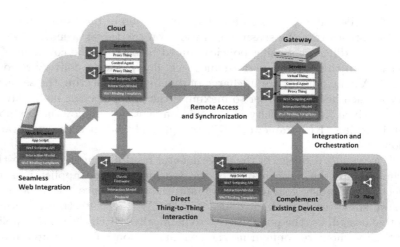

Fig. 1. The abstract architecture of W3C WoT (source: [10]). The image shows the internal blocks and the multiple interactions patterns among the Things.

can be a device, a logical component of a device, a local hardware component, or even a logical entity such as a location" [10].

- *WoT Thing Description (TD)*: this represents the metadata of the Thing, including its interactions, data models, communication protocols and security mechanisms. By default, the TD is serialized with the JSON-LD language and following the Properties, Actions, and Events paradigm.
- *WoT Binding Templates*: this is the metadata describing the communication strategies that the Thing is able to implement. For instance, a possible strategy could be the following: Machine-to-Machine (M2M) over the MQTT protocol, with TLS security mechanism enabled.
- *WoT Scripting API*: this is a WoT interface allowing scripts to perform main operations on a Thing, like adding properties, reading properties, or retrieving its TD.

All the blocks above are implemented within a software runtime named *Servient*, which can indifferently act as a Server or as a Client. In the first case, the Servient is said to host and *expose* Things, i.e. it takes the TD as input and creates a software object serving the requests like accessing the exposed properties, actions and events. In the second case, the Servient is said to *consume* Things, i.e. it creates a runtime resource model that allows accessing the properties, actions and events exposed by the server Thing on a remote device.

Figure 1 depicts the abstract W3C architecture for the WoT, including the blocks within each Thing and their possible interactions. In particular, the W3C working group identified a short list of interaction patterns that are general enough to cover most of the existing IoT deployments, regardless of the application domain. The simplest one is the Client-Thing interaction, i.e. a Web application that invokes actions on a remote Thing, after having consumed it.

Due to the recent appearance of the W3C WoT standard, few real-world applications and testbed have been proposed so far in the literature. A demo showing the possibility to query a W3C WoT sensor device from a mobile phone is sketched in [11]. In [12], an interesting application of the W3C WoT architecture to the automotive industry is described; more specifically, the authors illustrate how to describe the car signals data with a semantic ontology, and how to make them available to external applications through the W3C WoT interaction patterns. Security risks and vulnerabilities presented by WoT metadata are discussed in [13]. Versioning mechanisms for the TD metadata are proposed in [14]. Finally, in [15], we proposed the WoT Store, a W3C WoT-compliant framework that enables the semantic Thing discovery and the seamless distribution and execution of WoT applications. The WoT Store constitutes the natural execution environment for the mash-up applications considered in this study: we plan to explore such feature in a future work.

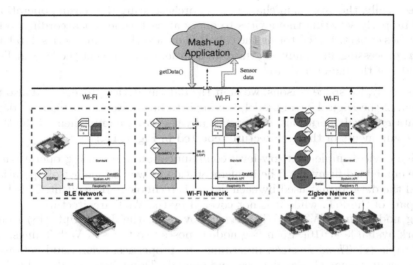

Fig. 2. The IoT/WoT monitoring system deployed in this study.

3   The W3C WoT Testbed: Architecture and Components

The goal of this study is to investigate the suitability - both in terms of ease of deployment and of performance- of the W3C WoT architecture for Industry 4.0 applications. To this purpose, we consider a generic IoT monitoring system of a production site, characterized by the presence of heterogeneous sensors using different communication technologies. The overall architecture of the testbed, depicted in Fig. 2, is structured on three tiers:

– **Edge layer**. This layer is composed of three Wireless Sensor Networks (WSNs), operating over the same environment: an IEEE 802.15.4 WSN network, a IEEE 802.11 Wi-Fi WSN network and a BLE device. The 802.15.4

network includes four devices (*Arduino Xbee* boards), with one Coordinator and three Leaf nodes equipped with sensing units (*ThinkerKit* temperature sensor). The Wi-Fi network includes three devices (two *NodeMCU* and one *Arduino WiFly* board), all provided with a direct link toward the Access Point (AP) and with a *DHT11* temperature/humidity sensor. Finally, the BLE WSN consists of one *ESP32* board, provided with a *DHT11* sensor.

- **Fog layer.** The 802.15.4 coordinator, the BLE and the Wi-Fi devices are connected to the corresponding Fog node, via USB cable links (for the BLE and the 802.15.4 Coordinator) or Wi-Fi links (for the IEEE 802.11 devices). Each fog node is constituted by a *Raspberry PI3B+* board and it is in charge of exposing the corresponding Web avatar (i.e. the Web Thing) for each managed device and WSN.
- **Processing layer.** This layer implements the logic of the monitoring system. It is constituted by a Linux server running the mash-up applications further defined in Sect. 4, and connected to the Fog nodes via Wi-Fi links. More specifically, the layer is in charge of: (*i*) orchestrating the sensing operations, by properly selecting the devices to query at each time slot according to the policies of Sect. 4; (*ii*) storing the collected data within a time-series database; (*iii*) processing and analyzing the data in order to implement the Digital Twin model of the monitored site.

In this study, for space reasons, we omit the data analytics process, and also the creation of the Digital Twin model, leaving it to future works. Instead, we detail the data retrieval operations, and specifically the way we implemented the WoT W3C components of the architecture reported in Fig. 1, i.e.:

- Edge devices implement low-level communication and sensing operations in the embedded firmware. The implementation as well as the list of operations and the data format used by each device is technology dependent. This layer is part of the IoT, while it is not covered by the WoT architecture.
- Fog nodes run a W3C WoT Servient, by using the JavaScript (JS) framework available at [16]. Each Fog node exposes two types of Web Things, i.e.: multiple (*i*) *Thing Devices*, describing the properties, events and actions of physically managed edge devices, and one (*ii*) *Thing Network*, describing the overall performance of the virtual WSN composed by the list of connected Thing Devices. Moreover, we consider three possible protocol bindings for each Thing, i.e. interaction modes with the Things, based on the HTTP (default choice), the CoAP or the MQTT protocols. The System APIs are implemented in Javascript, and further structured into two layers, i.e.: (*i*) a *Device Query* level, that is in charge of issuing request-response communication with the Edge device, based on the wireless technology and the protocol stack supported by this latter (e.g. UDP socket for the WiFi devices, Serial socket for the Zigbee Coordinator, BLE connected mode for the BLE device), (*ii*) an *Inter-Process Communication* (IPC) level, that makes the sensor data available to the upper Scripting APIs via IPC facilities (in our case, implemented in the ZeroMQ library[1]).

---

[1] ZeroMQ Project Website, http://zeromq.org.

Table 1. Example of Properties, Actions, and Events described in a Thing Description of a Device Thing.

Name	Type	Description
DeviceID	Property	Device identifier in the network
NetworkID	Property	Network identifier the device belongs to
Temperature	Property	Last temperature value
State	Property	Current state of the device
GetData	Action	Get the temperature data
Start	Action	Start sending data at each time-slot
Stop	Action	Stop sending data
NewData	Event	This event is fired when a new sensor data is produced
ChangeState	Event	This event is fired when the connection state changes

- Finally, the Processing node interacts with each Fog node/Servient in order to consume Things, e.g. by periodically *invoking* the `getData` *action* from the Things selected according to the actual mash-up policy.

Table 1 shows some of the properties, actions, and events described in the Thing Description (TD) for a Device Thing. The TD of a Network Thing includes only properties that are referred to the average network performance (i.e. the delay, the packet delivery ratio and the throughput) and actions that can be invoked from the entire network, like for instance the *getAllData()*. Similarly, the snippet below shows a code fragment of the mash-up application, specifically the way we query a sensor device in order to read its temperature value. We can notice that - through the WoT architecture- the mash-up application is agnostic on the wireless access technology in use, and retrieves data from heterogeneous sensors by means of a common API regardless of the WSN implementation. The rationale of the sensing applications is presented in the Listing 1.1.

Listing 1.1. Example code for discovering and invoking actions on Things.

```
let type = "http://wots.unibo.it/labWireless/testbed"
let THINGS = []
//get Thing Descriptions from the discovery service
for(var t in discovery.discoverByType(type)) {
    //Consume things
    let thing = await consumer.consumeThing(t);
    //Set http as protocol required
    thing.getClients().set('http', http_client);
    THINGS.push(thing)
}
for(var i = 0; i < lambda; i++) {
    //invoke the getData action for collecting data
    let thing = THINGS[i%THINGS.length];
    var res = await thing.actions['getData'].invoke();
}
```

4   The W3C WoT Testbed: The Mash-up Sensing Policies

We implemented multiple mash-up sensing policies, and we tested the capability of switching among them in a seamless way in Sect. 5. To this purpose, let D be the set of available devices, and $W(d_i)$, $\forall d_i \in D$, be the function describing the WSN type. In our testbed, $W : D \rightarrow \{WiFi, BLE, Zigbee\}$. We assume the time to be divided into discrete time-slot, i.e. $T = \{t_0, t_1, ...\}$, corresponding to sensing events when the mash-up application is issuing `getData` command toward a selected subset of the available devices. Let $t_{interval}$ be the temporal interval between two measurements, i.e. the time difference between t_{i+1} and t_i, assumed constant. Moreover, let $\kappa : D \times T \rightarrow \{0, 1\}$ the function indicating whether device d_i is active, i.e. it is used at time slot t_j (in this case, $\kappa(d_i, t_j) = 1$, otherwise $\kappa(d_i, t_j) = 0$). All sensing policies share a common rationale, i.e.: they keep the area covered higher than a predefined threshold, while maximizing a performance index I. In our case, the area coverage is expressed in terms of number of active devices (M) at each time-slot. More formally, all policies address the optimization problem formally defined below:

$$\text{Goal} : \text{Maximize } I$$
$$\text{Constraint} : \sum_{d_i \in D} \kappa(d_i, t_j) = M, \forall t_j \in T \tag{1}$$

The performance I can vary according to sensing policy in use. We implemented and tested four different metrics:

– Static *Energy-aware* policy (P_0). The mash-up application selects the M active devices at each time-slot according to a pure round-robin scheme, in order to discharge them with the same rate.
– Dynamic *Delay-aware* policy (P_1). The mash-up application takes into account the average delay required to issue a `getData` command and to receive the corresponding reply message. The M devices with the lowest Round Trip Time (RTT) are selected at each time slot.
– Dynamic *PDR-aware* policy (P_2). The mash-up application takes into account the communication reliability of each sensor expressed in terms of average Packet Delivery Ratio (PDR), i.e. the ratio of received replies over the total number of `getData` requests sent toward each d_i. Specifically, the M devices with the highest PDR values are selected at each time slot.
– Dynamic *Delay-PDR-aware* policy (P_3). The mash-up application takes into account both the delay and the PDR, as better explained in the following.

Excluding P_0, all the other policies compute the M sensors to query at each time-slot based on the current traffic loads and network conditions. For this reason, we employ a dynamic, learning-based scheme based on the Reinforcement Learning (RL) framework [2]. In brief, this latter refers to a class of machine learning algorithms where an agent learns over time the optimal sequence of actions

---

[2] For space shortage, we do not provide an in-depth illustration of the RL framework. Interested readers can refer to [17] for a detailed discussion on the topic.

needed to perform a task, by dynamically interacting with the environment and by receiving a numeric reward at each interaction. More formally, the RL framework can be represented as a Markov Discrete Process (MDP) $< S, A, R, TR >$ where: S is the set of States, A is the set of Actions, $R : \{S, A\} \rightarrow \mathbb{R}$ is the Reward function, expressing a numeric reward received by the agent when executing action $a_j \in A$ in state $s_i \in S$, and $TR : \{S, A\} \rightarrow S$ is the transition function, expressing the next state s_j after performing action a_j from state s_i (a deterministic environment is assumed). The goal of the RL agent is hence to determine the optimal policy function $\tau : S \rightarrow A$ that indicates the optimal action to execute at each state, so that the long-term reward is maximized. In our modeling, we omit the state function S, while the list of action A coincides with the list of devices D. The immediate reward $R(d_i)$ is computed when issuing a `getData` command on sensor d_i, according to the policy in use:

- P_1: this is the RTT for each `getData` command. Only successful requests (i.e. reply messages are received) are considered.
- P_2: this is a positive value (+1) if the `getData` is successful, 0 otherwise.
- P_3: similarly to P_1, however a penalty equal to $t_{timeout}$ is applied in case no reply is sent back after a timeout.

Each time a `getData` is issued on d_i, and the immediate reward $R(d_i)$ is computed, we also update the Q-value entry at time slot t for d_i as follows:

$$Q_t(d_i) = Q_{t-1}(d_i) + \alpha \cdot (R(d_i) - Q_{t-1}(d_i)) \tag{2}$$

where α is a learning rate, set equal to 0.7 in our experiments. Balancing the exploration and exploitation issue is a crucial issue in dynamic environments [17]. For this reason, we consider an ϵ-greedy exploration scheme, i.e.: each time a `getData` is executed, the policy selects with probability $1 - \epsilon$ the sensor with the k-th highest Q-value, and it performs a random selection over D otherwise (avoiding duplicates). We repeat the ϵ-greedy selection M times at each time slot, since all policies need to guarantee an M-coverage of the scenario (in other words, the k above varies between 0 and $M-1$). The ϵ parameter is progressively discounted at each time slot, i.e. $\epsilon_t = \epsilon_{t-1} \cdot \psi$, with $0 < \psi < 1$, in order to reduce the exploration over time. At the same time, the ϵ parameter cannot decrease below a minimal threshold (ϵ_{min}), i.e. a default exploration rate is kept anyway in order to detect any possible change in the scenario, and to adapt the system policy accordingly. We set $\epsilon = 0.8$, $\psi = 0.97$, $\epsilon_{min} = 0.1$ in our testbed.

5   The W3C WoT Testbed: Experimental Results

In this Section, we report a subset of experimental results collected through the WoT testbed described above. The experimental analysis is divided in three stages: (i) first, we characterize the overall performance of different WSNs and sensors; (ii) second, we evaluate the four different mash-up policies of Sect. 4; (ii) finally, we demonstrate the possibility of dynamic mash-up policy replacement

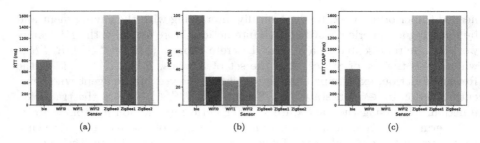

(a)   (b)   (c)

Fig. 3. The average per-device RTT and PDR is shown in Fig. 3(a) and (b), respectively. The per-device RTT for the CoAP protocol is shown in Fig. 3(c).

and quantify the overhead introduced by the W3C WoT architecture. Fig. 3(a), (b) and (c) refer to the first analysis. Specifically, Fig. 3(a) and (b) show respectively the average RTT and PDR for each device and WSN type, when the HTTP protocol is used to interact with each Web Thing. It is easy to notice that the Wi-Fi devices are producing the lowest RTT values. The PDR original results demonstrated that the Wi-Fi WSN is also the most reliable technology. However, in order to differentiate the mash-up policies, we introduced a probabilistic packet filter on the Wi-Fi Serviant, discarding the sensor data messages with a loss rate equal to 70% to emulate a congested access point. As a result, comparing Fig. 3(a) and (b), we can notice that the sets of $M=3$ nodes maximizing the RTT or the PDR depends on the selected performance index. Finally, Fig. 3(c) shows the per-device RTT when the CoAP protocol is used for data gathering. Only minimal differences can be noticed compared to the HTTP case (Fig. 3(a)).

In Figs. 4(a) and 5(a), we evaluate the performance of different mash-up policies. Figure 4(a) shows the RTT values of P_0, P_1, P_2, P_3 algorithms over time-slots; as expected, P_1 produces the lowest delay since it takes into account the per-packet RTT as immediate reward. Also, we can appreciate the learning phases of P_1: the RTT is high during the exploration phase and it is progressively reduced when increasing the amount of exploitation. After time-slot 1000, the RL algorithm has discovered the optimal set of sensors, however it keeps performing random actions for continuous, minimal exploration. This justifies the jagged shape of the plot. In Fig. 4(b) we depict the per-device ratio of utilization over time for the policy P_1. While during exploration all the devices are equally used, after time-slot 1000 the mash-up policy is mostly exploiting the three Wi-Fi devices since -in accordance with Fig. 3(a)- they are associated to the lowest RTT values. Figure 4(c) compares the policies in terms of PDR. Here, the optimal policy is P_2; form Fig. 5(a) we can notice that, after the exploration phase, the three Zigbee devices are maximally used, hence conversely to Fig. 4(b) but again in accordance with Fig. 3(b). We tested the dynamic policy replacement in Fig. 5(b); i.e. from time-slot 1 to 3000, policy P_1 is used (delay minimization), then P_2 from 3001 to 6000 (PDR maximization), finally we switch to P_3 (delay-PDR trade-off) from instant 6001. We remark that the policy replacement is

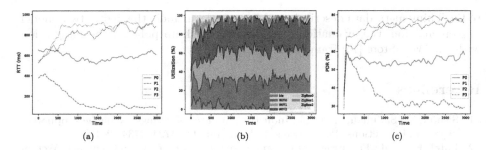

Fig. 4. The RTT an PDR values for the four mash-up policies are shown in Fig. 4(a) and (c). The device utilization ratio for the P_1 policy is shown in Fig. 4(b).

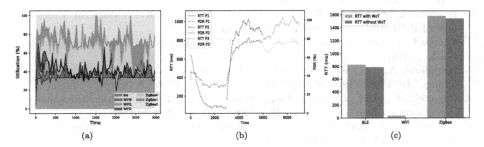

Fig. 5. The device utilization ratio for the P_2 policy is shown in Fig. 5(a). The RTT and PDR values when replacing the active policy at runtime in shown in Fig. 5(b). The RTT when enabling/disabling the WoT approach is shown in Fig. 5(c).

simply implemented as the shut-down of a JS process and the execution of a new one, thanks to the abstraction provided by the W3C WoT architecture; no hardware or software re-configuration of the WSNs is required. Finally, we evaluate in Fig. 5(c) the overhead introduced by the W3C WoT deployment, and specifically by the WoT servient: to this aim, we compute the RTT required to perform a sensor request directly at the System API level. We can notice that most of the overhead is due to the channel access and the processing at the firmware level, while the overhead introduced by the Servient and by the additional communication with the Web Thing is negligible.

6   Conclusions and Future Works

In this paper, we have described the deployment and evaluation of a W3C-based WoT system for generic site monitoring applications. In order to stress the interoperability issue, we have realized a testbed composed of three heterogeneous WSNs and mash-up applications orchestrating the sensing operations over the monitored area. We have discussed how the different WoT components have been instantiated on the target scenario, and we have demonstrated the capability of decoupling the sensing policy from the low-level networking operations, thanks to the Thing meta-data description. Future works include: the digital twin model implementation, the evaluation of additional mash-up policies, the integration with the WoT Store [15] framework.

References

1. Sisinni, E., Saifullah, A., et al.: Industrial Internet of Things: challenges, opportunities, and directions. IEEE Trans. Industr. Inf. **14**, 4724–4734 (2018)
2. Patel, P., et al.: From raw data to smart manufacturing: AI and semantic Web of Things for industry 4.0. IEEE Intell. Syst. **33**(4), 79–86 (2018)
3. McKInsey Global Institute: The Internet of Things: Mapping the value beyond the hype. Executive Summary (2015)
4. Blackstock, M., Lea, R.: Toward interoperability in a Web of Things. In: Proceedings of IEEE UbiComp, Zurich, Switzerland (2013)
5. Guinard, D., Trifa, V.: Building the Web of Things. Manning Publications, Shelter Island (2016)
6. Kamilaris, A., Ali, M.I.: Do "Web of Things platforms" truly follow the Web of Things? In: Proceedings of IEEE WF-IoT, Reston, USA (2016)
7. Paganelli, F., et al.: A Web of Things framework for RESTful applications and its experimentation in a smart city. IEEE Syst. **10**(4), 1412–1423 (2016)
8. Mainetti, L., Mighali, V., Patrono, L.: A software architecture enabling the Web of Things. IEEE IoT J. **2**(6), 445–454 (2015)
9. Mingozzi, E., Tanganelli, G., Vallati, C.: CoAP proxy virtualization for the Web of Things. In: Proceedings of IEEE CloudCom, Singapore (2014)
10. WoT W3C Architecture. http://www.w3.org/TR/wot-architecture/
11. Ji, Y., Ok, K., Suk Choi, W.: Demo Abstract: Web of Things based IoT standard interworking test case. In: Proceedings of ACM BuildSys, Shenzen, China (2018)
12. Klotz, B., Datta, S.K., Wilms, D., et al.: A car as a semantic Web Thing: motivation and demonstration. In: Proceedings of IEEE GIoTS, Bilbao, Spain (2018)
13. McCool, M., Reshetova, E.: Distributed security risks and opportunities in the W3C Web of Things. In: Proceedings of IEEE DISS, San Diego, USA (2018)
14. Blank, M., Kaebisch, S., Lahbaiel, H., Kosch, H.: Role models and lifecycles in IoT and their impact on the W3C WoT thing description. In: Proceedings of IEEE IoT, Santa Barbara, USA (2018)
15. Sciullo, L., Aguzzi, C., Di Felice, M., Cinotti, T.S.: WoT Store: enabling things and applications discovery for the W3C Web of Things. In: Proceedings of IEEE CCNC, Las Vegas, USA (2019)
16. Eclipse ThingWeb. https://projects.eclipse.org/proposals/eclipse-thingweb
17. Barto, A., Sutton, R.S.: Reinforcement Learning: An Introduction. MIT Press, Cambridge (1998)

Adaptive Guard Time for Energy-Efficient IEEE 802.15.4 TSCH Networks

Alex Mavromatis[1], Georgios Z. Papadopoulos[2], Atis Elsts[1,3],
Nicolas Montavont[2], Robert Piechocki[1], Theo Tryfonas[1], George Oikonomou[1],
and Xenofon Fafoutis[4(✉)]

[1] University of Bristol, Bristol, UK
{alex.mavromatis,r.j.piechocki,theo.tryfonas,g.oikonomou}@bristol.ac.uk
[2] IMT Atlantique, Rennes, France
{georgios.papadopoulos,nicolas.montavont}@imt-atlantique.fr
[3] Institute of Electronics and Computer Science (EDI), Riga, Latvia
atis.elsts@edi.lv
[4] Technical University of Denmark (DTU), Kgs. Lyngby, Denmark
xefa@dtu.dk

Abstract. Several Internet of Things (IoT) applications have strict performance requirements, in terms of reliability and power consumption. IEEE 802.15.4 Time Slotted Channel Hopping (TSCH) is a recently standardised Medium Access Control (MAC) protocol that supports these requirements by keeping the nodes time-synchronised. In order to ensure successful communication between a sender and a receiver, the latter starts listening shortly before the expected frame's arrival. This time offset is called guard time and it aims to reduce the probability of missed frames due to clock drift. This paper investigates the impact of the guard time on the energy consumption and proposes a scheme for the decentralised adaptation of the guard time in each node depending on its hop-distance from the sink. Simulations and test-bed experiments demonstrate that guard time adaptation can reduce the energy consumption by up to 50%, without compromising the reliability of the network.

Keywords: IEEE 802.15.4 · TSCH · Internet of Things

1 Introduction

The Internet of Things (IoT) consists of smart, uniquely identifiable and connected objects that construct a network of things suitable for wireless industrial-type of scenarios. Nowadays, industry is considering IoT technologies to accelerate the fourth industrial revolution, also called the Industry 4.0 [22]. It consists of applying the IoT automations to reduce the operational and management cost, to simplify the production chains, to ease the deployments and to allow for adaptability in the factories [13]. Applications such as e-health, cargo transportation, smart buildings, automotive industry or airport logistics, all share hard performance requirements, such as ultra-low energy consumption, latency

---

This work was partially supported by EPSRC, Grant EP/K031910/1.

© IFIP International Federation for Information Processing 2019
Published by Springer Nature Switzerland AG 2019
M. Di Felice et al. (Eds.): WWIC 2019, LNCS 11618, pp. 15–26, 2019.
https://doi.org/10.1007/978-3-030-30523-9_2

and jitter, as well as high network reliability. Yet, the currently available IoT technologies straggle to provide such services, since they are extremely costly in terms of energy consumption. Therefore, in order to realise the vision of the IoT, the current standards must consider energy-efficient algorithms and solutions within the functionality of the wireless infrastructure to provide stable and predictable performance. This study focuses on reducing the energy consumption, without compromising the Packet Delivery Ratio (PDR).

The IEEE 802.15.4-2015 standard [2], published in 2016, aims to offer a certain quality of service for applications with an industrial-level of performance requirements. Among the Medium Access Control (MAC) protocols defined in this standard, Time Slotted Channel Hopping (TSCH) is designed for low-power and reliable networking in Low-power Lossy Networks (LLNs). In TSCH, the nodes in the network must remain synchronised throughout the deployment lifetime. Indeed, the nodes maintain a level of synchronisation by periodically compensating for the clock drifts. To avoid the loss of synchronisation between the synchronisation events, a TSCH receiver wakes up before the scheduled transmission by a fixed period of time. This period of time is called guard time and is responsible for significant energy wastage in idle listening. In previous work [15,17,18], we highlighted the effect of guard time on a TSCH network and identified that, when employing the 6TiSCH minimal schedule, most of the energy consumed is wasted in idle listening.

Unlike other types of synchronous sensor networks [3], in TSCH the guard time is typically configured statically and, therefore, needs to account for the worst case scenario, not only in terms of clock drift, but also in terms of network size. Instead, this work demonstrates that TSCH could operate more energy-efficiently by adapting the guard time in a decentralised manner. To this aim, this paper first proposes a decentralised heuristic algorithm for guard time adaptation in multi-hop TSCH networks, implemented for Contiki OS. The performance evaluation, which includes simulations and test-bed experiments, demonstrates that adapting the guard time on each node can significantly improve the energy consumption of TSCH networks (*i.e.*, by up to 50%) without compromising their reliability.

To summarise, this paper extends our earlier works [15,17,18] with the following contributions. Firstly, different to our preliminary works, we evaluate and quantify the benefits of guard time adaptation in multi-hop line topologies and random multi-hop topologies and under various application-layer traffic conditions via a series of COOJA (a simulator for Contiki OS) simulations. Secondly, we implement and experimentally evaluate the proposed algorithm in test-bed experiments, conducted in the SPHERE house test-bed [8], a deployment of CC2650-based sensor nodes [10] in a real residential environment in the city of Bristol, UK. The test-bed experiments also consider multi-hop topologies. Lastly, this paper evaluates the robustness of the proposed scheme on temperature differences that severely affect the clock drifts [7]. In particular, adaptive guard time is experimentally evaluated in the SPHERE house test-bed [8] in links with temperature difference (indoors-to-outdoors). Overall, this paper extends our preliminary works with extensive experimentation, and hence, strengthens and generalises our findings in a wide range of realistic scenarios.

2   Background and Related Work

TSCH is among the MAC protocols defined in the IEEE 802.15.4-2015 standard, and promises performance levels that are competitive to industrial standards, such as ISA [11], WirelessHART [1]. This section provides the necessary background information about the mechanics of TSCH and reviews the related work.

2.1   IEEE 802.15.4-2015 TSCH

TSCH achieves high level of network reliability and low-power operation by combining channel hopping and time synchronisation. Packet transmissions are organised by a deterministic scheduling scheme and the continuous time is divided into timeslots of equal size, while a set of timeslots form a slotframe which continuously repeats over time. At each timeslot, a node may transmit a packet and receive an acknowledgement. The timeslots are either contention-free (i.e., dedicated) or contention-based (i.e., shared). Finally, each timeslot comes with Absolute Slot Number (ASN) variable which indicates the number of timeslots since the beginning of the TSCH network.

Typically the clocks of the devices drift relatively their neighbours' due to production spread, as well as temperature changes. In TSCH, a node may re-synchronise to its time source neighbour according to either a frame-based or acknowledgement-based scheme [20]. To re-synchronise, the receiver node computes the offset, i.e. the relative de-synchronisation time. Then, under frame-based synchronisation, the offset is handled at the receiver side, while in ACK-based, it is applied to the transmitter's timing. The nodes regularly transmit Enhanced Beacon (EB) packets to re-synchronise their clocks and, consequently, to remain time-synchronised during the network's lifetime. In addition, data packets may also be employed to calculate the clock drifts [5]. EB packets contain the channel hopping sequence, the current ASN and information related to the initial link and slotframe. Finally, by receiving the EB packets, new nodes may join an existing TSCH network.

Each TSCH receiver activates its radio before the scheduled transmission by a fixed amount of time to avoid the loss of synchronisation between the synchronisation events. This guard time controls a performance trade-off. A longer guard time yields better resilience to loss of synchronisation, and therefore higher PDR. Yet, this comes at the cost of higher energy consumption, as more energy is lost in idle listening.

2.2   Related Work

Previous works improve the energy efficiency of TSCH networks either by improving the scheduler [14,16] or the synchronisation process. In this section, we briefly discuss the latter.

In [19], the authors present an adaptive synchronisation technique, and suggest that in a TSCH network the resynchronisation frequency should be reduced while the nodes are synchronised. In order to keep synchronisation, the nodes measure their clock drift rates relative to their time source neighbours. Later, the nodes periodically perform a time correction based on the previously calculated offset. As a result, this frequency reduction technique allows for lower duty cycle and longer network lifetime. In [4], the authors propose an adaptive compensation method that enables synchronisation between nodes, without exchanging any control or data packet. To this aim, the proposed algorithm compensates the clock drift error by regularly adjusting the interval of resynchronisation (*i.e.*, local clock) of each node to improve the accuracy of the clock drift.

In [5], the authors propose an adaptive synchronisation scheme which allows the nodes to learn and predict how their clocks are drifting relative to their neighbours. Later, they coordinate the instants at which the nodes will re-synchronize. To this aim, an additional field in the EB and ACK packets is introduced to inform the neighbour node about the synchronised time. The authors evaluated the proposed technique in a TSCH multi-hop topology. In [9], the authors improve the level of synchronisation of TSCH networks by one order of magnitude in comparison to [5]. This is achieved by improving the resolution of measurement of the drift via keeping the high- and low-frequency clocks of a sensor node synchronised. This high level of synchronisation allows the reduction of the guard time and, therefore, the reduction of the energy consumption. In [7], the authors extend this algorithm with temperature calibration and provide an solution for temperature-resilient time synchronisation. In [12], the authors present a detailed analysis of the main factors contributing to the energy-consumption of Wireless HART standard, a Time Division Multiple Access (TDMA)-based and frequency hopping protocol [1]. Similar to TSCH protocol, under Wireless HART, the nodes listen the medium for certain time before the reception of control or data packets. The authors demonstrated that in addition to the radio transmission and reception states, the listening state in data and control timeslots has a significant impact of the energy consumption of a node.

Directly or indirectly, the above works improve the energy efficiency of TSCH by enhancing the process of synchronisation. Indeed, these works demonstrate that significant energy savings can be achieved through tighter time synchronisation. Yet, all the above works keep the guard time static throughout the network. Different to the related work, this paper proposes the adaptation of the guard time at a node level in a fully distributed fashion. This technique exploits the individual properties of each node, such as the distance to the sink. Indeed, adaptive guard times can be used together with adaptive synchronisation techniques for combined benefits.

3   Guard Time Adaptation

As the number of hops increases, the aggregated relative clock drift increases as well [9]. Therefore, multi-hop TSCH networks require longer guard times to maintain their synchronous operation. By employing the default version of TSCH in a multi-hop network, all nodes homogeneously operate with a static guard time configuration (*i.e.*, 2200 μs for CC2420, 1800 μs CC2650) [6]. Indeed, the nodes that are closer to the sink forward more packets and, thus, synchronise more frequently than leaf nodes. Therefore, the nodes that are closer to the sink require shorter guard times to maintain synchronisation.

This paper proposes a fully-distributed guard time adaptation algorithm for improving the energy efficiency of TSCH without compromising its reliability. Following a heuristic approach, each node adapts its guard time according to its runtime hop-distance to the time source (sink node). The runtime hop-distance is defined as the number of hops required to reach the sink node, according to the respective topology of the routing layer. In particular, the proposed scheme operates as follows. During an off-line calibration phase, the scheme constructs an empirical look-up table of optimum guard times, according to the number of hops from the root. At the end of the calibration process, shown in Algorithm 1, the look-up table contains the minimum guard times that do not break time synchronisation. At runtime, once the RPL [21] Direction-Oriented Directed Acyclic Graph (DODAG) is successfully constructed and, thus, each node in the network obtain all the necessary information related with its rank, each node adjusts its guard time according to the look-up table, as shown in Algorithm 2. It is straightforward that the nodes closer to the DODAG root will maintain shorter guard times, since they frequently participate in the routing procedure and, thus, they constantly re-synchronise their clocks, while the leaf nodes will have longer guard times. Finally, the nodes reconfigure their guard time in a decentralised and local manner, and the runtime overhead is minimal, $i.e.$, $O(1)$.

In this paper, we propose guard time adaptation according to the hop-distance to the sink. This technique can be combined with other guard time adaptation techniques that are based on other parameters that affect synchronisation, such as the temperature [7].

4   Performance Evaluation

In order to evaluate the benefits of guard time adaptation, as well as the impact of the guard time in the energy consumption of a TSCH network, a series of simulations are conducted in COOJA, the network simulator distributed as part of the Contiki OS, emulating the CC2420-based Z1 motes. In addition, a series of test-bed experiments are executed in the SPHERE house test-bed [8], a deployment of CC2650-based sensor nodes [10] in a real residential environment in the city of Bristol, UK. This section presents a thorough performance evaluation for both statically configured guard times and the proposed adaptive guard time scheme. The details of the simulation and test-bed setup are given in Table 1, unless explicitly stated otherwise.

4.1   Simulation: Multi-hop Line Topologies

The next series of simulations evaluate guard time adaptation in a 9-hop multi-hop chain topology, shown in Fig. 1. The traffic rate of each node is set to one packet per minute. The simulations focus on a worst case scenario for time

---

Algorithm 1. Calibration

Data: Step, GuardTimeMax, Duration
Result: GuardTime look-up table
foreach Hop **do**
  GuardTime[Hop] ← GuardTimeMax;
  while GuardTime[Hop] > 0 **do**
    SyncLoss ← Simulate(GuardTime, Duration);
    if SyncLoss = False **then**
      | GuardTime[Hop] ← GuardTime[Hop] − Step;
    else
      | GuardTime[Hop] ← GuardTime[Hop] + Step;
      | break;
    end
  end
end

Algorithm 2. Runtime

Data: GuardTime look-up table
Result: AppliedGuardTime
foreach *Routing Change* **do**
  Rank ← getRankfromRPL();
  AppliedGuardTime ← GuardTime[Rank];
end

---

synchronisation: odd nodes have positive clock drift and even nodes have negative clock drift. Moreover, the nodes use the 6TiSCH minimal schedule. Finally, the duration of each simulation is 60 m.

The goal of the first set of simulations is to identify the minimum guard time that yields 100% PDR in each layer of the network. The empirically-derived minimum guard time for each hop is illustrated in Fig. 1 and used as a look-up table for the implementation of guard time adaptation in Contiki. The results verify that nodes closer to the sink require a smaller guard time as opposed to the leaf nodes. The empirically-derived network-wide optimum guard time is 1200 μs. Therefore, this static configuration is used as a benchmark for the evaluation of the proposed adaptive guard time scheme.

The following simulations quantify the benefits of adapting the guard time according to the hop-distance to the sink. A set of simulations evaluates the proposed scheme in various application-layer traffic rates, focusing on the 9-hop line topology. Figure 2 shows that the adaptation of the guard time improves the energy efficiency of the TSCH network, by reducing the radio duty cycle. This reduction is more significant (*i.e.*, up to 50%) for TSCH networks that run low-throughput applications and drops as the traffic increases. This happens because in high traffic scenarios the radio is primarily used for transmissions.

Table 1. Simulation & Experimental Setup

	Simulation	Experiments
Multi-hop Line Topology		
Number of devices	From 2 to 10	10
Node spacing	100 m	2 m–6 m
Multi-hop Random Topology		
Number of devices	15	–
Node spacing	random	–
Maximum number of hops	6	–
Indoor-to-Outdoor Link		
Number of devices	–	2
Node spacing	–	2 m
Duration, Network and Traffic parameters		
Duration	1 h	1-hop: 24 h
		Multi-hop: 1 h
Traffic rate	1–512 pkt/60 s	1 pkt/60 s
Packet size	102 bytes	102 bytes
Routing	RPL [21]	RPL [21]
MAC	TSCH	TSCH
Schedule	6TiSCH minimal	Collision-free
TSCH-specific parameters		
EB frequency	3.42 s	4 s
Slotframe length	7	17
Timeslot length	15 ms	10 ms
Guard time	$(0-2200)\,\mu s$	$(0-1600)\,\mu s$
Clock drift	± 20 ppm	Natural drift
		up to ± 20 ppm
Hardware configuration		
Radio hardware	CC2420	CC2650
Radio frequency	2.4 GHz	2.4 GHz
TX power	0 dBm	5 dBm

4.2 Simulation: Multi-hop Random Topologies

The following simulations evaluate the proposed algorithm in multi-hop random topologies of 15 nodes to further validate its efficiency in realistic TSCH networks. Similarly to the previous simulations the clock drift is fixed to ±20 ppm, while 1 data packet was transmitted per minute. The simulations demonstrate that the guard time of the receiver nodes can be reduced without compromising the reliability of the network (100% PDR). Indeed, as depicted in Fig. 3, the

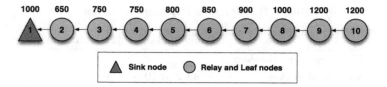

Fig. 1. The simulated line topology. The number above each node corresponds to the minimum configuration that maintains 100% network reliability (in μs).

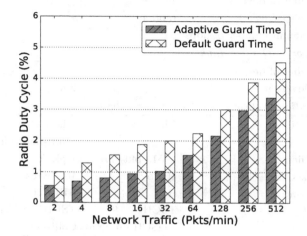

Fig. 2. Average radio duty cycle for various application-layer traffic rates.

average radio duty cycle is reduced by approximately 20%. Moreover, the consistency of the results in 10 random networks demonstrate the robustness of the proposed algorithm to the network topology.

4.3 Experiment: Multi-hop Line Topology

Next, guard time adaptation is evaluated in experiments, conducted in the SPHERE house test-bed [8]. The SPHERE house test-bed is a wireless sensor network deployed in a 2-storey residential environment in the city of Bristol, UK, shown in Fig. 4. In particular, the house is deployed with TI CC2650-based sensor nodes [10] (Fig. 5); a platform that is supported by the Contiki OS. All of the deployed nodes are equipped with the FC-135 low-frequency crystal, using it to schedule the wake-up events. This crystal has a frequency error $e_f \in [-20, 20]$ ppm and a parabolic dependence on temperature (parabolic coefficient value $B = 0.04$ ppm/°C^2). The channel conditions in the SPHERE house are typical for an urban residential neighbourhood, with occasional 2.4 GHz interference from the neighbouring houses. The nodes are sufficiently close to form a single-hop star topology. Yet, for the purposes of this experiment, the nodes use a static schedule that enforces a 9-hop line topology, similar to Fig. 1.

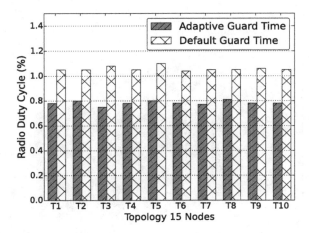

Fig. 3. Guard time adaptation evaluated in 10 random multi-hop topologies of 15 nodes

In this setting, the proposed adaptive guard time scheme is compared against the Contiki default fixed guard time in two 1-hour experiments. Figure 7 summarises the experimental results, which show the reduction of the radio duty cycle in each of the 10 nodes in the test-bed. The experiments verify the simulations presented in Sect. 4.1, indicating an average 15% reduction in the radio duty cycle without sacrificing the reliability (100% PDR). The experiments show that nodes that are closer to the sink (*i.e.*, shorter hop-distance) relay more traffic, and hence, synchronise with their parent node more frequently. Thus, a smaller guard time is sufficient and energy can be saved by adapting it.

4.4   Experiment: Indoors-to-Outdoors

Clock drifts are also dependent on temperature [7]. This section presents an experiment that considers a link with temperature differences, *i.e.*, the sender is indoors (22 °C room temperature) while the receiver is outdoors and, therefore, exposed to outdoor temperatures. The proposed adaptive guard time algorithm is, again, compared against the default configuration in 24-hour experiments. Figure 6 summarises the results of the experiment. In particular, Fig. 6(a) plots the radio duty cycle over the course of the 24-hour experiment. Both approaches demonstrate a fairly constant duty cycle, yet present a periodicity that is attributed to the temperature variations, shown in Fig. 6(b). Despite these temperature variations, both configurations operate robustly in this 24-hour experiment, yielding 100% PDR. Yet adaptive guard time reduces the radio duty cycle, and thus, the energy consumption of the radio by approximately 25%.

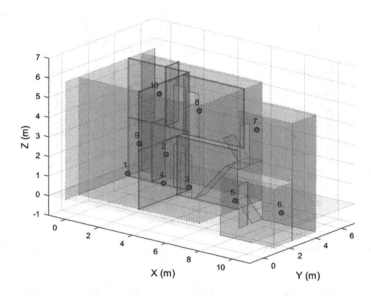

Fig. 4. The SPHERE house test-bed is a deployment of C2650-based nodes in a two-storey residential environment in Bristol, UK [8].

Fig. 5. Experiments were conducted on the SPES-2 [10] sensing platform; a environmental sensor that is equipped with the TI CC2650 radio.

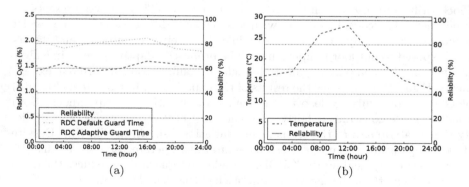

Fig. 6. Adaptive guard times reduce the average radio duty cycle without compromising the reliability (a) despite the temperature differences (b). In this 24-hour experiment, the sender is indoors (room temperature) whilst the receiver is exposed to various outdoor temperatures.

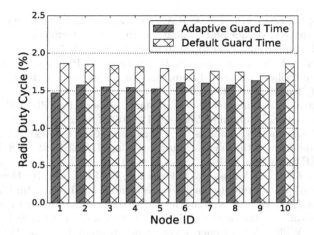

Fig. 7. The practical benefits of guard time adaptation in the SPHERE house test-bed (9-hop line topology). The PDR is 100% in all the experiments.

5 Conclusions

This paper investigates the impact of guard time on IEEE 802.15.4 TSCH networks and proposes a decentralised guard time adaptation algorithm for reducing the energy consumption of TSCH-based multi-hop networks. The proposed technique follows the formation of the network topology and allows each node to assign its own guard time according to its distance in hops from the sink node. This dynamic procedure allows the network nodes to reduce the time they spend in idle listening; therefore, the energy consumption is significantly reduced. The proposed algorithm is implemented in Contiki OS and evaluated with an extensive set of simulations, which include several types of topologies, such as multi-hop line and random topologies. In addition, the proposed algorithm is also evaluated on the SPHERE test-bed. The results of the simulations and test-bed experiments demonstrate the advantage of adapting the guard time instead of using a static configuration.

References

1. WirelessHART Specification 75: TDMA Data-Link Layer. Std., Rev 1 (2008)
2. IEEE Standard for Low-Rate Wireless Personal Area Networks (LR-WPANs). IEEE Std 802.15.4-2015 (Revision of IEEE Std 802.15.4-2011), April 2016
3. Brzozowski, M., Salomon, H., Langendoerfer, P.: On efficient clock drift prediction means and their applicability to IEEE 802.15.4. In: 2010 IEEE/IFIP International Conference on Embedded and Ubiquitous Computing, pp. 216–223, December 2010
4. Chang, T., Wang, Q.: Adaptive compensation for time-slotted synchronization in wireless sensor network. Int. J. Distrib. Sens. Netw. **10**, 540397 (2014)
5. Chang, T., Watteyne, T., Pister, K., Wang, Q.: Adaptive synchronization in multi-hop TSCH networks. Comput. Netw. **76**, 165–176 (2015)

6. Duquennoy, S., Elsts, A., Nahas, B.A., Oikonomou, G.: TSCH and 6TiSCH for contiki: challenges, design and evaluation. In: 13th International Conference on Distributed Computing in Sensor Systems (DCOSS) (2017)
7. Elsts, A., Fafoutis, X., Duquennoy, S., Oikonomou, G., Piechocki, R., Craddock, I.: Temperature-resilient time synchronization for the internet of things. IEEE Trans. Industr. Inf. **14**(5), 2241–2250 (2018)
8. Elsts, A., et al.: Enabling healthcare in smart homes: the SPHERE IoT network infrastructure. IEEE Commun. Mag. **56**(12), 164–170 (2018)
9. Elsts, A., Duquennoy, S., Fafoutis, X., Oikonomou, G., Piechocki, R., Craddock, I.: Microsecond-accuracy time synchronization using the IEEE 802.15.4 TSCH protocol. In: IEEE SenseApp (2016)
10. Fafoutis, X., Elsts, A., Vafeas, A., Oikonomou, G., Piechocki, R.: Demo: SPES-2 - a sensing platform for maintenance-free residential monitoring. In: EWSN (2017)
11. ISA-100.11a-2011: Wireless systems for industrial automation: process control and related applications. International Society of Automation (ISA) Std. 1, May 2011
12. Khader, O., Willig, A.: An energy consumption analysis of the Wireless HART TDMA protocol. Comput. Commun. **36**, 804–816 (2013)
13. Koutsiamanis, R.A., Papadopoulos, G.Z., Fafoutis, X., Fiore, J.M.D., Thubert, P., Montavont, N.: From best effort to deterministic packet delivery for wireless industrial IoT networks. IEEE Trans. Industr. Inf. **14**(10), 4468–4480 (2018)
14. Matsui, T., Nishi, H.: Time slotted channel hopping scheduling based on the energy consumption of wireless sensor networks. In: 2018 IEEE 15th International Workshop on Advanced Motion Control (AMC), pp. 605–610, March 2018
15. Mavromatis, A., Papadopoulos, G.Z., Fafoutis, X., Elsts, A., Oikonomou, G., Tryfonas, T.: Impact of guard time length on IEEE 802.15.4e TSCH energy consumption. In: Proceedings of the IEEE SECON (2016)
16. Ojo, M., Giordano, S., Portaluri, G., Adami, D., Pagano, M.: An energy efficient centralized scheduling scheme in TSCH networks. In: 2017 IEEE International Conference on Communications Workshops (ICC Workshops), pp. 570–575, May 2017
17. Papadopoulos, G.Z., et al.: Guard time optimisation and adaptation for energy efficient multi-hop TSCH networks. In: IEEE WF-IoT, pp. 301–306 (2016)
18. Papadopoulos, G.Z., et al.: Guard time optimisation for energy efficiency in IEEE 802.15.4-2015 TSCH links. In: Proceedings of the EAI International Conference on Interoperability in IoT (InterIoT) (2016)
19. Stanislowski, D., Vilajosana, X., Wang, Q., Watteyne, T., Pister, K.S.J.: Adaptive synchronization in IEEE802.15.4e networks. IEEE Trans. Ind. Inf. **10**(1), 795–802 (2014)
20. Thubert, P.: An Architecture for IPv6 over the TSCH mode of IEEE 802.15.4. draft-ietf-6tisch-architecture-20, March 2019
21. Winter, T., et al.: RPL: IPv6 Routing Protocol for Low-Power and Lossy Networks. RFC 6550 (2012)
22. Xu, L.D., He, W., Li, S.: Internet of things in industries: a survey. IEEE Trans. Industr. Inf. **10**(4), 2233–2243 (2014)

Assessment and Hardening of IoT Development Boards

Omar Alfandi[2(✉)], Musaab Hasan[1], and Zayed Balbahaith[2]

[1] University of Science and Technology of Fujairah, Fujairah,
United Arab Emirates
m.mohammad@ustf.ac.ae
[2] Zayed University, Abu Dhabi, United Arab Emirates
{omar.alfandi, M80007225}@zu.ac.ae

Abstract. Internet of Things (IoT) products became recently an essential part of any home in conjunction with the great advancements in internet speeds and services. The invention of IoT based devices became an easy task that could be performed through the widely available IoT development boards. Raspberry Pi is considered one of the advanced development boards that have high hardware capabilities with a reasonable price. Unfortunately, the security aspect of such products is overlooked by the developers, revealing a huge amount of threats that result in invading the privacy and the security of the users. In this research, we directed our study to SSH due to its extensive adoption by the developers. It was found that due to the nature of the Raspberry Pi and development boards, the Raspberry Pi generates predictable and weak keys which make it easy to be utilized by MiTM attack. In this paper, Man in The Middle (MiTM) attack was conducted to examine the security of different variations provided by the SSH service, and various hardening approaches were proposed to resolve the issue of SSH weak implementation and weak keys.

Keywords: IoT · Raspberry Pi 3 · Man-in-the-middle attack ·
Remote authentication · SSH keys · OpenSSH

1 Introduction

The great advancements in the internet and its extremely high speeds revealed a huge amount of innovative inventions that are based on the internet, releasing the Internet of Things (IOT) term and even the Internet of Everything (IoE) [1]. These products that depend on their operation mainly on the internet started to be an essential part of any home [2]. Recently, the development of internet-based products become not limited to specialized manufacturers only but became on hand to small developers with limited resources due to the widely available development boards that could be bought from the market with high hardware specifications and low cost [3]. IOT has continuously filled all aspects of contemporary human life, such as learning, healthcare, and business, involving the warehouse of sensitive data about people and companies, commercial data, product development, and marketing [4]. The cluster appropriation of the internet of things (IOT) is a multibillion-dollar chance for product companies, An

© IFIP International Federation for Information Processing 2019
Published by Springer Nature Switzerland AG 2019
M. Di Felice et al. (Eds.): WWIC 2019, LNCS 11618, pp. 27–39, 2019.
https://doi.org/10.1007/978-3-030-30523-9_3

expected 30 billion devices or things will be connected to the internet by 2020, with a cost expected to be $1.7bn [5]. In future, IOT will ultimately improve our living behaviors and allow people and devices to interact anytime, anyplace, with any device under typical circumstances using any network and any service [6].

The main purpose of IOT is to produce a better environment for humans in future [7]. IOT computation different hardware-based components and platforms, in the modern times, hardware devices identified as single board computers have been improving into affordable, powerful, and skilled machines, the most popular at the time is the Raspberry Pi, which produced by Dr. Eben Upton and the Raspberry Pi foundation in 2010 [8].

The Raspberry PI device formed to facilitate for people to explore computing and to learn programming languages like Python and Scratch [9]. Since its beginning, the device has moved on to be adopted in home projects as well being practiced by education institutes to be assistance in educating student's computer science concepts. This small size computer device can arrange everything that a normal computer can do from browsing the net, enjoying video games, forming word files, etc. [10]. Raspberry PI has a processor, memory and graphics driver for output HDMI. It has the ability of plug-in on a computer screen, keyboard and mouse. It can also be utilized in various apps requiring interacting with the outside world [11]. Raspberry PI matches all the characteristics of being an IOT device which can be configured to produce a different kind of functionalities per user conditions. This small device has been employed in various and several applications and can be incorporated into networks, which has to commence to questions concerning about security weaknesses regarding such device [9].

The widespread distribution of devices in the IOT has created tremendous demand for strong security in response to the increasing demand of billions of connected devices and services [12]. A number of threats are rising every day, and attacks have been on the rise in both number and complexity, also the tools accessible to potential attackers are also growing more complex, productive and efficient [13]. IOT challenges an amount of threats that need to be noticed for protecting actions to be taken. Unluckily, the majority of these devices and apps are not outfitted to manage the security and privacy attacks and it raises a lot of security and privacy concerns in the IOT networks [14]. An assessment reveals that 70% of the IOT devices are very easy to attack; therefore, an effective mechanism is greatly required to secure the devices connected to the internet against hackers and intruders [15]. Security requirements in the IOT context are not dissimilar from any other ICT systems; therefore, for IOT devices to reach the completest potential, it needs protection against threats and vulnerabilities [16].

In the Raspberry PI, a security issues of generation a predictable secure shell (SSH) keys have risen as a hot topic in this field, SSH is a vital communication protocol and no way to neglect it uses from IoT devices. The research problem focusing on Raspberry Pi devices which affected by a security issue arising from the Raspbian operating system which makes generating of SSH keys weak and predictable.

The rest of this paper is organized as follows. Section 2 presents a related work for our study. The Problem and motivation is discussed in Sect. 3. In Sect. 4, the security evaluation of using different versions of Raspbian operating system and SSH server was presented and discussed thoroughly. The experimental procedures steps and actions performed are presented in Sect. 5. Next, the discussion of the results and the findings of the experimental procedures are presented in Sect. 6. Finally, we conclude the paper with future work in Sect. 7.

2 Literature Review

Previous related works in the field of IoT, man in the middle attack and SSH have been studied to gain a full understanding of what have been conducted out in this field by previous researchers.

Xiaohong et al. [17] studied how to detect and defeat the man in the middle attack to reduce the loss under the MITM attacks since avoidance of the MITM attacks shows an incredible responsibility. They started the work by offering a defense strategy against MITM attacks, and then they show the communication among the attacker and the defender under Stackelberg security game framework and use the Strong Stackelberg Equilibrium (SSE) as the strategy for the defender. After that they implement a novel way to defeat the searching scope of calculating the optimal defense strategy. On the final step, they assess their ideal defense strategy by comparing it with non-strategic defense strategies. The correlation of the simulated results concludes for them that the suggested theoretic defense strategy exceeds than nonstrategic defense strategies in terms of reducing the total losses on MITM attacks. The limitation of the paper based on the focusing only on one singular service and assuming it applies to all other services without real examination.

Mauro et al. [18] provided a huge study of the literature on the man in the middle attack to examine and characterize the range of MITM attacks and classified them based on the position of an attacker in the network, environment of a transmission channel, and impersonation ways. After that, based on their analysis, they recognize some potential directions for future researchers based on the large number of literatures studied, and they suggest a categorization of MITM prevention mechanisms as follow: (1) Use secure interactive authentication to constantly validate endpoints of any communications channel and exchange public keys using a reliable channel. (2) Use few stable channels for checking if data has not been discredited and signify public keys by a certified authority. (3) Use certificate pinning and encrypt the communication by employing cryptography. (4) Check the conventional behavior of communicating endpoints, according to the allowed communication protocol.

Shubh and Sharma [19] analyzed the ways that man in the attacks works and they indicates the way it intercept the network to collect information even without outside party knowing it. They focus on their study at attacking SSL across HTTP which identified as HTTPS. The conclusive goal of their recommended system is to build a secure channel over a vulnerable network. They applied a combination of Diffie-Hellman and blowfish algorithm, Diffie-Hellman for key generation and blowfish for encryption which is improving the data security over SSL and HTTPS. Also they explained a scheme to strengthen the SSL by utilizing a Firefox add-on which can recognize any fraudulent SSL certificates. They conducted a real examination of a man in the middle attack against bank website by applying their proposed model and they were successful to detect of MITM attack and their suggested recommendation shows an efficient method to avoid the MITM attack.

Yaoqi et al. [20] performed a methodical interpretation of browser cache poisoning attacks on HTTPS connections that expose the victim web sessions with the target site by poisoning the victim's browser cache wherein a web attacker completes a man in the middle attack on a user's HTTPS session and exchanges cached sources with malicious entireties. Their experimental study of such attack was held on 5 desktop browsers and 16 common mobile browsers and they noticed that the experimented browsers are extremely variable in their caching strategies for storing resources over SSL connections with fallacious certificates and they achieved that 99% of the tested browsers induced by BCP attacks to an immense amount. They presented guidelines for users and browser vendors to overcome BCP attacks. They have recorded their conclusions to browser vendors and approved the vulnerabilities of them and some of them have settled the problem based on their suggestion.

Esmaeil et al. [21] studied Brute-force attacks for SSH carried out on six separated universities campus networks by applying Honeypot techniques in attempts to obtain remote access to a system using information obtained from their SSH honeypots using the help of the tools and techniques employed. On the first phase, they used open VZ software with Kojoney honeypot and POf fingerprinting tool to log innumerable details about the attacks. Secondly, they configured the firewall to allow the SSH service to be available on the web using its public static IP address. A Brute-force attack used to list the usernames and passwords that are publicly assigned and they successfully obtain remote access to SSH Honeypots and collect numerous data. They assessed the effectiveness of a variety of techniques intended to defend the systems against these attacks. They conclude the paper with an amazing table that recommending 17 lists for the protection of SSH servers.

Alsaadi and AlKubaisi [22] performed penetration testing on remote secure OpenSSH running on version 7.1p2 On Raspberry Pi 2 running Kali Linux version 3.2–4.4. Their study focused on the vulnerabilities discovered in exchange keys in SSH protocol which creates multiple CRLF injections and admits to conduct man in the middle attack to allow remote users bypass shell-command constraints via crafted X11 forwarding data. They approached an efficient security model based on an experimentation attack formed on various scenarios that can resolve the problems of enabling remote authentication access using SSH protocol exchange keys without hitting the encrypted protocols communications. They injected the secure shell session on port 22 of Kali Linux OS with the produced SSH keys which enabled them to achieve full entrance to device information. The limitations can be shown in missing of real testing attack on their suggest model structure and what they proposed maybe will suffer difficulties with newer versions of Raspberry Pi and SSH.

3 Problem and Motivation

Internet of Things (IOT) operates as one of the biggest potentials for human life transformation. It strongly becomes the quickest growing market but the more notable concern is that this growth is moving fast while there are major problems occurring within it causing these devices to offer well-known vulnerabilities for hackers to exploit them. IOT devices configured through the network and SSH is essential for that but the dilemma resides on SSH problematic because the likelihood of generating weak keys. IOT devices and especially Raspberry PI devices were discovered to be generating predictable and weak keys which make these devices easy to be utilized by MiTM attack when owning the weak keys and by performing weak algorithm implementations these devices could be exploited. The motivation remains on the continuous use of SSH as communication protocol but we want to maintain its security and make sure it's secure and perfect.

4 Security Evaluation of Raspbian and SSH Various Versions Implementation

In this section, the evaluation of using various versions of Raspbian and SSH server among the different versions of the Raspberry Pi developments boards is presented. Keeping in mind that the same Raspbian image that is being used for the Raspberry Pi3 could be used directly with the Raspberry Pi 1 as most of the advancements that are presented on the boards are focused on providing higher processing speeds and extra functionalities [25].

As SSH is considered a necessary service to be used by developers to configure their Raspberry Pi developments boards, it was provided as a built-in service on the operating system image without the need to install it after starting the operating system. Raspberry Pi Debian through all its versions was implementing the OpenSSH as SSH server software [8]. The most interesting thing about the SD card that holds the operating system image is that it can be used directly with any version of the Raspberry Pi boards starting from the version 1 reaching the latest Raspberry Pi 3 Model B [9]. However, as Raspbian was being released since 2013-09-10 and at the time the first release was announced, the Raspberry Pi 2 & 3 were not yet released and thus the versions earlier than 2015-01-31 doesn't support the Raspberry Pi 2. In the same manner, the versions of Raspbian that are earlier than 2016-02-26 doesn't support Raspberry Pi 3 [23]. Through the different versions, it was noticed that the newer the version, the more packages, and services are being installed and kept with it. For example, starting from 2014-09-09 Raspbian release, multiple extra packages were built in the default image including Minecraft that is a game that most developers don't use for their IoT implementations. Another important notice for the same release that a downgrading was performed for Java from version 8 to version 7 exposing the system to an outdated packages security risk [24]. The 2015-09-25 release faced a huge transfer towards including a big number of preinstalled packages including games and utilities making the operating system more like regular Linux desktop distributions. Having various tools preinstalled on the development board may present a handy operating system for users that are using the board as their desktop and not an operating system for IoT device and again we are facing the same issue of having many preinstalled packages that could present a huge security breach [25]. The same approach was followed by the vendors by Raspberry to include more and more packages in the fresh operating system. An important notice about the 2016-09-23 release that it included a preinstalled RealVNC that allows remote connection to the Raspberry Pi device and that could be utilized by the hackers to attack the system and obtain remote access [26]. So as a conclusion the Raspbian operating system is being developed to create a more user-friendly environment for developers that wants everything to be working properly without the need for much configurations.

As there are no specific operating systems for the specific hardware of each Raspberry Pi version since the same Raspbian SD card could be inserted into both Raspberry Pi 2 or Raspberry Pi 3 and both of them will work properly without any issues. The SSH implementation through different versions could present unique possibilities of attacks that could be adopted by the hackers. According to the CVE Details database, OpenSSH was found to be vulnerable to almost 100 published vulnerabilities that are distributed among different categories including DoS, Code Execution Overflow, Memory Corruption, Directory Traversal, Http Response Splitting, Bypass something, Gain Information, Gain Privileges [27]. Among the various versions, it was noticed that Dos to be one of the main categories that most OpenSSH related vulnerabilities are published. Having that said could present the IoT device to shut down or stopping the service causing the device to stop its intended action. This issue could create a big threat especially if the device was used for a critical function such as medical applications [28]. The second most common attack through all the versions was Bypassing one of the mechanisms that are used to start and initiate the SSH connection which could result in reducing the security as each one of the mechanisms and steps that are adopted by OpenSSH are meant to maintain the security as this is the main purpose of using SSH over the clear text telnet services [29]. Gaining the privileges was the third most common vulnerability on the OpenSSH through its all versions. Gaining privileges is an extremely dangerous issue as having a non-root user gaining higher privileges will allow him to experiment a huge amount of open possibilities to manipulate the system and obtain full access and control over the system [30]. As it is always recommended to perform the updates for all the packages and tools including OpenSSH it is worth mentioning that the released versions of the OpenSSH in 2017 were having in total around six various vulnerabilities that are distributed over various categories [29]. At the same time, the 2015 OpenSSH releases recorded no published vulnerabilities at all. This issue could be explained by the fact that the higher the version, the more options, and services are available in the implementation exposing the system to further exploitation vulnerabilities [27]. Another explanation could be that the latest versions of the OpenSSH are designed to provide backward compatibility including, for example, the support for the SSH V1 that is considered to be weak and crackable communication by the widely available tools [30].

5   Implementation and Analysis

The main focus of this research was about performing Man in The Middle (MiTM) attack to examine the security of the different variations provided by the SSH service. In Raspberry Pi, most of the time the SSH 22/tcp port is found to be open by the developers as it allows them to configure the development board through the network without the need of connecting it to a monitor. This section is divided into two main subsections where the first one shows the examination process for the different variations of SSH and the second one shows the proper approaches for making the usage of SSH more secure.

5.1   Security Examination of Various SSH Implementations

The examination of the various implementations of SSH was performed on this research work by implementing each variation separately while examining the traffic through the Man in The Middle (MiTM) machine. Figure 1 Shows the detailed process followed in achieving this task and the rest of this subsection explains each part of the descried steps.

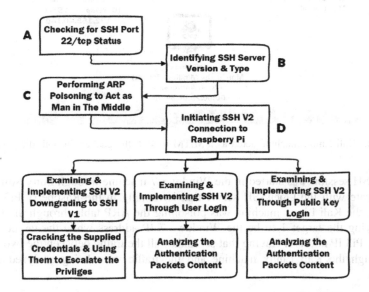

Fig. 1. Framework for performing the security examination on various SSH implementations.

(A) Checking for SSH Port 22/tcp Status
Having a port open in any target reveals a significant amount of information and possibilities for attacks [13]. As a start for our examination process the open ports in the newly installed fresh RASPBERRY PI DEBIAN JESSIE (2017-06-22) operating system was performed through n map on the Raspberry PI IP address that showed the port 22/tcp as the only open port in the device.

(B) Identifying SSH Server Version & Type
The version and the type of SSH server specifies the algorithms and procedures followed by the server to implement the service. It could also identify if it is susceptible to published vulnerabilities. Metasploit framework was used to lunch the "*auxiliary/scanner/ssh/ssh_version*" against the IP address of the Raspberry Pi the version was identified to be OpenSSH 6.7 p1 which supports SSH V1 and SSH V2.

(C) Performing ARP Poisoning to Act as Man in The Middle

Attackers tend to perform ARP poisoning to stand in between the two victims. Figure [2] shows the actual scenario that was followed in performing the MiTM attack where the Kali Linux attacker machine spoofed the IP address of both Raspberry Pi3 and the Windows 7 machines and it worked as an interceptor that sniff the traffic then pass it to its actual direction.

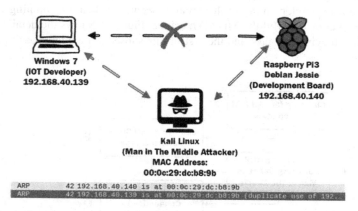

Fig. 2. Kali Linux machine acted as a MiTM to sniff the packets in both directions.

The SSH session was started in the Windows 7 machine through Putty Software to communicate with the OpenSSH server that is running in the Raspberry Pi3. At the same time the Kali Linux machine was poisoning the ARP table through the Ettercap by specifying the target 1 to be the Windows 7 IP address while the target 2 is the Raspberry Pi3 IP address. Having that set makes all the traffic between the two victims pass through the Kali Linux machine and the traffic were being analyzed through Wireshark.

(D) Initiating SSH V2 Connection to Raspberry Pi

In this part three variations of the SSH sessions were examined and analyzed. In the first scenario, the configurations for the SSH server on the Raspberry Pi were allowing the SSH V1 and SSH V2, knowing that SSH V1 is implementing weak algorithms that could be easily attacked [20]. The Kali Linux attacker machine was running Ettercap to perform ARP poisoning and implementing the ether filter that forces the SSH V2 requests to be downgraded to SSH V1 and attack the communication and reveal the user and password.

In the same way when SSH V2 communication was initiated while having the Raspberry Pi forcing only the SSH V2 and not allowing the SSH V1, Ettercap failed to downgrade or crack the credentials in both scenarios when the login is performed through user and password or through the authorized public key. The developer can select between two approaches to authenticate himself when using SSH V2. The first approach is to provide the name of one of the local users and his password and the authentication will be completed when correct credentials are provided [18]. The other approach, is to use to have the public key of the Windows 7 machine stored in the authorized public keys list in the Raspberry Pi " ∼/.ssh/authorized_keys" file. Then whenever the Windows 7 tries to authenticate itself for SSH V2 there will be no need to supply the password. The packets sequence retrieved by Ettercap MiTM scheme through Wireshark. This sequence of packets includes the negotiation about the algorithms and standards for the encryption.

As the generation process of the key pairs is based on pseudo random functions, a big risk appears for having weak predictable keys for the Raspberry Pi being generated. The issue raise there is a huge possibility of having predictable keys as the same process is followed in making the first boot process where the operating system image is copied to an SD card that is used to make the first boot with the same hardware making the pseudorandom functions behavior predictable and thus exposing the SSH V2 to the MiTM attacker that could launch similar attack to the one performed on SSH V1.

5.2   Hardening SSH Implementations

The communication through SSH could be hardened to ensure that it is not easily breakable or hackable. Figure [3] shows the considered three main sources of threat against SSH communication and the proposed solution.

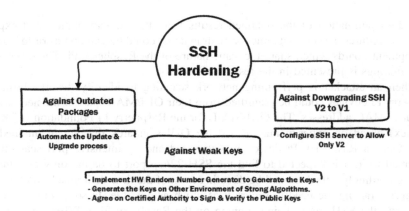

Fig. 3. Main threat sources to SSH communication and their proposed solutions.

Keeping in mind that each outdated package that is installed in the Raspberry Pi machine could present a big threat due to possible vulnerabilities. As an example, to that, an outdated version of OpenSSH could support only SSH V1 which is adopting weak algorithms that could be attacked easily making the communication not secure. Automating the update and upgrade process in the machine and using patch management tools could limit such type of threats. To prevent the downgrading of SSH V2 to SSH V1, the configuration file on the Raspberry Pi in "/etc./ssh/sshd_config" could be check to make sure only Protocol 2 is allowed. As the implementation of the Raspberry Pi OS makes it generating weak predictable keys, it is recommended to use well tested tools on other machines such as Putty in Windows environment to generate the key pair then add them to the Raspberry Pi SSH keys. Another solution to the weak keys issue, could be implementing an indirect way to use hardware random numbers generators through the following steps:

- Obtain the Raspberry Pi chipset number.
- Load the chipset related random number generator module.
- Install random number generator package and activate it.
- Now the entropy will be having a larger size of pool making the generation pseudo random numbers process more efficient.
- Remove old keys that were generated on the first boot and regenerate a new strong pair of keys and use them.

Even when the presence of the weak key, a good solution could be implemented to have a certified authority that signs the public keys of both parties to ensure that they are not the public key of the MiTM attacker machine. In that way, both parties don't start the SSH communication unless they verify that the public keys are genuine and not belonging to unknown party.

6   Results and Discussion

Upon the examination of the obtained results from the implementation and experimental procedures, a set of outcomes were drawn that could be valid on most IoT based development boards which share the same nature of the Raspberry Pi. The discussion of the findings is presented in the rest of this section.

When an attacker is performing network scanning to identify the live host, the Raspberry Pi devices could be identified from their OUI/MA-L part of the networking interfaces MAC addresses. The OUI/MA-L for the Raspberry Pi Foundation is B8-27-EB (hex) based on experimentation and the OUI standards that are maintained by IEEE. Once a Raspberry Pi device is discovered and an intensive port scanning is performed to it, it is expected to find the SSH 22/tcp port to be the only port that is open. Accordingly, attackers will be directing most of the time their attacks on this port and service raising the need to secure it as much as possible. In some other cases in addition to the SSH server being running on the Raspberry PI, a WEB server is the second most probably service that could be running as well to allow the communication and control for the users through WEB portals that are based on the Raspberry PI.

As operating system installation was the main issue that caused the Raspberry Pi to generate weak keys that are predictable, the same threat could be valid to other IoT development boards. Most development boards, uses an SD card that is having an image of the operating system to run its hardware leading to similar environments that could result in predictable keys. In other words, if two development boards with the same hardware and were booted from exactly similar SD card images while not having a big entropy pool for the random numbers generation process as the first boot then the big chance of generating similar predictable keys could be happening. Accordingly, the generated keys from the first boot must be regenerated with strong keys before stating to use the SSH service.

As it was proved earlier that Ettercap was successful in performing MiTM attack and crack the SSH V1 communication revealing the user and password in plain text, it is extremely important to prevent SSH server from allowing this version of SSH as it will be exposing the communication and credentials to the attackers.

Having an attacker granted an SSH session to the device even if was with a user that is having limited privileges could expose the system to an endless exposure. Many exploits are available that allow privilege escalation and many Linux versions are vulnerable to them. An example of privilege escalation was performed on the Raspberry Pi 3 device through the DirtyCow exploit that changes the root password from when running the DirtyCow script file from any non-root user.

When an attacker is performing MiTM attack on a SSH session, he will be providing his own public key so that the other side used it to encrypt the data instead of the destination public key. It is recommended that the public key of the administrator machine being hardcoded or another trusted certification authority is involved that signs the public keys to verify their authenticity.

7 Conclusions and Future Work

IoT devices draw a clear plan towards the future, which requires us to measure all the risks that can be exposed to these devices and propose solutions that will improve the operation of this process toward the best use without compromising privacy and security of people. In this paper, we have examined the security of SSH on Raspberry Pi Debian Jessie device and we discovered to be generating weak key pair in the first boot due to not implementing hardware number generators. It's recommended to change the default first boot key pair on any device since the randomization process and pool were not yet efficient leading to weak and predictable keys. Based on that we proposed various solutions to harden SSH on its various communication scenarios since we cannot abandon it due to its importance for communicating with the device. Thus our proposed solutions could be summarized in four points through (1) checking the configuration file on the Raspberry Pi in "/etc./ssh/sshd_config" and guarantee only Protocol 2 is allowed. (2) Using well-tested tools on other machines such as Putty in Windows environment to generate the key pair then add them to the Raspberry Pi SSH keys. (3) Implementing an indirect way to use hardware random numbers generators through suitable suggested steps. (4) Having a certified authority that signs the public keys of both parties to ensure that they are not the public key of the MiTM attacker machine.

As a future work, a controlled experiment could be conducted on multiple Raspberry Pi development boards to examine and predict the behavior of the generated first boot key pairs. After obtaining the behavior that predicts the possible key pairs, this behavior can be used to test other multiple Raspberry Pi development boards but after implementing our proposed approach in adopting hardware random number generator. As an extension to that, a script could be written to perform MiTM attack between two targets that are communicating through SSH and use the predicted key pairs to crack the communication.

References

1. Ramirez, J., Pedraza, C.: Performance analysis of communication protocols for internet of things platforms. In: 2017 IEEE Colombian Conference on Communications and Computing (COLCOM), pp. 1–7 (2017)
2. Junaid, M., Shah, M.A., Satti, I.A.: A survey of internet of things, enabling technologies and protocols. In: 2017 23rd International Conference on Automation and Computing (ICAC), pp. 1–5 (2017)
3. Pan, J., McElhannon, J.: Future edge cloud and edge computing for internet of things applications (2017)
4. Hassan, R., Jubair, A.M., Azmi, K., Bakar, A.: Adaptive congestion control mechanism in CoAP application protocol for internet of things (IoT). In: 2016 International Conference on Signal Processing and Communication (ICSC), pp. 121–125 (2016)
5. Lei, W., Xu, L.: Research and implementation of access control model of internet of things. In: 2016 5th International Conference on Computer Science and Network Technology (ICCSNT), pp. 102–106 (2016)
6. Ren, Z., Liu, X., Ye, R., Zhang, T.: Security and privacy on internet of things. In: 2017 7th IEEE International Conference on Electronics Information and Emergency Communication (ICEIEC), pp. 140–144 (2017)
7. Prabavathy, S., Sundarakantham, K., Shalinie, S.M.: Decentralized secure framework for social collaborative internet of things. In: 2017 Fourth International Conference on Signal Processing, Communication and Networking (ICSCN), pp. 1–6 (2017)
8. Marot, J., Bourennane, S.: Raspberry Pi for image processing education. 2017 25th European Signal Processing Conference (EUSIPCO), pp. 2364–2366 (2017)
9. Bhave, S., Tolentino, M., Zhu, H., Sheng, J.: Embedded middleware for distributed raspberry Pi device to enable big data applications. In: 2017 IEEE International Conference on Computational Science and Engineering (CSE) and IEEE International Conference on Embedded and Ubiquitous Computing (EUC), vol. 2. pp. 103–108 (2017)
10. Sanada, A., Nogami, Y., Iokibe, K., Khandaker, M.A.A.: Security analysis of raspberry Pi against side-channel attack with RSA cryptography. In: 2017 IEEE International Conference on Consumer Electronics - Taiwan (ICCE-TW), pp. 287–288 (2017)
11. Tavade, T., Nasikkar, P.: Raspberry Pi: data logging IOT device. In: 2017 International Conference on Power and Embedded Drive Control (ICPEDC), pp. 275–279 (2017)
12. Dowling, S., Schukat, M., Melvin, H.: A ZigBee honeypot to assess IoT cyberattack behaviour. In: 2017 28th Irish Signals and Systems Conference (ISSC), pp. 1–6 (2017)
13. Eigner, O., Kreimel, P., Tavolato, P.: Detection of man-in-the-middle attacks on industrial control networks. In: 2016 International Conference on Software Security and Assurance (ICSSA), pp. 64–69 (2016)
14. Dowling, S., Schukat, M., Melvin, H.: Using analysis of temporal variances within a honeypot dataset to better predict attack type probability. In: Proceedings of the IEEE World Congress on Internet Security, (WorldCIS 2016) (2017)
15. Song, I.-A., Lee, Y.-S.: Improvement of key exchange protocol to prevent man-in-the-middle attack in the satellite environment. In: 2016 Eighth International Conference on Ubiquitous and Future Networks (ICUFN), pp. 408–413 (2016)
16. Saqib, N.: Key exchange protocol for WSN resilient against man in the middle attack. In: 2016 IEEE International Conference on Advances in Computer Applications (ICACA), pp. 265–269 (2016)
17. Li, X., Hao, J., Feng, Z., An, B.: Optimal personalized defense strategy against Man-In-The-Middle attack. vol. 2 (2017)

18. Conti, M., Dragoni, N., Lesyk, V.: A survey of man in the middle attacks. IEEE Commun. Surv. Tutorials **18**(3), 2027–2051 (2016)
19. Shubh, T., Sharma, S.: Man-In-The-Middle-Attack prevention using HTTPS and SSL, vol. 5, no. 6, pp. 569–579 (2015)
20. Chen, Y., Dong, X., Saxena, P., Mao, J., Liang, Z.: Man-in-the-browser-cache: persisting HTTPS attacks via browser cache poisoning. Comput. Secur. **55**, 62–80 (2015)
21. Kheirkhah, E., Amin, S., Sistani, H., Acharya, H.: An experimental study of SSH attacks by using Honeypot Decoys, vol. 612, pp. 5567–5578 (2013)
22. Alsaadi, H., AlKubaisi, M.: Penetration Testing of Remote Secure OpenSSH On Raspberry Pi 2. Unpublished manuscript (2016)
23. De Luca, G.E., Carnuccio, E.A., Garcia, G.G., Barillaro, S.: IoT fall detection system for the elderly using intel Galileo development boards generation I. In: 2016 IEEE Congreso Argentino De Ciencias De La Informática y Desarrollos De Investigación (CACIDI), pp. 1–6 (2016)
24. Valverde, M.P., González, J.: A software controlled hardware acceleration architecture for image processing using an embedded development board. In: 2016 IEEE 36th Central American and Panama Convention (CONCAPAN XXXVI), pp. 1–5 (2016)
25. Mischie, S., Muntean, A.: Distance estimation through stereoscopy using BeagleBoneBlack and RaspberryPi. In: 2017 International Symposium on Signals, Circuits and Systems (ISSCS), pp. 1–4 (2017)
26. Sukvichai, K., Wongsuwan, K., Kaewnark, N., Wisanuvej, P.: Implementation of visual odometry estimation for underwater robot on ROS by using RaspberryPi 2. In: 2016 International Conference on Electronics, Information, and Communications (ICEIC), pp. 1–4 (2016)
27. Coonjah, I., Catherine, P.C., Soyjaudah, K.M.S.: Performance evaluation and analysis of layer 3 tunneling between OpenSSH and OpenVPN in a wide area network environment. In: 2015 International Conference on Computing, Communication and Security (ICCCS), pp. 1–4 (2015)
28. Coonjah, I., Catherine, P.C., Soyjaudah, K.M.S.: A VPN framework through multi-layer tunnels based on OpenSSH. In: International Conference on Computing, Communication & Automation, pp. 1395–1401 (2015)
29. Studiawan, H., Pratomo, B.A., Anggoro, R.: Clustering of SSH brute-force attack logs using k-clique percolation. In: 2016 International Conference on Information & Communication Technology and Systems (ICTS), pp. 39–42 (2016)
30. Sadasivam, G.K., Hota, C., Anand, B.: Classification of SSH attacks using machine learning algorithms. In: 2016 6th International Conference on IT Convergence and Security (2016)

IEEE 802.11 Latency Modeling with Non-IEEE 802.11 Interfering Source

Patrick Bosch[✉], Steven Latré, and Chris Blondia

University of Antwerp - imec, Antwerp, Belgium
{patrick.bosch,steven.latre,chris.blondia}@uantwerpen.be
https://www.uantwerpen.be/en/research-groups/idlab/

Abstract. IEEE 802.11 network deployments are ubiquitous and provide connectivity to millions of users. Interference that originates from other technologies, like simple Radio Frequency (RF) equipment, severely degrades the performance of those networks. To effectively manage wireless networks, the interference needs to be modeled and predicted. The current state of the art models are insufficient to model performance correctly. In this letter, we describe the interference as an interrupted Poisson process and use a decomposition approach to predict the latency of an interfered client from the latency of a non-interfered client. This novel approach allows for fast and easy prediction of latency in an interfered network. The results show that our method gets as close as 6% of the real value.

Keywords: IEEE 802.11 networks · Interference · Latency prediction

1 Introduction

Since the beginning of IEEE 802.11 networks, interference from overlapping networks degrades the performance, especially in large and dense deployments [3,10]. The main reason for this degradation is the Carrier Sense Multiple Access with Collision Avoidance (CSMA/CA) Listen-Before-Talk (LBT) protocol of IEEE 802.11. It uses Carrier Sense (CS) and Energy Detection (ED) to detect whether the channel is busy and defers from sending when it is. A failed attempt results in an increased random back-off and in the end to a dropped packet. With recent technologies, the spectrum of IEEE 802.11 becomes severely crowded, which has an impact on the performance, especially when they do not adhere to an LBT protocol. Many daily appliances with RF capabilities like baby phones, television screens, or microphones, can have an impact [5,11,14]. The more such appliances are employed, for example at a concert, the more impact they have. However, also Long-Term Evolution (LTE) in the unlicensed band can lead to up to 98% throughput loss if no LBT protocol is employed [1,6]. This severe performance degradation makes network management increasingly difficult and a solution to predict latency depending on the interference is needed.

© IFIP International Federation for Information Processing 2019
Published by Springer Nature Switzerland AG 2019
M. Di Felice et al. (Eds.): WWIC 2019, LNCS 11618, pp. 40–50, 2019.
https://doi.org/10.1007/978-3-030-30523-9_4

Several studies analyzed the latency of IEEE 802.11 networks. Initially, the focus was throughput, but soon it became broader and included latency, jitter, packet loss, and error-prone channels as well [2,7,8,13]. The main component of all of these works is the Markov chain to model the IEEE 802.11 back-off mechanism. While this allows for an accurate representation thereof, it also makes computation slow as it is needed to solve it numerically. These works all lack to assess the impact of non-IEEE 802.11 interference though, which can have a significant impact [4]. The base performance, however, or the one obtained from a real setup without interference, can be used to calculate the performance when interference is present.

In this article, we propose a fast and accurate analytical model that can predict the latency with an interfering source present from latency when no interfering source is present. We use an interrupted Poisson process as a model for the interfering source. Taking into account three characteristics of the IEEE Medium Access Control (MAC), we can accurately describe the latency in such a system. Our measurement results show that the latency we observe correlates with the latency of our prediction. This is especially useful when deploying wireless networks in challenging environments like large concerts or conferences.

2 Characterizing an Interfering Source

To correctly model the interfering source, we take an on/off process with exponentially distributed on and off periods as a basis. The interruptions of the medium access by the interfering source, which generates energy above the ED threshold, occurs according to a Poisson process with rate ν. Different sources can be modeled in this form, for example, a microwave oven or baby phone [12]. We assume that during an ongoing interruption no new interruptions occur. The variable u denotes the random variable representing the length of the interruptions. We assume that u is exponentially distributed with mean $E[u]$. With the Poisson assumption in mind, the average time that the interfering source is inactive is given by $\frac{1}{\nu}$. In contrast, the fraction of the time the interfering source is active is given by:

$$p_a = \frac{E[u]}{E[u] + \frac{1}{\nu}} \tag{1}$$

3 Modeling Latency

3.1 Description of the Latency Components

An interfering source has three major effects on the operation of the IEEE 802.11 MAC protocol.

The first is based on the ED function of an IEEE 802.11 station which senses for energy on the channel before it tries to send a packet. When the interfering source becomes active, the station detects energy on the channel and defers from transmitting a packet for $E[u]$ seconds on average.

Next, when the interfering source becomes active at the time a packet is being transmitted, the packet collides with the signal of the interfering source and is lost. Not only a re-transmission of the packet is the result, but it also adds additional latency in the form of a doubled contention window for the next back-off phase.

Third, stations with a packet at the head of the queue during the time the interfering source is active will sense the medium busy. As soon as the interfering source stops transmitting, the stations will enter in a back-off phase. If a station is in the back-off phase during the activity of the interfering source, it has to stop the process and needs to wait until the medium is considered free again.

3.2   Computing Average Latency in a System with Interference

We will first take the unavailability of the medium and the increased CW into account. Consider an IEEE 802.11 network with N stations, which are equally loaded. We model a station as a finite capacity single server queue with Poisson input with rate λ where the service time equals the sum of the IEEE 802.11 access latency and the transmission time itself. We will model the activity of the interfering source as service interrupts. Computing the latency in this M/M/1/K queue with service interruptions will result in the average packet latency of a station.

For a random variable d, we denote $D(t)$ its cumulative distribution, respectively $D^*(s)$ its Laplace-Stieltjes Transform (LST). $E[d]$ denotes its mean value. The service time of a packet consists of two major parts, access latency and the transmission time of the packet itself. The service time is denoted by b_{ni}, respectively b_{wi}, in the system without interference, respectively the system with interference. Let b denote the transmission time of a packet. We make the additional assumption that both b_{ni} and b_{wi} are exponentially distributed. This turns the model of a station in a system with and without interference into an M/M/1/K queue. Let d_{ni} and d_{wi} be the packet latency respectively in the system without interference and in the system with interference.

First, we derive a formula for the LST of the service time in a system with interference $B^*_{wi}(s)$, as a function of the LST of the packet latency in a system without interference $B^*_{ni}(s)$. We follow reasoning similar to the one by Fiems et al., where the service interruptions are the active periods of the interfering source [9]. We consider three cases, depending on the start of the first time the interfering source becomes active after a packet starts its service in relation to the different components of this service time.

First case: the interfering source does not become active during the service time. In this case, the service time in the system with interference is the same as the service time in a system without interference.

Second case: the interfering source becomes active during the access latency of a packet. In this case, the time the interfering source is active needs to be added to the service time in a system without interference.

Third case: the interfering source becomes active during the transmission time of a packet. In this case, not only the time the interfering source is active needs to be added to the service time, but also an additional time since the MAC protocol reacts on this interrupt of the transmission by doubling the contention window. Let a be the random variable representing the additional access latency of a packet whose transmission was interrupted by the interfering source. Note that this case includes the added latency of the paused back-off mechanism when a packet is at the head of the queue.

Assume that the service time in the system without interference is given by x.

1. No interrupt by the interfering source occurs during the service time, which happens with probability $e^{-\nu x}$. In this case

$$B^*_{wi}(s|x) = e^{-(\nu+s)x} \tag{2}$$

   where $B^*_{wi}(s|x)$ denotes the LST of b_{wi}, given that the service time in the system without interference is x.

2. An interrupt by the interfering source occurs during the access latency (i.e., during $[0, x - b[$). This happens with probability $1 - e^{-\nu(x-b)}$. In this case

$$B^*_{wi}(s|x) = \frac{\nu}{\nu + s} \cdot V^*(s) \cdot B^*_{wi}(s) \cdot (1 - e^{-(\nu+s)(x-b)}) \tag{3}$$

3. An interrupt by the interfering source occurs during the transmission time (i.e., during $[x - b, x[$). This happens with probability $e^{-\nu(x-b)} - e^{-\nu b}$. In this case

$$B^*_{wi}(s|x) = \frac{\nu}{\nu + s} \cdot V^*(s) \cdot A^*(s) \cdot B^*_{wi}(s) \cdot (e^{-(\nu+s)(x-b)} - e^{-(\nu+s)x}) \tag{4}$$

Combining the three cases, we obtain

$$\begin{aligned}
B^*_{wi}(s|x) &= e^{-(\nu+s)x} + \frac{\nu}{\nu + s} \cdot V^*(s) \cdot B^*_{wi}(s) \cdot (1 - e^{-(\nu+s)(x-b)}) \\
&+ \frac{\nu}{\nu + s} \cdot V^*(s) \cdot A^*(s) \cdot B^*_{wi}(s) \cdot (e^{-(\nu+s)(x-b)} - e^{-(\nu+s)x})
\end{aligned} \tag{5}$$

Integrating over all possible service times x leads to

$$\begin{aligned}
B^*_{wi}(s) &= B^*_{ni}(\nu + s) + \frac{\nu}{\nu + s} \cdot V^*(s) \cdot B^*_{wi}(s) \cdot (1 - e^{(\nu+s)b} \cdot B^*_{ni}(\nu + s)) \\
&+ \frac{\nu}{\nu + s} \cdot V^*(s) \cdot A^*(s) \cdot B^*_{wi}(s) \cdot (e^{(\nu+s)b} \cdot B^*_{ni}(\nu + s) - B^*_{ni}(\nu + s)) \quad (6)
\end{aligned}$$

Since

$$E[b_{wi}] = -\frac{d \cdot B^*_{wi}(s)}{ds}\Big|_{s=0} \tag{7}$$

we obtain that

$$E[b_{wi}] = \frac{1}{\nu \cdot B^*_{ni}(\nu)} \cdot (1 - B^*_{ni}(\nu)) \cdot (1 + \nu \cdot E[v]) + E[a] \cdot (e^{\nu b} - 1) \tag{8}$$

Given the assumption that b_{ni} is exponentially distributed, we obtain

$$E[b_{wi}] = E[b_{ni}] \cdot (1 + \nu \cdot E[v]) + E[a] \cdot (e^{\nu b} - 1) \tag{9}$$

Let us compute $E[a]$. The probability that the interfering source becomes active while a packet is being transmitted is given by

$$\int_0^b \nu e^{-\nu b} dt = 1 - e^{-\nu b} \tag{10}$$

with b being the time needed to transmit a packet.

Hence, the probability that the interfering source becomes active during each of the consecutive i re-transmissions of a packet and not during the $(i+1)^{\text{th}}$ is given by

$$(1 - e^{-\nu b})^i \cdot e^{-\nu b} \tag{11}$$

Assuming $CW_{min} = 63$, $CW_{max} = 1023$ and for the 5th and 6th re-transmission $CW = 1023$, the value of $E[a]$ is given by

$$E[a] = \sum_{i=1}^{5} 2^{4+i} \cdot (1 - e^{-\nu b})^i \cdot e^{-\nu b} + 2^9 \cdot [1 - \sum_{i=0}^{5} (1 - e^{-\nu b})^i \cdot e^{-\nu b}] \tag{12}$$

To take the increased latency of the paused back-off mechanism into account when the packet is at the head of the queue we consider the behavior of stations when the interfering source becomes active similar to their behavior when other stations transmit packets. Therefore, we express the activity of the interference source in terms of packet transmissions. The fraction of the time the interference source is active is given by p_a. Let n_{if} be the number of packets per second that could be sent during an active period of the interference source. Then

$$n_{if} = \frac{p_a}{b + c} \tag{13}$$

with c being the transmission time of an acknowledgment. For the latency computation with interference, the packet arrival rate is given by

$$\lambda_a = \lambda + \frac{n_{if}}{N} \tag{14}$$

and will be used to derive the performance measures for the system with interference.

To compute the average packet latency in a system with interference $E[d_{wi}]$, given the average packet latency in the system without interference $E[d_{ni}]$, using the relationship between $E[b_{wi}]$ and $E[b_{ni}]$ as established above, assume that the number of stations N and the packet arrival rate λ are given. Let K be the length of the MAC queue in a station. The random variables l_{ni} and l_{wi} denote the number of packets in a station without and with interference. Let

$$\rho_{ni} = \lambda \cdot E[b_{ni}] \tag{15}$$

respectively,

$$\rho_{wi} = \lambda_a \cdot E[b_{wi}] \tag{16}$$

be the load of a station without, respectively, with interference. Assume that we know the average latency $E[d_{ni}]$ of a packet in a system without interference and that a station in the system without interference is modeled as an M/M/1/K queue. Given Little's law, the average number of packets in the station is given by

$$E[l_{ni}] = \lambda_{eff_{ni}} \cdot E[d_{ni}] \tag{17}$$

where

$$\lambda_{eff_{ni}} = \lambda_a \cdot (1 - \frac{1 - \rho_{ni}}{1 - \rho_{ni}^{K+1}} \cdot \rho_{ni}^K) \tag{18}$$

is the effective packet arrival rate in the system without interference.

Then, the average number of packets, $E[l_{ni}]$, is also given by the formula

$$E[l_{ni}] = \rho_{ni} \cdot \frac{1 - (K+1) \cdot \rho_{ni}^K + K \cdot \rho_{ni}^{K+1}}{(1 - \rho_{ni}) \cdot (1 - \rho_{ni}^{K+1})} \tag{19}$$

From Eqs. 17 and 19 we derive the value of ρ_{ni}. This leads to

$$E[b_{ni}] = \frac{\rho_{ni}}{\lambda_a} \tag{20}$$

Now it is possible to compute $E[b_{wi}]$ using Eq. 9. Once $E[b_{wi}]$ is known, it is possible to compute

$$\rho_{wi} = \lambda \cdot E[b_{wi}]. \tag{21}$$

Using Eq. 19 for the system with interference, we derive $E[l_{wi}]$ and applying Little's formula leads to the average latency in a system with interference

$$E[d_{wi}] = \frac{E[l_{wi}]}{\lambda_{eff_{wi}}} \tag{22}$$

with

$$\lambda_{eff_{wi}} = \lambda \cdot (1 - \frac{1 - \rho_{wi}}{1 - \rho_{wi}^{K+1}} \cdot \rho_{wi}^K) \tag{23}$$

4   Results

4.1   Experimental Setup

For our experimental study, the w-ilab.t[1] lab facility, a large-scale emulation platform with wireless nodes allowing extensive experiments, has been used. Configurations of 15, 20, and 25 stations on the 5 GHz band with IEEE 802.11a were used. All stations are connected to a single access point (AP), and a test

---

[1] http://doc.ilabt.imec.be/ilabt-documentation/index.html.

includes transmitting packets for 60 s with a repetition of 5 times for each configuration. To generate interference according to the previously defined model in Sect. 2, we installed a Software Defined Radio (SDR).

Two modes of interference occurrence were used in the experiment: low occurrence with $\frac{1}{\nu}$ equal to $9 \cdot 10^{-4}$ s and high occurrence with $\frac{1}{\nu}$ equal to $1.8 \cdot 10^{-4}$ s. The duration of interference $E[u]$ was set to three different modes: low ($9 \cdot 10^{-5}$ s), medium ($4.5 \cdot 10^{-4}$ s), and high ($9 \cdot 10^{-4}$ s). The packets have a size of 1500 bytes and are sent at a fixed bit rate of 54 Mbps. The sending rate of packets per second had a minimum of 25 and a maximum of 200 packets per second with an interval of 25 packets per second. A continuous packet source was used to generate packets on the MAC layer according to a Poisson process. The queue length is given by $K = 64$.

4.2 Validation

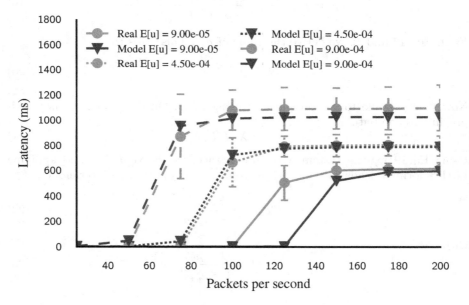

Fig. 1. Latency with interference $1/\nu = 9 \cdot 10^{-4}$ with 15 stations.

There are two significant elements to assess the accuracy of the model, the saturation point and the maximum average latency when the system is saturated. Saturation is the state when the maximum capacity of the wireless network is reached and depends on the number of stations, the number of packets per station, and the characteristics of the interfering source. Note that, as we only have measurement results with steps of 25 packets per second, interpolation was used when applying Eq. 17.

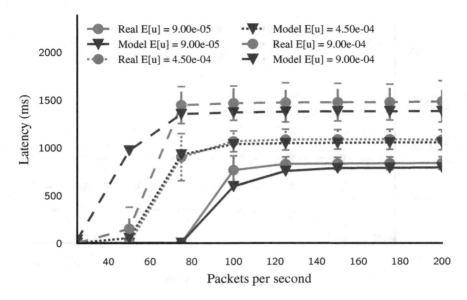

Fig. 2. Latency with interference $1/\nu = 9 \cdot 10^{-4}$ with 20 stations.

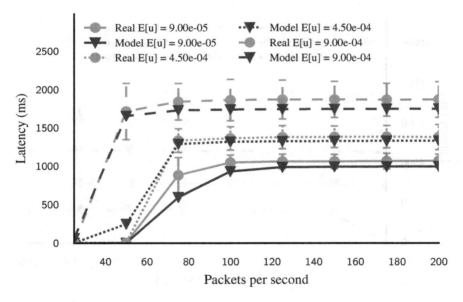

Fig. 3. Latency with interference $1/\nu = 9 \cdot 10^{-4}$ with 25 stations.

Low Occurrence. Figures 1, 2, and 3 present the graphs for 15, 20, and 25 stations and $1/\nu = 9 \cdot 10^{-4}$ s. In 8 out of 9 cases the saturation point is accurately matched. Only in the case of 15 stations and with the shortest duration was the saturation

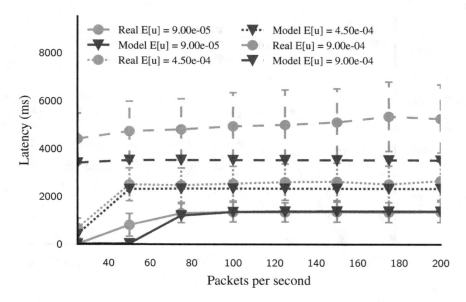

Fig. 4. Latency with interference $1/\nu = 1.8 \cdot 10^{-4}$ s with 15 stations.

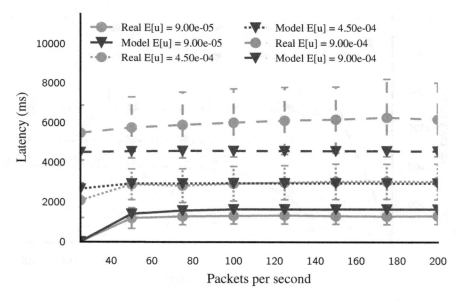

Fig. 5. Latency with interference $1/\nu = 1.8 \cdot 10^{-4}$ s with 20 stations.

point predicted too early. The latency prediction at saturation is within 6–7% of the average latency, while a higher number of stations leads to higher accuracy.

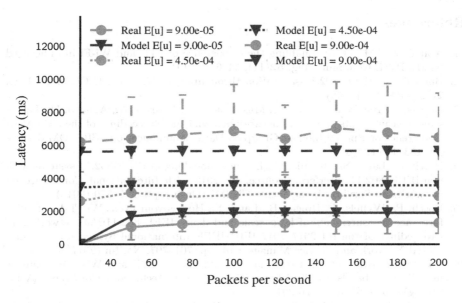

Fig. 6. Latency with interference $1/\nu = 1.8 \cdot 10^{-4}$ s with 25 stations.

High Occurrence. Figures 4, 5, and 6 show similar results for $1/\nu = 4.5 \cdot 10^{-4}$ s. The saturation point is accurately matched in 8 out of 9 cases, again except for 15 stations and the shortest duration, and the accuracy of the latency at saturation is within 13–50%. The high duration is an outlier with any number of station. The airtime usage of the interfering source amounts to 83% of the available airtime. The difficulty of prediction stems from the low amount of successful packets, as can be seen by the confidence interval.

The results show that the accuracy is high and that our proposed method can be used in further network management.

5   Conclusion

In this article, we developed an analytical model that allows predicting the average latency a station of an IEEE 802.11 network experiences in the presence of an interfering source assuming that the latency without interference is known. Three characteristics drive this model: the time the medium is busy during the activity of the interfering source, the interruption and increased CW of a station, and the additional latency of a station that has a packet ready to transmit when the source becomes active. We demonstrated the accuracy of our model using real-life measurements. The accuracy of the model increases with the number of stations, which is especially crucial for dense deployments.

Acknowledgment. Patrick Bosch is funded by FWO, a fund for fundamental scientific research, and the Flemish Government, under grant number 1S56616N.

References

1. Abinader, F.M., et al.: Enabling the coexistence of LTE and Wi-Fi in unlicensed bands. IEEE Commun. Mag. **52**(11), 54–61 (2014)
2. Bianchi, G.: IEEE 802.11-saturation throughput analysis. IEEE Commun. Lett. **2**(12), 318–320 (1998)
3. Biswas, S., Bicket, J., Wong, E., Musaloiu-E, R., Bhartia, A., Aguayo, D.: Large-scale measurements of wireless network behavior. In: Proceedings of the 2015 ACM Conference on Special Interest Group on Data Communication - SIGCOMM 2015, pp. 153–165 (2015)
4. Bosch, P., Latré, S., Blondia, C.: Latency modelling in IEEE 802.11 systems with non-IEEE 802.11 interfering source. In: 2018 14th International Conference on Network and Service Management (CNSM) (Cnsm), pp. 275–279 (2018)
5. Bosch, P., Wyffels, J., Braem, B., Latré, S.: How is your event Wi-Fi doing? Performance measurements of large-scale and dense IEEE 802.11n/ac networks. In: Proceedings of the IM 2017–2017 IFIP/IEEE International Symposium on Integrated Network and Service Management, pp. 701–707, No. Im (2017)
6. Cavalcante, A.M., et al.: Performance evaluation of LTE and Wi-Fi coexistence in unlicensed bands. In: 2013 IEEE 77th Vehicular Technology Conference (VTC Spring), pp. 1–6, No. April 2015 (2013)
7. Daneshgaran, F., Laddomada, M., Mesiti, F., Mondin, M.: Unsaturated throughput analysis of IEEE 802.11 in presence of non ideal transmission channel and capture effects. IEEE Trans. Wireless Commun. **7**(4), 1276–1286 (2008)
8. Felemban, E., Ekici, E.: Single hop IEEE 802.11 DCF analysis revisited: accurate modeling of channel access delay and throughput for saturated and unsaturated traffic cases. IEEE Trans. Wireless Commun. **10**(10), 3256–3266 (2011)
9. Fiems, D., Maertens, T., Bruneel, H.: Queueing systems with different types of server interruptions. Eur. J. Oper. Res. **188**(3), 838–845 (2008)
10. Fuxjäger, P., Valerio, D., Ricciato, F.: The myth of non-overlapping channels: interference measurements in IEEE 802.11. In: 2007 Fourth Annual Conference on Wireless on Demand Network Systems and Services, WONS 2007, pp. 1–8 (2007)
11. Gollakota, S., Adib, F., Katabi, D., Seshan, S.: Clearing the RF smog: making 802.11 robust to cross-technology interference. In: Proceedings of the ACM SIGCOMM 2011 Conference on SIGCOMM - SIGCOMM 2011, p. 170 (2011)
12. Kanemoto, H., Miyamoto, S., Morinaga, N.: Statistical model of microwave oven interference and optimum reception. In: 1998 IEEE International Conference on Communications, ICC 1998, Conference Record, Affiliated with SUPERCOMM 1998 (Cat. No. 98CH36220), vol. 3, pp. 1660–1664 (1998)
13. Raptis, P., Vitsas, V., Paparrizos, K.: Packet delay metrics for IEEE 802.11 distributed coordination function. Mob. Netw. Appl. **14**(6), 772–781 (2009)
14. Rayanchu, S., Patro, A., Banerjee, S.: Airshark: detecting non-WiFi RF devices using commodity WiFi hardware. In: Proceedings of the 2011 ACM SIGCOMM Conference on Internet Measurement Conference - IMC 2011, p. 137 (2011)

Security and Network Management

ChoKIFA: A New Detection and Mitigation Approach Against Interest Flooding Attacks in NDN

Abdelmadjid Benarfa[1], Muhammad Hassan[2]([⊠]), Alberto Compagno[3],
Eleonora Losiouk[2], Mohamed Bachir Yagoubi[1], and Mauro Conti[2]

[1] University of Laghouat, Laghouat, Algeria
{a.benarfa,m.yagoubi}@lagh-univ.dz
[2] University of Padova, Padova, Italy
{hassan,elosiouk,conti}@math.unipd.it
[3] Cisco Systems, Paris, France
acompagn@cisco.com

Abstract. Named-Data Networking (NDN) is a potential Future Internet Architectures which introduces a shift from the existing host-centric IP-based Internet infrastructure towards a content-oriented one. Its design, however, can be misused to introduce a new type of DoS attack, better known as Interest Flooding Attack (IFA). In IFA, an adversary issues non-satisfiable requests in the network to saturate the Pending Interest Table(s) (PIT) of NDN routers and prevent them from properly handling the legitimate traffic. Prior solutions to mitigate this problem are not highly effective, damages the legitimate traffic, and incurs high communication overhead.

In this paper, we propose a novel mechanism for IFA detection and mitigation, aimed at reducing the memory consumption of the PIT by effectively reducing the malicious traffic that passes through each NDN router. In particular, our protocol exploits an effective management strategy on the PIT which differentially penalizes the malicious traffic by dropping both the inbound and already stored malicious traffic from the PIT. We implemented our proposed protocol on the open-source ndnSIM simulator and compared its effectiveness with the one achieved by the existing state-of-the-art. The results show that our proposed protocol effectively reduces the IFA damages, especially on the legitimate traffic, with improvements that go from 5% till 40% with respect to the existing state-of-the-art.

Keywords: NDN · DDoS attack · IFA · PIT management · Congestion

1 Introduction

Numerous solutions have been proposed to narrow the gap between the Internet design and its current usage. One such potential Future Internet Architecture

© IFIP International Federation for Information Processing 2019
Published by Springer Nature Switzerland AG 2019
M. Di Felice et al. (Eds.): WWIC 2019, LNCS 11618, pp. 53–65, 2019.
https://doi.org/10.1007/978-3-030-30523-9_5

(FIA), sponsored by NSF, is Name Data Networking (NDN) [13]. NDN explicitly addresses the data (content) itself instead of its physical location (i.e., host) in the network, therefore, transforming data into the "first-class" entity. In NDN, consumer directly requests the name of the *content* by issuing an *interest*. The network then handles the request by efficiently finding and retrieving back the closest copy of the relevant content. This decoupling of time and space among request resolution and content transfer enables NDN to provide storage, mobility and security as native features belonging to the network architecture [13].

One of the key goals of NDN is "security by design", this paper addresses the most significant NDN-tailored DDoS attack: the *Interest Flooding Attack* (IFA) [6]. In IFA, adversary aims at flooding the network and blocking the network services received by legitimate users via abusing two fundamental NDN features [9], i.e., (i) forwarding grounded on the longest name-prefix match, and (ii) maintaining the record of outstanding forwarded interests in so-called *Pending Interest Table (PIT)* for efficient multicasting. In particular, the adversary issues unique requests for unsatisfiable content name targeting the name-space(s). As a consequence, one PIT entry is created for each request in each on-path NDN router. These entries stays in the PITs till they expire at the end. Succeeding to overload some or all PITs which leads to legitimate interest packets being dropped [6]. Regardless of the substantial quantity of research on NDN security, we identified that the proposed defence mechanisms for IFA [1,3,4,6,9] have one or more of the following limitations. First, the legitimate traffic is likely to be damaged, since most of the proposed countermeasures [1,3,12] limits the rate of incoming traffic and are not able to differentiate between legitimate and malicious packets, thus resulting in unfair punishments. Second, since each router has to perform first an attack detection and then attack mitigation, during the first phase (i.e., inaccurate), most of the approaches are likely to encounter harmful consequences. Finally, the proposed collaborative mechanisms [1,3,4,9] introduces unnecessary overhead given by the extra messages exchanged among routers.

We propose an efficient mechanism, named as Choose To Kill IFA (ChoKIFA), which mitigates the damages caused by IFA by differentiating the malicious traffic from the legitimate one, and by reducing the former, without any collaborative communication or global network monitoring. In order to do so, ChoKIFA exploits the Active Queue Management (AQM) scheme, i.e., CHOose and Keep for responsive flows, CHOose and Kill for unresponsive flows (CHOKe) [8], and without any delay penalizes the malicious traffic by dropping both the new incoming malicious interests and removing the ones already stored in the PIT. Thus, routers are able to independently detect and mitigate the attack in progress as-soon and as-close to the adversary as possible, while maintaining the simplicity of forwarding. We evaluate the effectiveness of ChoKIFA through extensive simulations on ndnSIM simulator [2], and by comparing it with the state-of-the-art mitigation approaches [1]. The results show that ChoKIFA effectively mitigates the adverse effects of IFA in the network. In particular, ChoKIFA is able to guarantee legitimate interest satisfaction rate up to 97% and it shows up to 40% less false positives in comparison with rate limiting mitigation approaches.

Organization: We present the overview of IFA in Sect. 2. Section 3 illustrates the existing mitigation approaches against IFA. Section 4 briefly describes the proposed protocol including system, adversary model and working methodology of ChoKIFA. Section 5 present the implementation, evaluation and comparison of ChoKIFA against IFA and state of the art. Finally, Sect. 6 concludes the paper.

2   Interest Flooding Attacks in NDN

In NDN, routers maintain per-packet state for each interest packet in PIT. Therefore, the immense amount of malicious interests can result in exhaustion of routers memory and resources, and prevent them from creating PIT entries for new incoming traffic, resulting in the disrupt of benign users services. In particular, IFAs are categorized on three types based on the type of content requested by the adversary [6]: (i) existing or static content, where adversary generates a large number of interests for an existing content that propagates through all intervening routers caches. In result, legitimate interests for the same content are not able to reach the producer(s) since they are being satisfied by the cached copies. This type of attack is quite restricted since in-network content *caching* provides a built-in countermeasure. (ii) Dynamically generated content, where adversary issues dynamic requests for existing content, therefore, all interests are propagated towards the producer(s), resulting in bandwidth consumption and PIT exhaustion. Correspondingly, targeted producer wastes considerable computational resources due to signing the content (i.e., per-packet operation). Lastly, (iii) non-existent content, where adversary requests for unique non-existent (unsatisfiable) content. These interests cannot be collapsed by routers, and are routed towards the producer(s). Such interest packets consume memory in router's PIT until they expire due to "interest lifetime". Thus, a massive number of non-existent interest packets in the PIT table leads to benign interest packets being dropped in the network [1,3,6].

We focus on the IFA where adversary generates unsatisfiable interests. Using a valid name *prefix*, there are many ways to generate these unsatisfiable interests, e.g., (i) by enabling the name of the interest to */prefix/nonce*, where the suffix *nonce* is a random value. Such interests are propagated throughout towards the producer and are never satisfied. (ii) By swapping the `Publisher Public Key Digest` [6] field to a random value. Subsequently, no public key would match this value, therefore, will never be satisfied. (iii) Lastly, by setting the `Interest Exclude filter` to exclude all existing content starting with */prefix*. In consequence, the interest can never be satisfied as it concurrently requests and excludes the same content.

3   Related Works

Several defense mechanisms against IFA are proposed which implements detection and reaction approach, similarly, in an independent or collaborative manner (unlike securing routing protocols in IP [10]). In independent systems, the detection of attack is largely based on network traffic analysis and(or) PIT usage, while the subsequent reaction mechanisms reduce the incoming/outgoing traffic, independently on each router. For instance, Afanasayev et al. [1] proposed four different methods to deal with IFA. The first method introduces a "simple limit" on the interfaces based on the physical capacity of the links, resulting in under-utilization of the network. The second method which is an alteration of "token fairness" algorithm, regulates the number of outgoing interests by limiting the assigned tokens to a specific outgoing interface. The drawback of this method is that it does not discriminate between benign and malicious traffic while assigning the tokens, and relatively admits a large number of malicious interests. The third method is based on the per-interface ratio between interests and their corresponding data packets for attack detection, namely "satisfaction-based". The work in [3,4,6] also adopts similar phenomena, where the mitigation is performed by reducing (or blocking) the requesting rate of detected nodes. The drawback of this method is that each router decides to forward/discard interest(s) using its local estimation of interest satisfaction ratio. Thus, the probability of benign interests being forwarded declines as the number of hops between the consumer and the producer increases [1]. The last method is a collaborative approach called as "satisfaction-based pushback". In this case, [1,3,4], each router sets an explicit limit value for each incoming interface, and announce this value to all downstream routers. This method has shown to be more effective than previous, but the legitimate stream is still influenced, especially when the path is long. Moreover, it creates unnecessary signalling overhead in the network.

In particular, all the countermeasures aims to limit the number of overall incoming interests (i.e., including benign and malicious), either at each interface [1,3] or router [4]. Therefore, results in performance degradation of legitimate users and requires further enhancements in terms of traffic differentiation between benign and malicious traffic.

4   Mitigation of IFA Exploiting AQM

In this paper, we take a footstep in the direction of identifying and differentiating malicious packets from the benign traffic during IFA. By exploiting the phenomena of AQM [8], we design an algorithm, i.e., CHOose to Kill malicious Interest, CHOose to keep genuine Interest for IFA (ChoKIFA) which aims to provide fairness among the benign interest packets that pass through the router. In particular, ChoKIFA utilizes the PIT state which forms adequate statistics regarding the incoming and outgoing interest packets and use it to identify and drop malicious interest packets.

4.1   System and Adversary Model

In our system model, we consider the topology illustrated in Fig. 1, as used by various authors [1,4]. Multiple benign consumers (C) issues Benign Interests

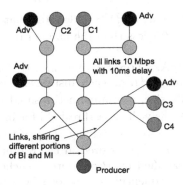

Fig. 1. Topology considered.

(BIs) for existing content towards a producer (P) which is publishing the content under specific name prefix $(prefix)$. BIs and the corresponding content packets traverse multiple routers (R) before being satisfied by P. Each router $r_i^j \in |R|$ has the default settings of NDN [13], where j is the interface of i-th router.

We assume that adversary (Adv) generates massive amount Malicious Interests (MIs) which have bogus names to request non-existing content (i.e., type three, see Sect. 2). The aim of Adv is to saturate R's PIT, in particular, by rapid generation of large numbers of MIs [1,3]. Once the PIT is completely full, incoming BIs are being dropped. Apart from that, this has more than a few consequences. First, the sending rate of MIs is not dependent on the allocated bandwidth [6]. Secondly, MIs cannot be replied back by the $R's$ caches. Lastly, if created sophisticatedly (i.e., with a random component at the end of each name-prefix such as $prefix/Rnd$) MIs are never collapsed until the interests decay. All these effects allows Adv to efficiently fill up $R's$ PIT, which makes the attack more damaging than type one and type two IFA. In addition, without the loss of generality, we assume that Adv is capable to corrupt set of C (i.e., botnet), through which it triggers the attack [1,3]. Lastly, the percentage of bots is taken 50% with the ratio of C in the whole network [1].

4.2 ChoKIFA: CHOose to Kill Interest Flooding Attack

In this section, we present the details our proposed mitigation mechanism for IFA. In order to be effective in defending against IFA, ChoKIFA exploits traffic flow as an attribute to differentiate and penalize the MIs from BIs. Unlike IP, where traffic flow measurement relates to the accountable attributes such as source/destination address, interface number, packets/bytes counts forwarded (source to destination), backward (destination to source) counts and so on. In NDN, following content oriented communication model, traffic flow is centered around series of packets that corresponds to specific piece of data [7]. Considering this, we design the three novel attributes to compare incoming traffic flow at each router: (i) name-prefix match, (ii) interface match, and (iii) level of interest satisfaction ratio, i.e., rate between incoming interests to outgoing content, denoted as $\delta(r_i^j)$. In particular, $\delta(r_i^j) > 1$ denotes that the number of content packets received at router r_i^j is less than the number of interests forwarded from the same interface.

In order to mitigate IFA, ChoKIFA dynamically computes the actual size of the PIT, denoted as $\rho_{size}(r_i^j)$, at each instance. Further, ChoKIFA marks two thresholds on the PIT size, a minimum threshold ($\rho_{th}^{min}(r_i^j)$) and a maximum threshold ($\rho_{th}^{max}(r_i^j)$), as well as, a threshold for interest satisfaction ratio, denoted as $\delta_{th}(r_i^j)$. For each interest arriving at r_i^j, if the actual PIT size is less than the $\rho_{th}^{min}(r_i^j)$, the interest gets stored in the router's PIT. If all the interests requested by C are satisfied by P or router's cache, then PIT size should not reach up to $\rho_{th}^{min}(r_i^j)$, frequently. In case of IFA, when the actual PIT size is greater than $\rho_{th}^{min}(r_i^j)$ and less than $\rho_{th}^{max}(r_i^j)$, each new incoming interest is compared with the randomly selected interest from PIT, named as *drop interest candidate*. If both the interests have the same traffic flow then both are dropped. This choice is motivated by the fact that all the entries in PIT are likely to be occupied by MIs (i.e., under IFA). On the other side, when the PIT size goes more than $\rho_{th}^{max}(r_i^j)$, all the new incoming interest are being dropped. This leads the PIT occupancy back to below $\rho_{th}^{max}(r_i^j)$.

The key attributes to identify the traffic flow of each new incoming interest are three subsequent conditions: (i) if it holds the same prefix as of drop interest candidate, (ii) if it is coming from the same incoming interface as of *drop interest candidate*, and (iii) if both the above conditions holds true, then router compares if the current $\delta(r_i^j)$ exceeds $\delta_{th}(r_i^j)$. In contrast, if the new incoming interest is not having the same traffic flow as of drop interest candidate then the randomly selected interest is remained stored in PIT, and the incoming interest is dropped/accepted with the probability (P_b) which depends on the average PIT size ($\rho_{avg}(r_i^j)$), as illustrated in Eq. 1 [5].

$$P_b = \frac{P_{max} * (\rho_{avg}(r_i^j) - \rho_{th}^{max}(r_i^j))}{(\rho_{th}^{max}(r_i^j) - \rho_{th}^{min}(r_i^j))}, \tag{1}$$

here P_{max} denotes the maximum probability[1]. As the average PIT size varies from $\rho_{th}^{min}(r_i^j)$ to $\rho_{th}^{max}(r_i^j)$, the interest dropping probability P_b varies from 0 to P_{max}. In particular, the interest dropping probability is computed by exploiting the mechanism of packet dropping probability of Random Early Detection (RED) [5]. A detailed flow chart of ChoKIFA is given in Fig. 2.

4.3 Parameters Setting

The parameters, $\rho_{avg}(r_i^j)$, $\rho_{th}^{min}(r_i^j)$ and $\rho_{th}^{max}(r_i^j)$ are essential as they directly impact on the interest dropping probability. Below we illustrate few rules for parameter's setting which give effective performance for ChoKIFA under variety of traffic conditions while mitigating the attack.

---

[1] We take the value of maximum probability (P_{max}) to be one.

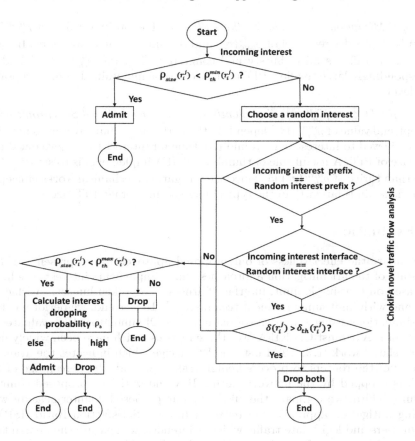

Fig. 2. ChoKIFA algorithm flowchart.

Ensure Adequate Calculation of the Average PIT Size: ChoKIFA calculates the average PIT size using an exponential weighted moving average (EWMA). The use of EWMA for calculating $\rho_{avg}(r_i^j)$ makes sure that the short term increase in PIT size which may result from a burst of benign incoming interests (e.g., which are not satisfied due to network congestion/delay from the producer) do not result in the significant increase of average PIT size. Equation 2 illustrates the calculation of the $\rho_{avg}(r_i^j)$ where w_ρ is the weight factor for calculating EWMA and $\rho_{size}(r_i^j)$ is the current/actual PIT size [5].

$$\rho_{avg}(r_i^j) = (1 - w_\rho) * \rho_{avg}(r_i^j) + w_\rho * \rho_{size}(r_i^j). \tag{2}$$

Note that the calculation of average PIT size can be made particularly efficient when w_ρ is set as a negative power of two[2]. If w_ρ is too large, then the averaging procedure will not filter out the temporary congestion of PIT.

---

[2] In our simulations, we take w_ρ equal to 0.001.

Setting a Minimum Threshold for the PIT Size: The optimal value of $\rho_{th}^{min}(r_i^j)$ depends on the desired level of $\rho_{avg}(r_i^j)$ and default network conditions. In case, the typical traffic is fairly bursty and congested, then the $\rho_{th}^{min}(r_i^j)$ should be correspondingly large to allow PIT utilization to be maintained at an acceptably high level.

Setting $\rho_{th}^{max}(r_i^j) - \rho_{th}^{min}(r_i^j)$ Sufficiently Large to Avoid Global Synchronization: The optimal value of $\rho_{th}^{max}(r_i^j)$ depends in the part of maximum average delay that can be allowed to interest (e.g., round trip time for interest to retrieve data) and total size of PIT. A useful rule of thumb ChoKIFA implements is to set $\rho_{th}^{max}(r_i^j)$ more than thrice of $\rho_{th}^{min}(r_i^j)$ [5], since the mitigation mechanism works efficiently when max-min is larger than the typical increase in average PIT size.

5   Evaluation

We evaluate the effectiveness of our proposed approach in the presence of IFA and state of the art mitigation approaches which implements interest rate limiting based on the simple limit, interface fairness using token bucket, satisfaction ratio and with limit announcement technique [1]. To this end, we perform extensive simulations using the open-source ndnSIM [2] simulator. We evaluate the impact of IFA against ChoKIFA over three metrics which have been widely used in the related work [1,3,4,9]. First, the PIT usage which indicates the available capacity of the routers to process benign traffic. Second, the percentage of BIs and MIs dropped by the network during IFA and with the proposed countermeasure. Third, we compare the efficiency our proposed countermeasure with existing mitigation approaches in terms of Interest Satisfaction Ratio (ISR) of benign users and legitimate traffic which is intended to measure the benign traffic received by users. Precisely, the lower the ISR refer, the greater amount of false positives made by the mitigation approach while distinguishing between the MIs and BIs.

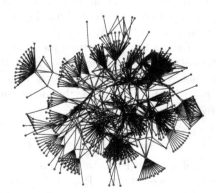

Fig. 3. Internet-like topology: 296 clients (red), 108 gateways (green), 221 backbone (blue). (Color figure online)

Test Setup: We ran our simulations (with 100 s of simulation time for each experiment) on two different network topologies: a tree topology [4] (see Fig. 1) and a more realistic large-scale ISP-like topology, i.e., AS-7018 [11] (see Fig. 3). The selection of tree topology is because it represents one of the worst case to defend IFA [1], while the larger ISP topology reflects the performance of mitigation approach when deployed on the real Internet. The topology consist of a single P and number of consumers, including four honest clients (C) and four adversaries (Adv) connected with multiple ICN routers. Adv requests for non-existing content (i.e., MI), which exhibits distinct suffix (/*good*/*rnd*) compared to valid content (/*good*/*data*) with frequency of 1000 interests/s. C requests the interests (BI) for valid content which are entitled to P at a rate of 30 interests/s. The total PIT size of R, i.e., 600 kbyte, thus we set the $\rho_{th}^{max}(r_i^j)$ and $\rho_{th}^{min}(r_i^j)$ equal to 3/4 and 1/8 of total PIT capacity (i.e., 450 and 75), respectively.

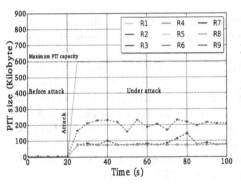

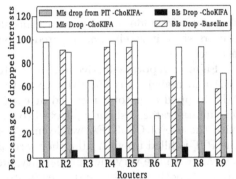

Fig. 4. PIT usage, base-line (solid lines) and ChoKIFA (dotted lines).

Fig. 5. BI and MI drop, base-line and ChoKIFA.

5.1 Small-Scale Simulation

In this section, we present the results of tree topology to evaluate the impact of attack and effectiveness of ChoKIFA. Figure 4 reports PIT usage of all the routers as a function of the simulation time under IFA for the base-line scenario (i.e., with no countermeasure) and, when the proposed countermeasure is active. In our simulations to evaluate and compare ChoKIFA under IFA, adversaries launches the attack at different time, i.e., starting from the 20th s, while the benign users starts to request for existing content from the beginning (see Fig. 4). Because of the design of CHoKIFA, approach allows the IFA to fill the PIT of all the routers till 75 kilobyte before being able to start traffic flow comparison, i.e., minimum threshold of PIT. In contrast, after exceeding the minimum threshold, ChoKIFA's traffic flow comparison and interest dropping probability does not allow PITs to exceed certain level (i.e., slightly higher than 75) which depends on the dropping probability related to average PIT size. Results show (see Fig. 4)

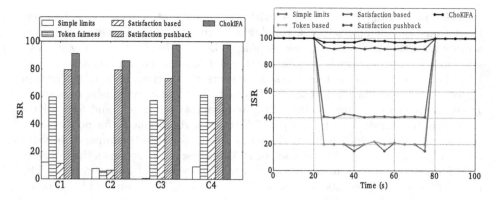

Fig. 6. Benign consumers ISR in small topology.

Fig. 7. Global legitimate ISR in AS-7018.

that gateway node to producer attains slightly higher PIT size than the rest of routers since it receives aggregated amount of malicious traffic from the whole network.

Figure 5 reports effectiveness of ChoKIFA under IFA, in terms of legitimate (BI) and malicious traffic (MI) drop. It shows the percentage of total BIs and MIs dropped over total received at each router, respectively. In particular, the legitimate traffic is slightly affected (only 4% of BIs are dropped on an average) with the use of ChoKIFA, while in base-line 90% of BIs are dropped. Because the PIT is filled up with MIs, therefore, the drawn random interest from PIT is also MI with the very high probability, and in consequence ChoKIFA drops only MIs, i.e., both incoming and already stored in the PIT (see Fig. 5).

Figure 6 reports the ISR of benign users which can be achieved when enabling ChoKIFA. We also compare these results with four different mitigation approaches [1]. The first three approaches are lightweight and stateless nevertheless not effective in legitimate ISR. Results show (see Fig. 6) that Satisfaction-based pushback is slightly effective than previous methods but it also induces unnecessary signaling overhead by sending rate limiting announcements continuously in the whole network [1]. In particular, Fig. 6 reports that ChoKIFA outperforms all four approaches in terms of all benign users ISR, remarkably. In particular, ChoKIFA is able to main 97% of all benign users ISR, moreover, induces 20 to 60% less false positives comparing to all four approaches while mitigating the attack.

5.2 Large-Scale Simulation

In this section, we evaluate the performance of ChoKIFA by implementing a real ISP-like topology (AS 7018) which is measured by the Rocket fuel project [11] (see Fig. 3). To study the performance of ChoKIFA in ISP-like topology and under a range of conditions, we varied the percentage of adversary in the network and the frequency with which adversary is sending malicious interests.

Figure 7 confirms that rate limiting approaches [1] are not able to maintain acceptable ISR for benign users in bigger topology as well. In particular, the result shows the percentage of global ISR of all legitimate interests generated in the network, where ChoKIFA maintains almost 97% of ISR during the attack. Note that the attack duration, in this case, is from 20 to 80 s. Figure 8 shows the ISR percentage of legitimate interests when we varied the percentage of attackers in the network, precisely, the values ranged from 6% attackers to over 50% attackers in the network. The results are as expected—for ChoKIFA and all four state of the art mitigation algorithms. As the number of attackers in the network increases, the lower is the ISR ratio for legitimate interests. For instance, in the case of the token bucket with per interface fairness, only 3 attackers can halve the quality of service for the remaining 13 legitimate users. While the two intelligent attack mitigation algorithms also show a decline in legitimate service quality as the percentage of attackers increases. Although ChoKIFA outperforms all mitigation algorithms and shows a very minor reduction in ISR ratio (i.e., approximately 3%) even when the attacker's percentage is raised more than 50%.

Figure 9 shows the aggregated legitimate ISR ratio when we increased malicious interest sending rate from 100 interests/s to 10000 interests/s. The result shows that ChoKIFA remains almost unaffected even with huge amount of increase in malicious interest frequency, while among all state of the art approaches only Satisfaction-based pushback shows satisfactory results.

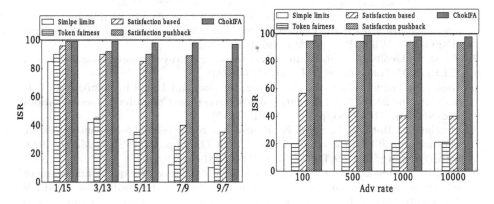

Fig. 8. Legitimate ISR with increasing adversary.

Fig. 9. Legitimate ISR with increasing malicious traffic.

6 Conclusion

In this paper, we address the interest flooding-based DDoS over NDN, which is explicitly named as IFA. More specifically, we have found that several proposed countermeasures, that adopt detection and reaction mechanisms based on interest rate limiting, are not highly effective and also damage the legitimate traffic.

In our solution, we exploited an active queue management scheme to propose an efficient detection and mitigation mechanism against IFA, which stabilizes the router PIT. The proposed approach penalizes the unresponsive flows generated by adversarial traffic by dropping malicious interests generated during the IFA. We implemented the proposed protocol on the open-source ndnSIM simulator and compared it with the state-of-the-art. The results report that our proposed protocol effectively mitigates the adverse effects of IFA and shows significantly less false positives in comparison to the state-of-the-art IFA mitigation approaches.

References

1. Afanasyev, A., Mahadevan, P., Moiseenko, I., Uzun, E., Zhang, L.: Interest flooding attack and countermeasures in named data networking. In: IFIP Networking Conference, pp. 1–9. IEEE (2013)
2. Afanasyev, A., Moiseenko, I., Zhang, L.: ndnSIM: NDN simulator for NS-3. Technical Report NDN-0005, NDN, October 2012. http://named-data.net/techreports.html
3. Compagno, A., Conti, M., Gasti, P., Tsudik, G.: Poseidon: mitigating interest flooding DDoS attacks in named data networking. In: 2013 IEEE 38th Conference on Local Computer Networks (LCN), pp. 630–638. IEEE (2013)
4. Dai, H., Wang, Y., Fan, J., Liu, B.: Mitigate DDoS attacks in ndn by interest traceback. In: 2013 IEEE Conference on Computer Communications Workshops (INFOCOM WKSHPS), pp. 381–386. IEEE (2013)
5. Floyd, S., Jacobson, V.: Random early detection gateways for congestion avoidance. IEEE/ACM Trans. Netw. 1(4), 397–413 (1993)
6. Gasti, P., Tsudik, G., Uzun, E., Zhang, L.: DoS and DDoS in named data networking. In: 2013 22nd International Conference on Computer Communications and Networks (ICCCN), pp. 1–7. IEEE (2013)
7. Oueslati, S., Roberts, J., Sbihi, N.: Flow-aware traffic control for a content-centric network. In: 2012 Proceedings IEEE INFOCOM, pp. 2417–2425, March 2012. https://doi.org/10.1109/INFCOM.2012.6195631
8. Pan, R., Prabhakar, B., Psounis, K.: Choke-a stateless active queue management scheme for approximating fair bandwidth allocation. In: Proceedings of the IEEE Nineteenth Annual Joint Conference of the IEEE Computer and Communications Societies, INFOCOM 2000, vol. 2, pp. 942–951. IEEE (2000)
9. Salah, H., Wulfheide, J., Strufe, T.: Coordination supports security: a new defence mechanism against interest flooding in NDN. In: 2015 IEEE 40th Conference on Local Computer Networks (LCN), pp. 73–81, October 2015
10. Singla, G., Kaliyar, P.: A secure routing protocol for manets against byzantine attacks. In: Chaki, N., Meghanathan, N., Nagamalai, D. (eds.) Computer Networks and Communications (NetCom). LNEE, pp. 571–578. Springer, New York (2013). https://doi.org/10.1007/978-1-4614-6154-8_56
11. Spring, N., et al.: Measuring ISP topologies with Rocketfuel. IEEE/ACM Trans. Netw. 12, 2–16 (2004)

12. Vassilakis, V.G., Alohali, B.A., Moscholios, I., Logothetis, M.D.: Mitigating distributed denial-of-service attacks in named data networking. In: Proceedings of the 11th Advanced International Conference on Telecommunications (AICT), Brussels, Belgium, pp. 18–23 (2015)
13. Zhang, L., et al.: Named data networking. ACM SIGCOMM Comput. Commun. Rev. **44**(3), 66–73 (2014)

Application-Level Traceroute: Adopting Mimetic Mechanisms to Increase Discovery Capabilities

Chiara Caiazza[1,2] [iD], Enrico Gregori[3], Valerio Luconi[3] [iD], Francesco Mione[1,2,3], and Alessio Vecchio[2(✉)] [iD]

[1] University of Florence, Florence, Italy
[2] Dip. di Ingegneria dell'Informazione, University of Pisa, Pisa, Italy
`chiara.caiazza@phd.unipi.it, alessio.vecchio@unipi.it`
[3] IIT-CNR, Pisa, Italy
`{enrico.gregori,valerio.luconi}@iit.cnr.it`

Abstract. Traceroute is a popular network diagnostic tool used for discovering the Internet path towards a target host. Besides network diagnostic, in the last years traceroute has been used by researchers to discover the topology of the Internet. Some network administrators, however, configure their networks to not reply to traceroute probes or to block them (e.g. by using firewalls), preventing traceroute from providing details about the internal structure of their networks. In this paper we present *camouflage traceroute* (camotrace), a traceroute-like tool aimed at discovering Internet paths even when standard traceroute is blocked. To this purpose, camotrace mimics the behavior of a popular TCP-based application-level protocol. We show preliminary results that confirm that camotrace is able to obtain additional information compared to standard traceroute.

1 Introduction

The typical traceroute application, in its many forms, sends IP packets with increasing time-to-live (TTL) to discover the network path towards a destination. Traceroute relies on the fact that when a router receives an IP packet with TTL equal to 1, the router should discard it and send to the source address an ICMP packet indicating that the TTL has expired before arriving at the destination (ICMP Time Exceeded) [19]. From that ICMP packet, traceroute is able to discover the IP address of the router at that distance from the source.

Originally designed as a diagnostic tool, traceroute has been widely used by researchers to discover Internet paths at various levels of abstraction, e.g. IP interface, router, point-of-presence, and autonomous system (AS) [7,14,17,20]. The effectiveness of traceroute depends on the response rate to traceroute packets of routers across the Internet and it can be limited by several factors [16]. First, not all routers always send ICMP packets when receiving a datagram with TTL equal to 1. Some may be configured to never send ICMP packets, some others

© IFIP International Federation for Information Processing 2019
Published by Springer Nature Switzerland AG 2019
M. Di Felice et al. (Eds.): WWIC 2019, LNCS 11618, pp. 66–77, 2019.
https://doi.org/10.1007/978-3-030-30523-9_6

may be configured to give low priority to this operation, and send ICMP packets only when their load is low. In these cases, traceroute is not able to discover part of the path. Another relevant factor that could affect traceroute performance is the presence of modern firewalls, traffic shapers, or similar machines. These devices are able to recognize traffic as belonging to different applications, basing classification on the pattern or the payload of traversing packets (via deep packet inspection). Then, certain classes of traffic can be blocked, shaped, or throttled according to the network operator's policies (in the EU this practice is prohibited as it goes against the network neutrality principles [4]). Some operators configure their firewalls to block incoming and/or outgoing traceroute traffic. Since traceroute does not belong to any end-to-end application, they consider it useless (as it wastes the bandwidth available for other traffic), or even potentially dangerous (e.g., DDoS attacks). If this happens, the last part of the Internet path between a source and a destination will be unreachable by measurement probes.

We devised *camouflage traceroute* (*camotrace*), a traceroute variant whose aim is to bypass firewalls and shapers and to possibly discover those parts of the network that are inaccessible to conventional traceroute tools. Camotrace mimics the behavior of common application-level protocols to confound traffic classification tools and avoid being blocked by firewalls. The idea is to establish a TCP connection between the measurement source and a server inside a firewall-protected domain, and then vary the TTL of some TCP packets during communication to discover the intermediate routers. We ran a validation measurement campaign that showed that the output of camotrace is correct. In addition, we ran a set of experiments on the Italian Internet that show that camotrace is able to obtain additional information in comparison with classic traceroute.

2   Related Work

The traceroute tool has been firstly developed for network diagnostic purposes by Van Jacobson. This original traceroute uses UDP probes with high destination port number, to maximize the chance of not finding a used one. Each probe is sent with a TTL value increased by one with respect to the previous probe. According to the ICMP protocol RFC [19], once a probe reaches an intermediate router with a TTL value of 1, the router should discard it and send back to the source an ICMP Time Exceeded reply, which notifies that the probe has stopped on that router. On the destination, under the assumption that the destination port is not in use, an ICMP Port Unreachable is instead sent back. This is the implementation of the classic UNIX system's traceroute. On modern systems also an ICMP version of traceroute is available, based on ICMP Echo Request probes instead of UDP ones.

Besides diagnostic purposes, traceroute has been used in several studies of the past 15–20 years to infer Internet paths at various level of abstraction [6]: (i) IP interface level, (ii) router level upon alias resolution [15], and (iii) AS level upon IP-to-AS mapping [5]. Traceroute measurements have been used as a basis by several Internet mapping projects, such as CAIDA Ark [1, 7], iPlane [17], DIMES [20], or Portolan [9, 10, 13].

In the meanwhile, also some issues of the classic traceroute implementation have been discovered. In particular, bias in the outcome of Internet mapping measurements could be introduced because of the presence of load balancers, firewalls, or other evolved network equipment commonly referred to as middleboxes [2, 8]. Modern traceroute variants have been implemented to prevent or reduce the impact of such issues. For example, Paris traceroute [2] is designed to avoid known issues due to load balancers. The multipath detection algorithm (MDA) has been subsequently added to Paris traceroute to integrate its ability to discover all possible paths between a source and a destination in the presence of load balancers [3]. Tracebox is instead a tool which is able to discover the presence of middleboxes (i.e., machines that operate at levels higher than the network level) along the path between the source and the destination [8]. These tools however are not able to bypass firewalls specifically configured to block traceroute executions, which instead is the purpose of camotrace.

TCP traceroute has been developed to be able to bypass firewalls configured to block UDP- and ICMP- based probes. However, it must be noticed that TCP traceroute behavior is different from the one we propose. TCP traceroute's probes are just TCP SYN packets, but a connection between source and destination is never established. If the target host is not listening for incoming connections, a TCP RST will be generated to indicate to the other endpoint that the port is not open. Conversely, if the selected port on the target host is open, a TCP SYN+ACK will be sent back to the host running TCP traceroute. The latter terminates the connection with a TCP RST (the three-way handshake is never completed). This makes TCP traceroute easily identifiable by modern sophisticated firewalls. In camotrace instead, a TCP connection is first established and only after that TCP segments are used as probes by varying their TTL. Moreover, the payload of TCP segments contains the application-level data of the protocol currently in use by camotrace (i.e. HTTP). These differences are not marginal: since a connection is effectively established, packets can be considered by stateful firewalls as belonging to the same flow; since the payload of TCP segments contains real application-level data, this may help in making the flow being classified as non-diagnostic by deep packet inspection mechanisms.

3 Method

To better understand the behavior of camotrace, we briefly recall the main concepts upon which traceroute is based. Traceroute probes are IP packets with either UDP, ICMP, or TCP payload. These probes are sent without establishing a connection with the target host. For UDP probes, the payload is empty or random; ICMP probes are ICMP Echo Requests; TCP probes are instead TCP SYNs. Probes are sent cyclically with increasing IP TTL values, starting

---

Algorithm 1. Camouflage traceroute probing algorithm

```
 1: MAX_TTL ← System default TTL
 2: MAX_DEPTH ← 40
 3: MAX_ATTEMPT ← 3
 4:
 5: for all x ∈ {1..MAX_DEPTH} do
 6:     setTTL(x)
 7:     start timer
 8:     send an HTTP request
 9:     setTTL(MAX_TTL)
10:     nAttempt = 0
11:     while ICMP Time Exc. not received && nAttempt < MAX_ATTEMPTS do
12:         while True do
13:             try
14:                 listen for and consume ICMP Time Exceeded packets
15:                 if ICMP Time Exceeded packets arrive then
16:                     restart timer
17:                     break
18:                 end if
19:             catch timer expired
20:                 break
21:             end try
22:         end while
23:         if the server closes the socket then
24:             connect to the server
25:         end if
26:         nAttempt = nAttempt + 1
27:     end while
28: end for
```

---

from 1. Traceroute stops when the target host or a maximum TTL value (hereafter MAX_DEPTH) is reached. Common traceroute implementations use 30 as the default maximum TTL value[1]. At each iteration, a probe can reach either an intermediate router or the target host. Intermediate routers should send back an ICMP Time Exceeded packet, which indicates that the probe has reached the router with a TTL value of 1. The target host instead should respond with an ICMP Port Unreachable (if UDP probe), ICMP Echo Reply (if ICMP probe), or a TCP RST or SYN+ACK (if TCP probes), that will stop traceroute operations.

To disguise itself and bypass firewalls or other blocking entities, camotrace mimics the behavior of application-level protocols. In particular, we implemented camotrace to act as an HTTP speaker. Camouflage traceroute operates in two phases. In the first phase camotrace establishes a connection with the target host. Thus, to operate correctly, camotrace needs as a target for measurements a host listening for connections for the implemented protocol (i.e., an HTTP-based service or a Web-server). In its current implementation, to establish a connection, camotrace uses sockets of type stream, relying on the operating system support for the TCP protocol. In other words, to avoid implementing all the intricacies of TCP mechanisms, camotrace implementation uses just the functionalities offered by the stream socket interface. As a consequence, camotrace does not have the visibility at the packet level for both outgoing and incoming

---

[1] In some preliminary tests conducted using standard TCP traceroute, we observed that 30 hops may be insufficient to reach all destinations. For this reason, we set MAX_DEPTH to 40 hops for the experiments described in Sect. 5.

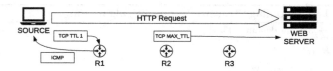

Fig. 1. Camotrace principle of operation.

traffic. The second phase is the probing phase. Once connected to the server, camotrace changes dynamically the TTL associated with outgoing data to discover routers along the path. In this phase, camotrace operates according to Algorithm 1. In detail, for values of x ranging from 1 to MAX_DEPTH camotrace executes the following steps: (i) the time-to-live (TTL) associated with the socket is set to x (this is done to discover the router at x hops from the sender); (ii) up to $MAX\_ATTEMPTS$ HTTP requests are sent through the socket: this data will elicit an ICMP error on the router at x hops from the sender (camotrace may stop before $MAX\_ATTEMPTS$ probes are sent if an ICMP error is received); (iii) the TTL associated with the socket is reset to its default value (MAX_TTL), this is done to retransmit the HTTP request with a TTL that makes it reach the other endpoint; (iv) ICMP errors are consumed; (v) the state of the socket is checked: if it has been closed by the server, a new connection is established. An overview of camotrace operations is shown in Fig. 1.

ICMP Time Exceeded errors are handled in a `while` cycle to cope with possible TCP re-transmissions. The execution exits from the `while` cycle when a timer associated with the socket expires (`catch` block). In other words, if no ICMP Time Exceeded errors are received for a given amount of time, camotrace assumes that the router at x distance is not responding and it proceeds to the next hop. The payload of probes is an HTTP 1.1 GET request with the following simple format:

```
GET / HTTP/1.1
Host: <target_host_name>
Connection: keep-alive
```

It must be noticed that camotrace is able to detect a hop only if an ICMP packet is received. Since the destination host does not send any ICMP packet, camotrace is not able to determine if, and eventually when, the target is reached. Therefore, in its current implementation, the algorithm always continues until MAX_DEPTH is reached. The default values for MAX_DEPTH and $MAX\_ATTEMPTS$ are 40 and 3, respectively.

3.1 Performance Enhancements for Some Specific Cases

Since the Web server on the target machine is not under camotrace's control, the latter has to deal with arbitrary decisions that may affect the connection. To cope with these events we modified the basic camotrace algorithm presented in the first part of this section. In particular, two improvements were introduced.

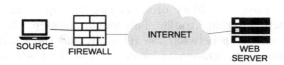

Fig. 2. Validation set up.

Managing Non Persistent Connections. To successfully operate, the connection between the sender and the target has to be persistent. The HTTP 1.1 standard states that the connection between client and server should be persistent [11]; however, some HTTP servers still close the connection immediately after completing to serve a request. To bypass this problem, we implemented a camotrace variant that, instead of sending a complete HTTP request at each step, sends only a portion of the request (few bytes at a time). More precisely, the operations illustrated in Algorithm 1 are changed by sending just a few bytes of an HTTP request and not a complete one (Line 8).

Managing Other Unexpected Connection Closures Performed by the Server. Even when adopting the above described mechanisms, the server may still unexpectedly close the connection. This could be due to several reasons, such as a high workload on the server or the presence of timers associated with connections. In fact, if a request is not completed in a given amount of time, or if the time between two consecutive requests is too long, the server can close the connection with the client. This issue may affect both the default camotrace algorithm and the variant previously described. To cope with this problem, when a connection-close is detected camotrace connects again to the target and restarts probing activities from the last hop reached during the previous run.

4   Validation

To validate camotrace both in terms of principle of operation and implementation we ran a two-step validation.

We first checked if camotrace is able to correctly discover the path from a source to a destination. We ran a measurement campaign with target belonging to the GARR network. GARR is the Italian public research network that connects all the Italian Universities and Research Centers [12]. The map of the GARR network is publicly available[2], thus we have been able to check if the paths found by camotrace were correct. We ran measurements towards 17 machines hosting the Web sites of University institutions and spread all over Italy. For all targets we checked that the Web server was actually hosted in the network of the considered institution. For all targets we successfully verified that the path found by camotrace was equal to the one available on the network map.

---

[2] https://gins.garr.it/xWeathermap/mapgen.php?slice=garrx_top.

Second, we checked the ability of camotrace to bypass firewalls that are configured to block traceroute traffic. This validation step was run in a controlled environment set up between the IIT-CNR and the University of Pisa. The machine running camotrace was located in the IIT-CNR network. In the same network a Palo Alto firewall was in execution [18]. Such device is able to recognize traffic at the application level via deep packet inspection, and then to block, shape, and forward traffic according to policies defined by administrators. We also set up a web server on a machine located at the University of Pisa. The validation environment is shown in Fig. 2.

The Palo Alto firewall was configured to block all traceroute applications between the machine hosted at IIT-CNR and the web server hosted at the University of Pisa. We ran three types of traceroute (UDP, ICMP, and TCP on port 80) and camotrace between the two hosts. The Palo Alto firewall was able to block all traceroute traffic except camotrace. Thus camotrace was the only traceroute application which always managed to discover the entire path between the source and the destination. In other words, camotrace was able to bypass the Palo Alto firewall configured to block traceroute.

5 Results

We evaluated the discovering capabilities of camotrace using a large set of Italian Web servers as targets. To generate the list of targets, we first collected from the Italian DNS system approximately one million domains belonging to the *.it* TLD. The list of domains was resolved to ~800 k IPv4 addresses (the remaining ~200 k names were registered but not associated with any IP address). We then removed duplicate addresses, thus obtaining a list of ~92 k unique IPv4 addresses. The significant reduction from ~800 k to ~92 k addresses is due to the fact that many websites are actually hosted by the same physical machine. Finally, we selected a single IP address for each AS in the list, and this produced a final set of 3 260 targets, which were used for the experiments described in the following. For performing IP-to-AS mapping we used the Whois service provided by Team Cymru [21]. The rationale for the last step was to be able to carry out experiments in a reasonable amount of time (collecting traceroute results is time consuming) while preserving heterogeneity. We suppose that traceroute filtering policies may be quite different from organization to organization, whereas policies can be reasonably homogeneous within a single organization. The significant reduction of the set of targets caused by the last filtering step is due to the fact that a large fraction of websites is managed by a relatively small number of hosting providers. For each of these destinations we executed both camotrace with the reconnect option and TCP traceroute. Both were configured to explore paths with $MAX\_DEPTH = 40$ hops. We compared camotrace with TCP traceroute only, as the latter is known to have better discovering capabilities in comparison to ICMP and UDP traceroute.

For 629 targets, camotrace was not able to successfully perform the connection to the server. There are several possible reasons behind this behavior:

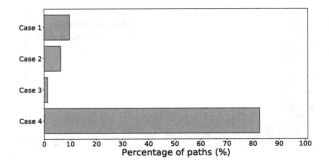

Fig. 3. Percentage of paths where camotrace finds more nodes (case 1), TCP finds more nodes (case 2), both find some nodes not found by the other but not all the nodes of the other (case 3), both find exactly the same nodes (case 4).

the target host may be disconnected, the target may be behind a completely blocking firewall, or a Web server may be unavailable on the target host. In fact, the presence of an entry in the DNS system does not imply that a Web server is necessarily running at that address. For 89.5% of the 629 targets, also TCP traceroute was unable to reach the destination machine (even though it was able to collect information about the intermediate nodes along the path), thus suggesting that the target IP address is not allocated. Since camotrace requires a Web server in execution at the target machine, this subset of targets has been discarded, and hereafter only the targets for which camotrace is able to successfully perform the connect operation will be taken into account.

Figure 3 shows the fraction of paths in which camotrace is able to find additional information on intermediate nodes with respect to TCP traceroute (case 1) and vice-versa (case 2). The third column shows the fraction of paths where each algorithm is able to find some more hops with respect to the other algorithm, but at the same time is unable to find all the hops of the other one (case 3). Finally, the last column shows the fraction of paths where the two algorithms find the same set of hops (case 4). More formally, let us call I_{cam} and I_{tcp} the sets of intermediate nodes found by the two algorithms along the path[3]. The first and second columns represent the fraction of targets where $I_{cam} \supset I_{tcp}$ and $I_{cam} \subset I_{tcp}$, respectively. The third column corresponds to the case when $I_{cam} \neq I_{tcp}$ and $I_{cam}, I_{tcp} \subset (I_{cam} \cup I_{tcp})$. Finally, the last column represents the case when $I_{cam} = I_{tcp}$.

For approximately 83% of probed paths, camotrace and TCP traceroute found the same set of intermediate nodes. This means, conversely, that in approximately 17% of the paths the chosen algorithm influences the set of discovered routers. In particular, case 1 accounts for $\sim$10%, whereas case 2 accounts for $\sim$6%, demonstrating that camotrace may be able to provide more information. Case 3 covers a limited number of paths ($\sim$1%).

---

[3] For example, $I = \{1, 4, 5\}$ when the first, fourth, and fifth routers are found.

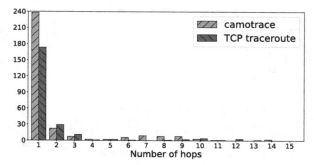

(a) Excluding the last occurrence of the destination address in TCP traceroute.

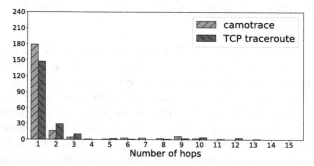

(b) Excluding all the occurrences of the destination address.

Fig. 4. Number of additional nodes.

The above results provide an indication on the number of paths where camotrace performs better than TCP traceroute and vice-versa, but they do not measure the amount of additional information that is discovered. Figure 4a shows the number of additional IP interfaces that each algorithm is able to find in the paths containing differences (which are, as mentioned, ∼17% of the total number of paths). For each number of additional IP interfaces, the number of occurrences for both camotrace and TCP traceroute are presented. As expected, camotrace is able to find a higher number of IP interfaces. For example, camotrace is able to find one additional IP interface in comparison to TCP traceroute on the path towards approximately 240 targets, while the opposite occurs approximately 170 times. For two and three additional interfaces TCP performs slightly better, then for higher numbers of interfaces camotrace is again better. In few cases, TCP traceroute finds almost all the IP interfaces along the path whereas camotrace is unsuccessful. This explains the long tail of the TCP traceroute distribution. These limited number of cases are due to some anomalous behaviors that are analyzed in Sect. 5.1.

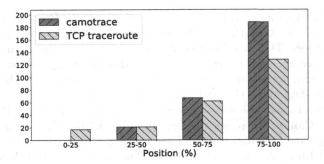

Fig. 5. Number of new IP interfaces, or groups, found by the two methods against the normalized position.

As previously mentioned, camotrace, differently from TCP traceroute, is not able to detect the target machine. Thus, the above results have been computed not considering the last hop found by TCP traceroute, i.e. the target itself. However, during the analysis, we noticed that in some cases some intermediate nodes were replying using the target's address. This could indicate that such hosts are behind a NAT connected to the public Internet using the target's address. We thus computed again the number of additional IP interfaces but excluding the target address, to show that this phenomenon marginally affects the previously discussed results (Fig. 4b).

In addition, we computed the position along the path of the additional (or groups of additional) IP interfaces found by the two methods (for groups, just the starting position is considered). Since the length of the path is different from target to target, the position is expressed as a percentage from the beginning of the path. Figure 5 shows that for camotrace the newly discovered IP interfaces are mostly in the second half of the path, and in particular in the last 25%. This is rather expected, as it is reasonable to suppose that the majority of classification and filtering systems are placed in non-transit networks. It must be noticed that in the first 25% of the considered paths, only TCP traceroute is able to discover more interfaces than camotrace, whereas the opposite does not occur. This situation takes place just a few times, for some atypical behaviors described in Sect. 5.1.

5.1   Analysis of Some Atypical Situations

Figure 4 includes a limited number of cases where TCP traceroute finds a rather large number of hops unseen by camotrace. We analyzed these cases in detail using a packet sniffing tool (Wireshark) and we found two main anomalous behaviors.

The first situation takes place right after the connection is established. The target server sends a TCP window update message that resets the TTL value to its maximum value. This means that subsequent messages are sent directly to the server and camotrace is unable to receive any ICMP message from the intermediate nodes. After the first message has been received these anomalous servers send a new TCP window update message or close the connection. This forces camotrace to open a new connection, thus starting the same behavior again. In the end, camotrace is not able to send any message with TTL lower than 64 and no hop along the path can be discovered.

In the second case, the server accepts the connection but an HTTP reply is never sent. Camotrace sends the first message with TTL = 1 receiving an ICMP message from the first router. Then it sends a message to the destination with TTL = 64 but no response is received. The underlying TCP layer starts to retransmit the packet and all following requests are queued. No ICMP message from the intermediate routers is received (with the exception of the first one). In some cases, after a while, the server sends a TCP reset and the connection can be re-established. However, since the server keeps being not responsive to HTTP requests, only an additional intermediate node can be discovered.

6   Conclusion

Traceroute is the most widely used tool for obtaining information about the topology of the Internet, and in the last decades it has been the cornerstone of countless research works. Camouflage traceroute tries to expand the amount of information collected in those portions of the network where operators apply restricting policies to diagnostic traffic. This is done by mimicking the behavior of application-level traffic, thus reducing the probability of being classified and consequently restricted. The main limitation of camotrace is that a server is required to be running on the target machine, as camotrace needs that a connection is open for delivering probes containing application-level traffic. Current implementation of camotrace only supports HTTP traffic, but other application protocols can be added to further improve its discovering capabilities and increase the set of possible targets.

Experiments carried out on the Italian Internet show that camotrace is able to provide more information than TCP traceroute in approximately 10% of the paths, while the opposite occurs in 6% of the paths. We believe that this is a good improvement, especially considering that the traceroute tool is well consolidated. Moreover, it is possible to conceive a tool that first operates as the classical TCP traceroute and then as camotrace, to finally produce a set of intermediate routers that corresponds to the union of the results obtained by the two methods.

Future work will focus on studying how to cope with camotrace limitations, mainly the ability to discover the target IP address. In addition, we plan to execute a world-wide measurement campaign to evaluate both the soundness of camotrace and the diffusion of traceroute blocking mechanisms at a planetary scale.

Acknowledgment. This work was partially funded by the University of Pisa (project PRA 2017_37 - "IoT e Big Data"), and the Italian Ministry of Education and Research (MIUR) in the framework of the CrossLab project (Departments of Excellence).

References

1. The Cooperative Association for Internet Data Analysis Archipelago Measurement Infrastructure (CAIDA Ark). http://www.caida.org/projects/ark/
2. Augustin, B., et al.: Avoiding traceroute anomalies with paris traceroute. In: Proceedings of the ACM SIGCOMM IMC, pp. 153–158 (2006)
3. Augustin, B., Friedman, T., Teixeira, R.: Multipath tracing with Paris traceroute. In: Proceedings of the IEEE/IFIP E2EMON 2007, pp. 1–8 (2007)
4. BEREC Guidelines on the Implementation by National Regulators of European Net Neutrality Rules (2016). http://berec.europa.eu/eng/document_register/subject_matter/berec/download/0/6160-berec-guidelines-on-the-implementation-b_0.pdf
5. Chang, H., Jamin, S., Willinger, W.: Inferring AS-level internet topology from router-level path traces. In: Proceedings of the SPIE ITCom 2001, pp. 196–207 (2001)
6. Cheswick, B., Burch, H., Branigan, S.: Mapping the internet. IEEE Comput. **32**(4), 97–98, 102 (1999)
7. claffy, k., Hyun, Y., Keys, K., Fomenkov, M., Krioukov, D.: Internet mapping: from art to science. In: Proceedings of the CATCH 2009, pp. 205–211 (2009)
8. Detal, G., Hesmans, B., Bonaventure, O., Vanaubel, Y., Donnet, B.: Revealing middlebox interference with tracebox. In: Proceedings of the IMC 2013, pp. 1–8 (2013)
9. Faggiani, A., Gregori, E., Lenzini, L., Luconi, V., Vecchio, A.: Smartphone-based crowdsourcing for network monitoring: opportunities, challenges, and a case study. IEEE Comm. Mag. **52**(1), 106–113 (2014)
10. Faggiani, A., Gregori, E., Lenzini, L., Mainardi, S., Vecchio, A.: On the feasibility of measuring the Internet through smartphone-based crowdsourcing. In: Proceedings of the WiOpt 2012, pp. 318–323 (2012)
11. Fielding, R., et al.: Hypertext Transfer Protocol - HTTP/1.1. RFC 2616 (1999)
12. Consortium GARR Home Page. https://www.garr.it/
13. Gregori, E., Lenzini, L., Luconi, V., Vecchio, A.: Sensing the internet through crowdsourcing. In: Proceedings of the PerMoby 2013, pp. 248–254 (2013)
14. Gregori, E., Luconi, V., Vecchio, A.: Studying forwarding differences in European mobile broadband with a net neutrality perspective. In: Proceedings of the 24th European Wireless Conference, pp. 81–87, May 2018
15. Keys, K., Hyun, Y., Luckie, M., Claffy, K.: Internet-scale IPv4 alias resolution with MIDAR. IEEE/ACM Trans. Netw. **21**(2), 383–399 (2013)
16. Luckie, M., Hyun, Y., Huffaker, B.: Traceroute probe method and forward IP path inference. In: Proceedings of the ACM SIGCOMM IMC 2008, pp. 311–324 (2008)
17. Madhyastha, H.V., et al.: iPlane: an information plane for distributed services. In: Proceedings of the USENIX OSDI 2006, pp. 367–380 (2006)
18. Palo Alto Networks. https://www.paloaltonetworks.com/
19. Postel, J.: Internet control message protocol - DARPA internet program protocol specification. RFC 792 (1981)
20. Shavitt, Y., Shir, E.: DIMES: let the internet measure itself. ACM SIGCOMM Comput. Commun. Rev. **35**(5), 71–74 (2005)
21. Team Cymru: IP to ASN mapping. http://www.team-cymru.com/IP-ASN-mapping.html

A NAT Based Seamless Handover for Software Defined Enterprise WLANs

Arkadeep Sen and Krishna M. Sivalingam[(✉)]

Department of Computer Science and Engineering,
Indian Institute of Technology Madras, Chennai, India
arkadeep.sen87@gmail.com, krishna.sivalingam@gmail.com,
skrishnam@iitm.ac.in

Abstract. Various applications used by mobile users today need seamless connectivity for providing a good quality user experience. Enterprise Wireless Local Area Network (WLAN) is one of the technologies used by mobile devices to connect to the Internet in several environments. For providing seamless connectivity and communication, mobility management becomes an important aspect of such deployments. In this paper, we propose a client-unaware handover process for NAT (Network Address Translation) operation mode of the access points in a Software Defined Networking (SDN) based enterprise WLAN framework. The proposed mechanism has been implemented in simulation and the results show that the proposed mobility management mechanism is able to achieve seamless handover and provide uninterrupted connectivity and communication to the mobile devices.

Keywords: Enterprise wireless LANs · Mobility management · Software defined networks

1 Introduction

With the exponential increase in the number of mobile devices and applications, the mobile data traffic for the Internet has increased manifold. The mobile users use a myriad of mobile applications on a day-to-day basis and many such applications require seamless connectivity for a good quality user experience. Mobility management, thus, becomes a very important aspect of any wireless technology.

Enterprise wireless local area network (WLAN) technology provides Internet connectivity to mobile devices in several environments, such as building, campus. The deployment of such a network comes with its own set of requirements such

This work was supported in part of by India-UK Advanced Technology Centre of Excellence in Next Generation Networks, Systems and Services (IU-ATC). This work was also supported by an Institute Research & Development Awards (IRDA) grant from IIT Madras (2017–2020) and a Department of Science & Technology (DST) grant (EMR/2016/003016) from Government of India (2017–2020).

© IFIP International Federation for Information Processing 2019
Published by Springer Nature Switzerland AG 2019
M. Di Felice et al. (Eds.): WWIC 2019, LNCS 11618, pp. 78–90, 2019.
https://doi.org/10.1007/978-3-030-30523-9_7

as network security, load balancing, mobility management, etc. In this paper, we delve into the mobility management aspect of the enterprise WLANs.

In WLANs, the connection initiation and termination is taken care of by the mobile devices [2]. As a result, the handover process is mobile device driven. When the mobile device moves away from the current AP and the signal strength is not strong enough for communication, the mobile device disconnects from the current AP. It then searches for a suitable AP and finally connects with a new AP. This results in an interruption in the communication. Though IEEE 802.11r [1] reduces the handover delay, disruption in communication will still be there.

Thus, mobility management in WLANs is distributed in nature and because of this mobile devices encounter unnecessary disconnection while moving across the entire coverage area. A centralized mobility management mechanism, having a global view of the entire WLAN, can solve this problem. The network can track the movement of mobile devices and can also detect an imminent handover. Instead of the mobile devices, the network can initiate the handover and, as it has a global view, it can also choose the AP which the mobile device should connect with after the handover. This process will significantly reduce the handover delay, and the ongoing communication will not get interrupted.

The advent of SDN [12–16] has paved a way for centralized network design and control. This has been achieved by decoupling the data plane and the control plane of a switch (router) and placing the control plane in a centralized controller. Such a design allows the controller to have a global view of the entire network. SDN also enables network programmability by allowing the deployment of customized control applications at the controller. To reap the benefits of such a design, we have proposed a client-unaware, seamless handover process for NAT (Network Address Translation) operation mode of the access points (AP) in a Software Defined Networking (SDN) based enterprise WLAN framework. In this paper, we have considered the SDN based framework proposed in [17]. In [17], a non-NAT handover process is also proposed which creates tunnels in order to correctly deliver packets to the roaming STA after the handover. We have only used the SDN based framework in this paper. Additionally, we have extended the framework by adding features in order to aid the proposed NAT based handover mechanism. The additional features are providing a unique transport layer port number across all Light APs for the NAT entry of a flow by the SDN Controller, and tracking as well as storing of the NAT entries for the flows of each STA at the SDN Controller. The proposed handover process has been implemented in OMNeT++ simulator [19] and the results from the simulation show that the handover process is able to achieve seamless handover and provide uninterrupted communication to the mobile devices.

The rest of the paper is organized as follows. Section 2 presents the related work. Section 3 presents the proposed handover mechanism. Section 4 describes the simulation-based performance results. Section 5 concludes the paper.

2   Related Work

In this section, we discuss some of the proposed mobility management schemes for WLANs which try to reduce the delay during a handover process.

Handover management mechanisms for WLANs are proposed in [4,6,7,9,10]; however, the handover processes described in the papers are initiated by the mobile devices. As a result of this type of handover process, the communication of the ongoing sessions is disconnected and it can resume only after the handover is completed.

Mobility management mechanisms proposed in [5,8,18,20,21] are initiated by the network instead of the mobile devices. In [8], a mechanism is presented to migrate all the associated mobile devices of an AP to another one. However, this mechanism does not take into consideration that some of the mobile devices may not be in the coverage area of the second AP, thus resulting in disconnection of those mobile devices after the migration. Moreover, the proposed mechanism does not support the handover of an individual mobile device.

The Odin project [18] uses a Light Virtual AP (LVAP) for representing each mobile device. Each LVAP is configured with a unique basic service set identifier (BSSID). It is stored at the physical AP with which the mobile device is connected. In the paper, handover of a mobile device is handled by removing its LVAP from one AP and adding the LVAP to another one AP. Though this mechanism achieves client-unaware handover, it does not re-route the packets, which have the roaming mobile device as the destination, from the old AP to the new AP. As a result, the on-going communication may get disconnected, in certain situations, until the communication is re-established by the application, running on the mobile device. The paper also proposes unicasting of Beacon frames to each mobile device. For large WLANs, this will increase the wireless traffic leading to collisions with other frames.

In [20], a similar LVAP based approach is discussed. A handover mechanism is proposed which takes into consideration the signal strength, the load on the APs and the location of the mobile devices during taking a decision on the handover of the mobile devices. However, [20] has similar shortcomings as that of [18].

In [21], an SDN based framework is proposed, where the SDN controller detects an imminent handover and modifies flows at the old and new APs appropriately. The controller then proactively adds flows to the SDN enabled wired backbone to correctly deliver the data packets having the mobile device as the destination. This proactive route update may become a bottleneck for large WLANs. This is because of the added overhead of storing all the alternate paths at the controller and the number of flow modification messages required to be send for the route update.

In [5] Croitoru et al. propose that to have seamless mobility, the mobile devices should connect with all the available APs and the traffic should be split across them by using the Multi-path TCP (MPTCP) protocol. As the paper only takes care of TCP traffic, UDP traffic will not have an uninterrupted communication during handover. Moreover, the paper suggests multiple client-side modifications so that the throughput does not get severely affected in some scenarios. As a result, the clients without such modifications will suffer from low throughput.

In our proposed solution, we make modifications at the AP side only. The mobile devices do not require any changes. The SDN controller, in the proposed solution, detects imminent handovers and instructs the APs to initiate the handover processes. The data packets having the mobile devices as the destination are re-routed to the new APs by updating NAT entries after the handovers are completed. The proposed solution does not require the complete wired backbone to be SDN enabled. Moreover, the number of NAT entry updates remains the same even when scaling to large WLANs. Thus, we efficiently address the shortcomings of the above-mentioned work in our proposed solution.

3 Proposed Handover Mechanism for SDN Based Enterprise WLAN Framework

This section presents the proposed handover mechanism for SDN based enterprise WLAN. We have considered the SDN based enterprise WLAN framework proposed in [17]. Figure 1 depicts the SDN framework for the proposed NAT based handover mechanism.

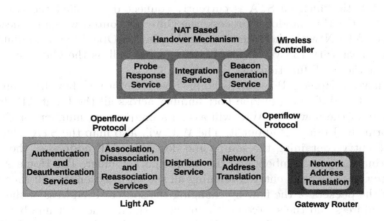

Fig. 1. Software defined enterprise WLAN framework.

In the framework, all the access points (APs) are SDN enabled. They all connect to the SDN Controller called the Wireless Controller (WiC) using the OpenFlow [16] protocol. The APs are called Light APs as the MAC management functionalities are split between the APs and the WiC. The WiC handles the Authentication and Deauthentication Services, the Association, Disassociation and Reassociation Services, and the Distribution Service and the Light APs handle the Probe Response Service, the Integration Service, and the Beacon

Generation Service. All the Light APs are configured to operate on the same channel. They are also configured with the same SSID and BSSID. Consequently, it will seem to the mobile stations (STAs) that only single AP is available. All the configurations are done centrally through the WiC.

The WiC has a global view of the entire enterprise WLAN because of the splitting of the MAC management functionalities. As a result of this design, the WiC can track and detect any imminent handover. Thus, the WiC can initiate the handover processes for the roaming STAs. Moreover, as the STAs are unaware of the availability of multiple APs, even after the completion of the handover, the STA will not be able to detect any change in its connectivity. As a result, the on-going sessions at the STAs will continue uninterrupted even during the handover. Additional features, such as providing a unique transport layer port number across all Light APs for the NAT entry of a flow by the WiC, and tracking as well as storing of the NAT entries for the flows of each STA at the WiC, are added to the SDN based framework proposed in [17]. These additional features aid in the operations of the proposed NAT based handover mechanism.

NAT Based Handover Mechanism. In this handover process, the WiC periodically checks whether any STAs are moving away from their corresponding Home APs and if so then the WiC initiates handover for all those STAs. The Light AP, with which an STA is currently connected, is called the Home AP of the STA. For this handover process, the Gateway router, which connects the enterprise WLAN with the Internet, should also be OpenFlow compliant and should connect with the WiC. The Light APs, as well as the Gateway router, implement the NAT functionality.

Whenever a Home AP receives the first packet of a new flow from an STA, it contacts the WiC for a unique port number across all the Light APs for the NAT entry of the flow. The WiC will assign a unique port number for the flow and inform the Home AP about it. The WiC will also map the STA address to the NAT entry containing the source and destination IP addresses, the source and destination port numbers and the unique port number. The Home AP will also store the same NAT entry containing all the information. It will then apply NAT on the packets of the flow by changing the source IP address of the Home AP's IP address and the source port number to the unique port number.

Whenever a data frame from any STA is received by a Light AP, including its Home AP, the signal strength of the frame is reported to the WiC by the Light APs. For each STA, the WiC keeps track of the Light AP, which is currently receiving the maximum signal strength from that STA.

The WiC periodically calls the handover process, described in algorithm 1, and checks the handover criterion for each STA. That is, if the Home AP of the STA is not the Light AP (max AP) currently receiving the maximum signal strength from that STA, then the handover process for the STA is initiated.

If there exist any NAT entries corresponding to the STA at the WiC, it will send OpenFlow Experimenter messages to add them to the max AP. This

Algorithm 1. NAT based Handover Mechanism

```
1: procedure HANDOVER
2:     for each STA do
3:         if STA→HomeAP ≠ STA→maxAP then
4:             for each NAT entry for STA do
5:                 Add NAT entry to STA→maxAP
6:             end for
7:             Change STA state to NOT_AUTHENTICATED in STA→HomeAP
8:             Change STA state to ASSOCIATED in STA→maxAP
9:             Set STA→HomeAP to STA→maxAP
10:            for each NAT entry for STA do
11:                At the Gateway update source address of NAT entry to
                   address of STA→maxAP
12:            end for
13:        end if
14:    end for
15: end procedure
```

will ensure any incoming packets from the Gateway router, belonging to any existing flows corresponding to the STA, will be properly routed by the max AP by applying NAT.

After this, the STA has to be migrated to the max AP from the Home AP without directly involving the STA. For achieving this, the Home AP and the max AP will be instructed by the WiC to change the state of the STA to *Not Authenticated* and *Associated* state respectively. The max AP now becomes the Home AP of the STA. As all the Light APs are configured with same SSID and BSSID, the STA will not detect any change in its connectivity after these operations.

The WiC then will send OpenFlow Experimenter messages to the Gateway router to update the NAT entries corresponding to the STA. The source IP address of those NAT entries will be changed to the IP address of the max AP. After the changes are made, if any packet, belonging to any existing flows corresponding to the STA, comes to the Gateway router from a remote host, the Gateway router will route the packet to the max AP which, in turn, will route the packet to the STA by appropriately applying NAT.

4   Simulation-Based Performance Study

The proposed handover process for NAT operation mode of APs has been implemented in the OMNeT++ simulator [19] (version 5.0). The INET framework [3] (version 3.4.0), which is an open-source OMNeT++ model suite for wired, wireless and mobile networks, and an OpenFlow extension to the INET framework [11] are used for the implementation.

4.1 Simulation Setup

The STAs and the APs are all configured to operate in IEEE 802.11n mode on the 2.4 GHz frequency band at a maximum data rate of 600 Mbps. All the APs connect to the remote hosts via the Gateway router. The STAs always move through the coverage area of the APs. Each STA randomly chooses a direction (right or left) towards which it will move. The STAs move in the chosen direction at a speed of 10 m/s until they reach an end of the simulation area and then start moving in the opposite direction with the same speed. This type of mobility model is chosen to ensure the occurrence of at least one handover per STA during the simulation.

We have compared the performance of the proposed handover process with the handover processes of the traditional enterprise WLAN and the Odin framework [18]. For the purpose of simplifying the routing process, static routes are pre-installed in all the network elements wherever required.

UDP and TCP applications are set up on the STAs and the remote hosts. Throughput, packet delivery ratio, and delay are measured for the performance study. Each STA sends a request to a remote host and the remote host sends traffic to the STA at the rate of 1.024 Mbps. In one simulation scenario, the STAs send UDP traffic request and in another one, the STAs send TCP traffic request. Each STA sends the request at a randomly chosen time between 5 s and 10 s of simulation time. The remote hosts, after receiving the request, keep sending the traffic till the end of the total simulation time. The sender application continues to send packets even if there is a disconnection during the handover process. If the receiver application detects that there is a disconnection, to reconnect, it sends a request packet to the sender application. The request is sent again because in the cases of traditional enterprise WLAN and Odin framework, there might occur disconnections during handovers. If the receiver application does not send a request packet after detecting a disconnection, then the subsequent packets sent by the remote host will not reach the STA. All the experiments are run for a total of 45 simulation seconds to ensure the occurrence of at least one handover per STA during the simulation.

4.2 Performance Evaluation Results for Fixed Number of APs

The parameters used for running the next set of simulations are summarized in Table 1.

Figure 2a and b present the average UDP throughput and packet delivery ratio experienced by the STAs. The UDP throughput and packet delivery ratio decrease as the number of STAs increases because, as the number of STAs increases the chance of interference and collision increases, resulting in higher packet loss. The average UDP throughput for the proposed handover process reaches 1.024 Mbps for 10 STAs and the reduction in throughput is almost negligible as the number of STAs increases from 10 to 80. From the packet delivery ratio plot, we can see that for the proposed handover process negligible loss is experienced for the case of 10 STAs and as the number of STAs increases,

Table 1. Simulation parameters for fixed no. of APs

Parameter	Value
No. of APs	10
No. of mobile stations	Varies from 10 to 80
Speed of mobile stations	10 m/s
Traffic at each mobile station	1 UDP application of 1.024 Mbps
	1 TCP application of 1.024 Mbps

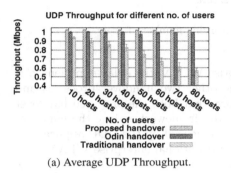 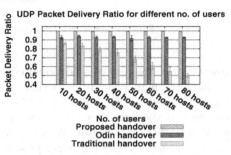

(a) Average UDP Throughput.   (b) Average UDP Packet Delivery Ratio.

Fig. 2. Throughput and packet delivery ratio for UDP applications for varying number of users.

the packet delivery ratio remains almost same. This shows that the proposed handover process is able to provide seamless handover for varying number of STAs and as a result, high throughput and high packet delivery ratio can be achieved. For the case of Odin framework, though for most of the cases the average throughput is almost 1 Mbps, the packet delivery ratio varies between 92% and 94%. This shows that though the handover process in Odin is able to reduce the handover delay, it fails to provide seamless handover, which results in packet loss during the handover. For the traditional enterprise WLAN framework, the throughput considerably reduces as the number of STAs increases. Even for the case of 10 STAs, the average throughput is below 1 Mbps. Similar results can be seen from the packet delivery ratio plot. The packet delivery ratio, for the case of 80 STAs, reduces to almost almost 50%. This shows that during handover there is high packet loss in the case of the traditional handover process and it increases with the increase in the number of STAs.

Figure 3 presents the per packet average UDP delay experienced by the STAs. It can be seen that the average delay increases as the number of STAs increases. Except for the case of 50 STAs, the average delay experienced by the STAs for the proposed handover process and the handover process in Odin framework are comparable (ranges between 3 ms and 10 ms). For the case of 50 STAs, the average delay experienced for the handover process in Odin framework (approx. 44 ms) is much higher than that of the proposed handover process (approx. 6 ms).

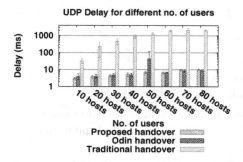

Fig. 3. Average UDP delay for varying number of users.

However, for the case of traditional enterprise WLAN, the delay experienced is significantly high compared to that of the other two handover processes and ranges between 33 ms and 2.13 s. This shows that both the proposed handover process and the handover process for the Odin framework reduce the handover delay because of which the average delay experienced by the UDP applications is less than that of the handover process for traditional enterprise WLAN.

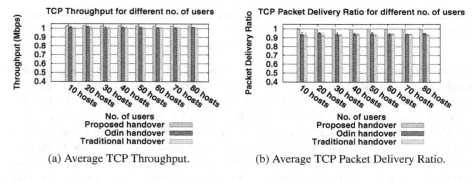

(a) Average TCP Throughput.   (b) Average TCP Packet Delivery Ratio.

Fig. 4. Throughput and packet delivery ratio for TCP applications for varying number of users.

Figure 4a and b present the average TCP throughput and packet delivery ratio per application experienced by the STAs. The TCP throughput and packet delivery ratio remain high for all the handover processes as TCP retransmits all the dropped packets, due to handover and interference, within a very short period of time. As a result, the overall average throughput and packet delivery ratio remain high in spite of packet loss during handover. We can see that even though the average TCP throughput for all the handover processes remains high (around 1 Mbps), the average throughput achieved for the proposed handover process is highest for all the cases. For all of the cases, it achieves a throughput of 1.024 Mbps. We can see that the packet delivery ratio achieved for the proposed handover process is also highest for all the cases with negligible packet loss. This shows that the proposed handover process is able to provide seamless handover for varying number of STAs and as a result, high throughput and high packet delivery ratio can be achieved. For the case of handover processes for the Odin framework and the traditional enterprise framework, even though they are able to achieve high throughput, still they suffer from packet loss which happens during the handover process (packet delivery ratio ranges between 93% and 95%).

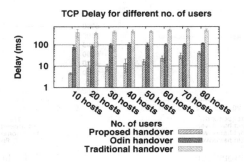

Fig. 5. Average TCP delay for varying number of users.

Figure 5 presents the per packet average TCP delay experienced by the STAs. The average delay increases as the number of STAs increases for the case of the proposed handover process and the handover process for the Odin framework, but the average delay for the proposed handover process is always less than that of Odin framework. This shows that though both handover processes reduce the handover delay, the handover process for the Odin framework does not achieve seamless handover which results in TCP retransmitting all the dropped packets. This, in turn, increases the total number of packets in the system thus resulting in higher average delay (more buffering). The average delay experienced in the case of the proposed handover process is also less than that of the handover process for traditional enterprise WLAN for all the cases. This shows that the handover delay is reduced by the proposed handover process and as a result, the TCP applications experience less delay.

4.3 Instantaneous Throughput Results

The parameters used for running the next set of simulations are summarized in Table 2.

Figure 6a and b present the instantaneous throughput of UDP and TCP applications respectively over the complete simulation time experienced by a randomly selected mobile station for all the three handover processes. The case of 4 APs and 10 STAs is chosen as in this case there will be little to no interference and we can clearly understand the effect of handover on throughput.

Table 2. Simulation parameters for checking instantaneous throughput.

Parameter	Value
No. of APs	4
No. of mobile stations	10
Speed of mobile stations	10 m/s
Traffic at each mobile station	1 UDP application of 1.024 Mbps
	1 TCP application of 1.024 Mbps

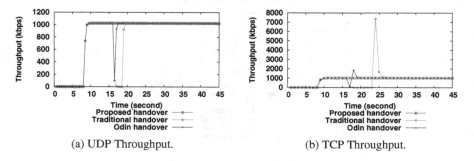

(a) UDP Throughput.   (b) TCP Throughput.

Fig. 6. UDP and TCP throughput experienced by a random mobile station.

For both UDP and TCP applications, there are interruptions during the handover processes for traditional enterprise WLAN and Odin framework but the communication in Odin framework resumes quickly compared to that of the traditional WLAN. This shows that even though Odin framework is able to reduce the handover delay, there still will be an interruption in the communication during the handover as the packets are not re-routed to the new AP after the completion of the handover process. The throughput of the TCP application spikes up just after the handover in the traditional enterprise WLAN and Odin framework. This is because, as soon as the connection is re-established all the packets, which were dropped during the handover, are retransmitted by the TCP layer at the remote host. However, for the UDP application, all the packets, sent during the handover, get dropped. Only when the connection is re-established after the handover, the UDP packets get delivered to the STA.

For the proposed handover process, the communication continues uninterrupted and the throughput, for both types of applications, remains high even during the handover. This shows that the proposed handover process is able to reduce the handover delay and also provide seamless handover to the roaming STA.

The simulation-based performance evaluation results show that the handover process is able to seamlessly handover the STAs with negligible handover delay. We can also see that the handover process is capable of serving a high number of STAs (10 to 80) with more network load and is still able to achieve high throughput with low packet loss. Thus, it can be said that the proposed handover process is well suited for enterprise WLAN environment.

5   Conclusions

Enterprise WLAN is used by mobile devices to connect to the Internet in various environments. Mobility management becomes an important aspect in an enterprise WLAN for providing seamless connectivity to the various mobile applications running on the mobile devices. In this paper, we have proposed a NAT based seamless mobility management mechanism for an SDN based enterprise WLAN framework. The performance study shows that the proposed mobility management mechanism is able to provide seamless, uninterrupted connectivity during handovers. Thus, high throughput and packet delivery ratio is achieved with the delay being within reasonable limits. As part of future work, this work can be extended to studies in a large-scale enterprise or campus environment to fully understand the potential benefits.

References

1. IEEE Standard for Information technology- Local and metropolitan area networks-Specific requirements- Part 11: Wireless LAN Medium Access Control (MAC) and Physical Layer (PHY) Specifications Amendment 2: Fast Basic Service Set (BSS) Transition. IEEE Std 802.11r-2008 (Amendment to IEEE Std 802.11-2007 as amended by IEEE Std 802.11k-2008), pp. 1–126, July 2008. https://doi.org/10.1109/IEEESTD.2008.4573292
2. IEEE Standard for Information technology-Telecommunications and information exchange between systems Local and metropolitan area networks-Specific requirements - Part 11: Wireless LAN Medium Access Control (MAC) and Physical Layer (PHY) Specifications. IEEE Std 802.11-2016 (Revision of IEEE Std 802.11-2012), pp. 1–3534, December 2016. https://doi.org/10.1109/IEEESTD.2016.7786995
3. INET Framework, February 2019. https://inet.omnetpp.org/
4. Chen, W., Yen, L., Chuo, C., Heish, T., Tseng, C.: SDN-enabled session continuity for wireless networks. In: Proceedings of the of IEEE ICC, pp. 1–6. IEEE (2017)
5. Croitoru, A., Niculescu, D., Raiciu, C.: Towards wifi mobility without fast handover. In: Proceedings of the NSDI, pp. 219–234 (2015)
6. Dai, Y., Li, F., Li, H., Wu, Q.: A core-stateless IP mobility management scheme based on OpenFlow protocol. In: Proceedings of IEEE IWCMC, pp. 1117–1122. IEEE (2016)
7. Dely, P., et al.: A software-defined networking approach for handover management with real-time video in WLANs. J. Mod. Transp. 21(1), 58–65 (2013)
8. Dely, P., Vestin, J., Kassler, A., Bayer, N., Einsiedler, H., Peylo, C.: CloudMAC - an OpenFlow based architecture for 802.11 MAC layer processing in the cloud. In: Proceedings of IEEE Globecom Workshops, pp. 186–191. IEEE (2012)
9. Feirer, S., Sauter, T.: Seamless handover in industrial WLAN using IEEE 802.11k. In: Proceedings of IEEE ISIE, pp. 1234–1239. IEEE (2017)
10. Guimarães, C., Corujo, D., Aguiar, R.L., Silva, F., Frosi, P.: Empowering software defined wireless networks through media independent handover management. In: Proceedings of IEEE Globecom, pp. 2204–2209. IEEE (2013)

11. Klein, D., Jarschel, M.: An OpenFlow extension for the OMNeT++ INET framework. In: Proceedings of the International Conference on Simulation Tools and Techniques, pp. 322–329 (2013)
12. Kobayashi, M., et al.: Maturing of OpenFlow and software-defined networking through deployments. Elsevier Comput. Netw. **61**, 151–175 (2014)
13. Masoudi, R., Ghaffari, A.: Software defined networks: a survey. Elsevier J. Netw. Comput. Appl. **67**, 1–25 (2016)
14. McKeown, N., et al.: OpenFlow: enabling innovation in campus networks. ACM SIGCOMM Comput. Commun. Rev. **38**(2), 69–74 (2008)
15. Nunes, B., Mendonca, M., Nguyen, X.N., Obraczka, K., Turletti, T.: A survey of software-defined networking: past, present, and future of programmable networks. IEEE Commun. Surv. Tutor. **16**(3), 1617–1634 (2014)
16. Open Networking Foundation: Openflow specifications, December 2014
17. Sen, A., Sivalingam, K.M.: An SDN framework for seamless mobility in enterprise WLANs. In: Proceedings of IEEE PIMRC, pp. 1985–1990 (2015)
18. Suresh, L., Schulz-Zander, J., Merz, R., Feldmann, A., Vazao, T.: Towards programmable enterprise WLANS with Odin. In: Proceedings of ACM HotSDN workshop, pp. 115–120 (2012)
19. Varga, A., Hornig, R.: An overview of the OMNeT++ simulation environment. In: Proceedings of International conference on Simulation tools and Techniques for Communications, Networks and Systems and Workshops, p. 60 (2008)
20. Zeljković, E., Marquez-Barja, J.M., Kassler, A., Riggio, R., Latré, S.: Proactive access point driven handovers in IEEE 802.11 networks. In: Proceedings of CNSM, pp. 261–267. IEEE (2018)
21. Zhao, D., Zhu, M., Xu, M.: SDWLAN: a flexible architecture of enterprise WLAN for client-unaware fast AP handoff. In: Proceedings of ICCCNT, pp. 1–6 (2014)

Proportional Fair Information Freshness Under Jamming

Andrey Garnaev[✉], Jing Zhong, Wuyang Zhang, Roy D. Yates,
and Wade Trappe

WINLAB, Rutgers University, North Brunswick, NJ, USA
garnaev@yahoo.com, jing.zhong@rutgers.edu,
{wuyang,ryates,trappe}@winlab.rutgers.edu

Abstract. The success of a UAV mission depends on communication between a GCS (Ground Control Station) and a group of UAVs. It is essential that the freshness of the commands received by UAVs is maintained as mission parameters often change during an operation. Ensuring the freshness of the commands received by UAVs becomes more challenging when operating in an adversarial environment, where the communication can be impacted by interference. We model this problem as a game between a transmitter (GCS) equipped with directed antennas, whose task is to control a group of UAVs to perform a mission in a protected zone, and an interferer which is a source spherically propagated jamming signal. A fixed point algorithm to find the equilibrium is derived, and closed form solutions are obtained for boundary cases of the resource parameters.

Keywords: Age of information · Jamming · Nash equilibrium · Proportional fairness

1 Introduction

In many Unmanned Aerial Vehicle (UAV) applications, a Ground Control Station (GCS) communicates with a group of UAVs to send instructions to control each UAV's mission. However, when such active communication faces the threat of hostile interference, the result can be delay or even interruption in getting such instructions. Larger periods of delay or interruption lead to reduced freshness of received instructions, and can decrease the probability of mission success. Thus we model the probability of mission success as a function of the age of the received information. Such considerations have been gaining prominence in the research literature lately, as reflected by interest in the age of information (AoI), a system delay performance metric that has been widely employed in different applications [1, 13, 23, 25, 26].

The pioneering paper, on the impact of hostile interference on age of information is [17]. Our work is based the model of [17] suggesting a relationship

© IFIP International Federation for Information Processing 2019
Published by Springer Nature Switzerland AG 2019
M. Di Felice et al. (Eds.): WWIC 2019, LNCS 11618, pp. 91–102, 2019.
https://doi.org/10.1007/978-3-030-30523-9_8

between SINR at the receiver and AoI of update packets. We employ this approach to model a scenario where a group of UAVs is cooperating to perform a
mission. A transmitter GCS employs directional antennas to control the UAVs
while jammer radiates a spherically symmetric interference intended to cause
the mission to fail. We model this problem via a game-theoretical approach. An
interesting feature of this problem is that the rivals have different structures for
their strategies. Specifically, the GCS's strategy is power allocation individually
between the UAVs, while the interferer's strategy involves assigning power to
jam the whole UAV group. While for most jamming games studied in literature
rivals strategies have the same structure: either power allocation for both rivals
[16,20,24] or assigning power level [7,12,17,22] for both rivals.

2   Model

We consider a group of n UAVs that, following their route/mission to a target
in a protected zone, must communicate with the GCS to get/verify position and
mission data. The GCS is equipped with n antennas (or n separate antenna
beams) to communicate with these UAVs. This communication can be damaged
by active interference that might lead to loss of navigation commands and failure of the mission. An interferer, located in the protected zone, is a source of
spherically symmetric interference intended to cause the UAV mission to fail.
As a metric for data updating in this paper, we consider AoI which reflects the
time that has passed since the last update. We assume that the probability π_S of
mission success is a function of the average age of information A, and this function is decreasing with A such that: (a) $\pi_S(0) = 1$, i.e., if the data is up-to-date
the mission succeeds with certainty; and (b) $\pi_S(A) \downarrow 0$ for $A \uparrow \infty$, i.e., if data is
never updated, then the mission fails with certainty. To model the probability of
mission success, we will use the ratio form contest success function. This is commonly used to translate involved resources into probability of winning or losing,
and has been widely applied in different economic and attack-defense problems
in the literature; see, for example, [5,9,11,19,21]. In our scenario, the metric
that dictates whether the mission is successful or fails, is age of information.
Specifically, in terms of positive constants a and b, the probability of mission
success is

$$\pi_S(A) = \frac{b}{b + aA}. \tag{1}$$

2.1   Age of Information

To model age of information, we will employ a generalization of the model introduced in [17]. For convenience of the readers, we give a brief description:

(i) The GCS can transmit at a rate that is proportional to the signal to inter-
    ference plus noise ratio (SINR) at the receiver. Following [17], when p_i and
    q are the powers of the transmitting signal by GCS to UAV i and interfering

signal, and h_i and g_i are the corresponding channel gains to the UAV, the packet transmission rate associated with power profile (p_i, q) is

$$\mu_i(p_i, q) = z_i \text{SINR}(p_i, q) = z_i \frac{g_i p_i}{N_i + h_i q}, \tag{2}$$

where N_i is background noise power and z_i is a positive constant.

(ii) Depending on the model for how update packets are delivered to the UAV, the age of information metric A_i takes on the form

$$A_i(p_i, q) = \frac{c}{\lambda_i} + \frac{d}{\mu_i(p_i, q)} \tag{3}$$

for packet arrival rate λ_i and constants $c \geq 0$ and $d > 0$. In particular, when $(c, d) = (1, 2)$ and fresh update packets are generated at the UAV as a rate λ Poisson process, the age metric $A(p, q)$ corresponds to the average peak age of an M/G/1/1 queue [3,10]. This is the age metric employed in [17].

We note that various other age metrics can be modeled by specifying (c, d) in (3). For example, with $(c, d) = (1, 1)$, $A_i(p_i, q)$ is the average AoI of an M/M/1/1 server supporting preemption in service [15]. Furthermore, with $(c, d) = (0, 2)$ and just-in-time arrivals (i.e., a fresh update goes into service precisely when the server would become idle) at a rate $\mu_i(p_i, q)$ memoryless server, $A_i(p_i, q)$ is again the average AoI [14]. Finally, with $(c, d) = (0, 3/2)$, $A_i(p_i, q)$ corresponds to just-in-time updates transmitted with deterministic service times at rate $1/\mu_i(p_i, q)$ [14]. In the following, we refer to $A_i(p_i, q)$ as the AoI for any $c \geq 0$ and $d > 0$.

2.2 Formulation of the Game

To define game we have to describe: (a) the set of players, (b) the set of feasible strategies of each player, and (c) the player's payoff [4]. In our scenario, there are two players: the interferer and the GCS. A strategy of the GCS is a non-negative power vector $\boldsymbol{p} = (p_1, \ldots, p_n)$, where p_i is the power employed to communicate with UAV i, and $\sum_{i=1}^{n} p_i = \bar{p}$ is the total power. Let Π_{GCS} be the set of all feasible GCS strategies. A strategy of the interferer is a power level q of the jamming signal. Let $\Pi_I = \mathbb{R}_+$ be the set of all feasible interferer's strategies. Note that the probability of mission success for UAV i is

$$\pi_S(A_i(p_i, q)) = \frac{b}{b + aA(p_i, q_i)} = \frac{bz_i g_i p_i}{(b + ac/\lambda_i)z_i g_i p_i + da(N_i + h_i q)}. \tag{4}$$

We now introduce the auxiliary notations:

$$\alpha_i = bg_i z_i, \ \beta_i = (b + ac/\lambda_i)g_i z_i, \ \gamma_i = dah_i, \delta_i = daN_i, \ \text{and} \ \Gamma_i(q) = \gamma_i q + \delta_i. \tag{5}$$

With this notation, (4) becomes

$$\pi_S(A_i(p_i, q)) = \frac{\alpha_i p_i}{\beta_i p_i + \Gamma_i(q)}. \tag{6}$$

As criteria for mission success we consider proportional fairness criteria [6,18] for mission success of each UAV, i.e.,

$$v_{\text{GCS}}(\boldsymbol{p}, q) = \sum_{i=1}^{n} \ln(\pi_S(A_i(p_i, q))). \tag{7}$$

This utility is the payoff for the GCS. For the interferer, the cost function is the sum of the GCS payoff and the involved cost of the effort, i.e.,

$$v_I(\boldsymbol{p}, q) = v_{\text{GCS}}(\boldsymbol{p}, q) + C_I q, \tag{8}$$

where C_I is the cost per unit of jamming power. The GCS wants to maximize its payoff, while the interferer aims to minimize its cost function. So, $-v_I$ is the payoff to the interferer. We are looking for Nash equilibrium. Recall that $(\boldsymbol{p}, q)$ is a Nash equilibrium [4] if and only if:

$$v_{\text{GCS}}(\tilde{\boldsymbol{p}}, q) \leq v_{\text{GCS}}(\boldsymbol{p}, q),$$
$$v_I(\boldsymbol{p}, q) \leq v_I(\boldsymbol{p}, \tilde{q}) \text{ for any } (\tilde{\boldsymbol{p}}, \tilde{q}) \in \Pi_{\text{GCS}} \times \Pi_I. \tag{9}$$

We denote this game by $\Gamma = \Gamma(v_{\text{GCS}}, \Pi_{\text{GCS}}; -v_I, \Pi_I)$.

Lemma 1. $v_{GCS}(\boldsymbol{p}, q)$ is concave in $\boldsymbol{p}$, and $v_I(\boldsymbol{p}, q)$ is convex in q.

Proof. Note that

$$\frac{\partial^2 v_{\text{GCS}}(\boldsymbol{p}, q)}{\partial p_i^2} = -\frac{\Gamma_i(q)(2\beta_i p_i + \Gamma_i(q))}{p_i^2(\beta_i p_i + \Gamma_i(q))^2} < 0,$$
$$\frac{\partial^2 v_I(\boldsymbol{p}, q)}{\partial q^2} = \sum_{i=1}^{n} \frac{\gamma_i^2}{(\beta_i p_i + \Gamma_i(q))^2} > 0,$$

and the result follows.   ∎

Lemma 1 and the Nash theorem [4] imply the following result.

Theorem 1. *In the game Γ there exists at least one equilibrium.*

3   Solution of the Game

In this section we design equilibrium strategies of the game Γ. By (9), $\boldsymbol{p}$ and q are equilibrium strategies if and only if each of them is the best response to the other, i.e., they are solutions of the equations:

$$\boldsymbol{p} = \text{BR}_{\text{GCS}}(q) = \text{argmax}\{v_{\text{GCS}}(\boldsymbol{p}, q) : \boldsymbol{p} \in \Pi_{\text{GCS}}\}, \tag{10}$$
$$q = \text{BR}_I(\boldsymbol{p}) = \text{argmin}\{v_I(\boldsymbol{p}, q) : q \in \Pi_I\}. \tag{11}$$

To solve these best response equations we will employ a constructive approach.

3.1 Best Response Strategies

In this section we derive the best response strategies.

Theorem 2. *The best response strategy p of the GCS to jamming power q is unique and given as follows:*

$$p_i = P_i(\Omega(q), q) \text{ for } i = 1, \ldots, n, \tag{12}$$

where for each fixed q, $\Omega(q) = \omega$ is the unique positive root of the equation

$$S_P(\omega, q) = \overline{p}, \tag{13}$$

with

$$S_P(\omega, q) \triangleq \sum_{i=1}^{n} P_i(\omega, q), \tag{14}$$

$$P_i(\omega, q) \triangleq \frac{\Gamma_i(q)}{2\beta_i} \left(\sqrt{1 + \frac{4\beta_i}{\Gamma_i(q)\omega}} - 1 \right). \tag{15}$$

Proof. Since, by Lemma 1, (10) is a concave NLP problem, to find the best response strategy p to q we have to introduce a Lagrangian depending on a Lagrange multiplier ω as follows: $L_\omega(p) = v_{GCS}(p, q) + \omega \left(\overline{p} - \sum_{i=1}^{n} p_i \right)$. Then, KKT Theorem implies that $p \in \Pi_{GCS}$ is the best response strategy to q if and only if the following condition holds:

$$\frac{\partial L_\omega}{\partial p_i} = \frac{\Gamma_i(q)}{p_i(\beta_i p_i + \Gamma_i(q))} - \omega \begin{cases} = 0, & p_i > 0, \\ \leq 0, & p_i = 0. \end{cases} \tag{16}$$

By (16), we have that $p_i > 0$ for any i. Thus, also $\omega > 0$, and

$$\frac{\Gamma_i(q)}{p_i(\beta_i p_i + \Gamma_i(q))} = \omega \text{ for any } i. \tag{17}$$

Solving this equation in p_i implies $p_i = P_i(\omega, q)$ as given by (15).

Since $p \in \Pi_{GCS}$ the ω is defined by the condition that the total power resource has to be utilized by the GCS, i.e., by Eq. (13).

Note that $P_i(\omega, q)$ given by (15) has the following properties:

(i) $P_i(\omega, q)$ is differentiable in ω and q
(ii) $P_i(\omega, q)$ is decreasing in ω from infinity for $\omega \downarrow 0$ to zero for $\omega \uparrow \infty$.
(iii) $P_i(\omega, q)$ is increasing in q to $1/\omega$ for $q \uparrow \infty$.

Note that (i) and (ii) straightforwardly follow from (15). By (15), for a fixed $\omega > 0$

$$\lim_{q \uparrow \infty} P_i(\omega, q) = 1/\overline{\omega} \tag{18}$$

Also, $P_i(\omega, q) = f_i(\Gamma_i(q))/(2\beta_i)$, where $f_i(x) = x(\sqrt{1 + m/x} - 1)$ with $m = 4\beta_i/\omega$. Since $\frac{df_i(x)}{dx} = \frac{2x+m}{2\sqrt{x^2+mx}} - 1 > 0$, $P_i(\omega, q)$ increases with q. This and (18) implies (iii). Then, (i) and (ii) yield existence of the unique root $\omega = \Omega(q)$ for Eq. (13). While (i)–(iii) and (18) imply that $\Omega(q)$ increases with q to $n/\overline{p}$. ■

Note that, $\Omega(q)$ can be found via bisection method and $\Omega(q)$ is differentiable for $q \geq 0$ and increasing from ω_0 for $q = 0$ to $n/\overline{p}$ for $q \uparrow \infty$, where ω_0 is the unique positive root of the equation:

$$S_P(\omega_0, 0) = \sum_{i=1}^{n} \frac{\delta_i}{2\beta_i} \left(\sqrt{1 + \frac{4\beta_i}{\delta_i \omega_0}} - 1 \right) = \overline{p}. \tag{19}$$

Theorem 2 straightforwardly implies the following result.

Corollary 1. *The inverse function $Q(\omega) = \Omega^{-1}(q)$ to $\Omega(q)$ is defined for $\omega \in [\omega_0, n/\overline{p}]$ and increases from $Q(\omega_0) = 0$ to $\lim_{\omega \uparrow (n/\overline{p})} Q(\omega) = \infty$. Moreover, $S_P(\omega, Q(\omega)) = \overline{p}$.*

Theorem 3. *The best response strategy q of the interferer to $\boldsymbol{p}$ is unique and given as follows:*

$$q = \begin{cases} 0, & \sum_{i=1}^{n} \dfrac{\gamma_i}{\beta_i p_i + \delta_i} \leq C_I, & \text{(20a)} \\[4mm] q_+, & \sum_{i=1}^{n} \dfrac{\gamma_i}{\beta_i p_i + \delta_i} > C_I, & \text{(20b)} \end{cases}$$

such that, when (20b) holds, q_+ is the unique positive root of

$$\sum_{i=1}^{n} \frac{\gamma_i}{\beta_i p_i + \Gamma_i(q_+)} = C_I. \tag{21}$$

Proof. Since, by Lemma 1, $v_I(\boldsymbol{p}, q)$ is a convex in q, by (11), q is the best response strategy to $\boldsymbol{p}$ if and only if the following condition holds:

$$\frac{\partial v_I(\boldsymbol{p}, q)}{\partial q} = -\sum_{i=1}^{n} \frac{\gamma_i}{\beta_i p_i + \Gamma_i(q)} + C_I \begin{cases} = 0, & q > 0, \\ \geq 0, & q = 0. \end{cases} \tag{22}$$

Since $\gamma_i/(\beta_i p_i + \Gamma_i(q))$ is decreasing in q, the result straightforward follows from (22). ∎

3.2   Equilibrium

In this section we establish threshold value of the jamming cost for the interferer to be active, derive the form the equilibrium has to have and design a fixed point algorithm to find the equilibrium.

Theorem 4. *(a) If*

$$\sum_{i=1}^{n} \frac{\gamma_i}{\delta_i \left(1 + \sqrt{1 + 4\beta_i/(\delta_i \omega_0)} \right)} \leq \frac{C_I}{2}. \tag{23}$$

then $(\boldsymbol{p}, q) = (\boldsymbol{P}(\omega_0, 0), 0)$ *is the unique equilibrium where* ω_0 *and* $\boldsymbol{P}$ *given by* (15) *and* (19) *correspondingly.*

(b) *If* (23) *does not hold then* $(\boldsymbol{p}, q) = (\boldsymbol{P}(\Omega(q), q), q)$ *is the equilibrium where* $\boldsymbol{P}$ *given by* (15) *and* q *is the positive root of the equation*

$$F(q) = C_I/2, \tag{24}$$

where

$$F(q) \triangleq \sum_{i=1}^{n} \frac{\gamma_i}{\Gamma_i(q)\left(1 + \sqrt{1 + 4\beta_i/(\Omega(q)\Gamma_i(q))}\right)}. \tag{25}$$

Proof. Let $(\boldsymbol{p}, q)$ be an equilibrium. By Theorem 2, $\boldsymbol{p} > 0$. Thus, only two cases arise to consider: (a) $q = 0$ and (a) $q > 0$.

(a) Let $q = 0$. Then, by Theorem 2, $\boldsymbol{p} = \boldsymbol{P}(\omega_0, q)$. Substituting this $\boldsymbol{p}$ into (20a) implies (20a).
(b) Let $q > 0$. Then, by Theorem 2, $\boldsymbol{p} = \boldsymbol{P}(\Omega(q), q)$. Substituting this $\boldsymbol{p}$ into (21) implies (24) and (25). By (21), q is decreasing in C_I. Thus, by (24) and (25), F also decreasing in C_I, and the result follows. ∎

By Theorem 2, we have that $\lim_{q \uparrow \infty} F(q) = 0$. Moreover, if (23) does not hold then $F(0) > C_I/2$. Also, note that (23) establishes the threshold on the jamming cost for the interferer to be active (i.e., for $q > 0$ to be an equilibrium) or non-active (i.e., for $q = 0$ to be an equilibrium). While the GCS is always active in communication with each of the UAVS. This remarkably differs with OFDM jamming problem where some of sub-subcarriers could be not involved in transmission [8] and network security problem where some not might be not protected [2].

Interestingly, the equilibrium q can be found using fixed point algorithm. To do so, note that, by Theorem 2 and Corollary 1, there is one-to-one correspondence between ω and q. That is why first in the following proposition we derive an equation for ω, and, then, in Theorem 5, we prove convergence of the fixed point algorithm to find the ω.

Proposition 1. *Equation* (24) *is equivalent to*

$$G(\omega) = \omega, \tag{26}$$

with $q = Q(\omega)$, *where*

$$G(\omega) \triangleq \frac{2C_I}{\sum_{i=1}^{n} \gamma_i \left(\sqrt{1 + 4\beta_i/(\omega\Gamma_i(Q(\omega)))} - 1\right)/\beta_i}. \tag{27}$$

Proof. Note that

$$\frac{\gamma_i}{\Gamma_i(q)\left(1 + \sqrt{1 + 4\beta_i/(\omega\Gamma_i(q))}\right)} = \frac{\gamma_i\left(\sqrt{1 + 4\beta_i/(\omega\Gamma_i(q))} - 1\right)}{4\beta_i/\omega}.$$

Substituting this into (24) and (25) imply the result.   ∎

The following theorem shows that Eq. (26) can be solved by fixed point algorithm.

Theorem 5. $G(\omega)$ *has the following properties:*

(i) $G(\omega_0) < \omega_0$;

(ii) $G(\omega)$ *is continuous and increasing on ω;*

(iii) *There is ω_* such that $G(\omega) < \omega$ for $\omega < \omega_*$ and*

$$G(\omega_*) = \omega_*; \tag{28}$$

(iv) *The fixed point ω_* of (28) can be found via fixed point algorithm:*

$$\omega^m = G^{-1}(\omega^{m-1}) \text{ for } m = 1, 2, \ldots \text{ with } \omega^0 \text{ is fixed.}$$

The algorithm converges to ω_* for any $\omega^0 \in (\omega_0, \omega_*)$.

Proof. (i) follows from (20b). (ii) follows from Corollary 1 and (27). (iii) follows from (i), (ii), Theorems 1, 4(b) and Proposition 1.

Since $\omega^0 < \omega_*$, by (ii) and (iii), $G(\omega^0) < \omega^0$. Then, (28) implies that there is the unique $\omega^1 \in (\omega^0, \omega_*)$ such that $G(\omega^1) = \omega^0$. Thus, $\omega^1 = G^{-1}(\omega^0)$. Similarly, there is the unique $\omega^2 \in (\omega^1, \omega_*)$ such that $G(\omega^2) = \omega^1$, and so on, i.e., there is the unique $\omega^m \in (\omega^{m-1}, \omega_*)$ with $m \geq 1$ such that $G(\omega^m) = \omega^{m-1}$. Thus, ω^m is increasing and upper-bounded. Thus, there exists $\lim_{m\uparrow\infty} \omega^m$, and, this limit is equal to ω_*.   ∎

Note that for boundary cases of the jamming cost and total transmission power the equilibrium strategies can be obtained in closed form:

Proposition 2. *(a) Let C_I be small. Then*

$$q \approx n/C_I \text{ and } p_i \approx \overline{p}/n \text{ for } i = 1, \ldots, n. \tag{29}$$

(b) Let $\overline{p}$ be small. Then $p_i \approx \overline{p}/n, i = 1, \ldots, n$ and

$$q \approx \begin{cases} 0, & \sum_{i=1}^{n}(\gamma_i/\delta_i) < C_I, & (30a) \\ q_*, & \sum_{i=1}^{n}(\gamma_i/\delta_i) > C_I, & (30b) \end{cases}$$

where q_* is the unique positive root of the equation

$$\sum_{i=1}^{n} 1/(q_* + \delta_i/\gamma_i) = C_I. \tag{31}$$

(c) Let $\bar{p}$ be large. Then $q = 0$ and

$$p_i \approx \frac{\sqrt{\delta_i/\beta_i}}{\sum_{j=1}^{n} \sqrt{\delta_j/\beta_i}} \bar{p} \text{ for } i = 1,\dots,n. \tag{32}$$

Proof. Let C_I be small. Then, by (20b), $q = q_+$. While, by (21), q_+ is large. Then, Eq. (21) can be approximated by $n/q_+ \approx C_I$. Thus, $q = n/C_I$. Substituting this q into (15) implies that $P_i(\omega, q) \approx 1/\omega$, and (a) follows. Let $\bar{p}$ be small. Then p_i also is small for any i. Substituting these p_i into (20a), (20b) and (21) and taking into account that $\boldsymbol{p} \in \Pi_{\text{GCS}}$ implies imply (b). Let $\bar{p}$ be large. Then p_i is large for at least one i. Then, by (20a), $q = 0$. Then, by (13) and (15), ω is small, and $p_i = P_i(\omega, 0) \approx \sqrt{\delta_i/\beta_i}/\sqrt{\omega}$. Then, since $\boldsymbol{p} \in \Pi_{\text{GCS}}$, (32) follows. ∎

If background noise can be neglected, then equilibrium strategies also can be found in closed form.

Proposition 3. *If $\delta_i = 0$ for all i, then,*

(a) if

$$\sum_{i=1}^{n} \sqrt{\gamma_i/\beta_i} \leq \sqrt{\bar{p}C_I} \tag{33}$$

then $q = 0$ is the unique interferer strategy, while there is a continuum of the GCS equilibrium strategies, namely, any strategy $\boldsymbol{p} \in \Pi_{GCS}$ such that:

$$\sum_{i=1}^{n} \gamma_i/(p_i\beta_i) \leq C_I. \tag{34}$$

(b) if

$$\sum_{i=1}^{n} \sqrt{\gamma_i/\beta_i} > \sqrt{\bar{p}C_I} \tag{35}$$

then q and $\boldsymbol{p}$ are uniquely defined as follows:

$$p_i = P_i(\omega) = \frac{\sqrt{(\bar{p}\omega/C_I)^2 + 4\bar{p}\beta_i/(\gamma_i C_I)} - \bar{p}\omega/C_I}{2\beta_i/\gamma_i} \text{ for } i = 1,\dots,n, \tag{36}$$

$$q = \omega\bar{p}/C_I, \tag{37}$$

where ω is the unique positive root of the equation: $\sum_{i=1}^{n} P_i(\omega) = \bar{p}$.

Proof. Since $\delta_i = 0$ for all i, if $q = 0$ then $\boldsymbol{p}$ is any feasible strategy such that $\sum_{i=1}^{n} \gamma_i/(\beta_i p_i) \leq C_I$. Such an equilibrium strategy exists if and only if

$$\min_{\boldsymbol{p} \in \Pi_{\mathrm{GCS}}} \sum_{i=1}^{n} \gamma_i/(\beta_i p_i) \leq C_I. \tag{38}$$

It is clear that left-side of (38) is a convex NLP problem, and straightforward applying the KKT theorem implies that its solution is

$$p_i = (\bar{p}\sqrt{\gamma_i/\beta_i})/\sum_{j=1}^{n} \sqrt{\gamma_j/\beta_i}.$$

Substituting this strategy into (38) implies (33), and (a) follows. While, if $q > 0$ then by (21) and (33) we have that $\sum_{i=1}^{n} \omega p_i/q = C_I$. This and the fact that $\boldsymbol{p} \in \Pi_{\mathrm{GCS}}$ implies (37). Substituting (37) implies that $\boldsymbol{p}$ is given by (36). Note that $\varphi(\omega) = \sum_{i=1}^{n} P_i(\omega)$ decreases with ω and tends to zero for $\omega \uparrow \infty$. Then, equation $\varphi(\omega) = \bar{p}$ has the positive root if and only if $\varphi(0) > \bar{p}$, and this condition is equivalent to (35). ∎

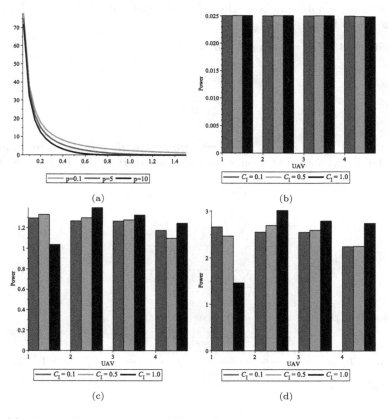

Fig. 1. (a) The equilibrium q for $\bar{p} \in \{0.1, 5, 10\}$, (b) the equilibrium $\boldsymbol{p}$ for $\bar{p} = 0.1$, (c) the equilibrium $\boldsymbol{p}$ for $\bar{p} = 5$ and (d) the equilibrium $\boldsymbol{p}$ for $\bar{p} = 10$.

Figure 1(a) illustrates a decrease in applied jamming power with an increase in jamming power cost and the total transmission power. Figure 1(b) illustrates that for $\bar{p}$ the GCS tends to serve the UAV uniformly. While an increase in $\bar{p}$ allows the GCS to serve in more individual form according to non-uniform power allocation (32). This makes the problem remarkably distinguish from OFDM transmission where uniform strategy arise for large total power resource [8]. This is caused by the fact that OFDM utility can be approximated by a superposition of logarithm and linear function of transmission power for large applied power while proportional fairness utility of the considered game can be approximated similar way for small applied power.

4 Conclusions

The problem to maintain freshness of the commands received by a group of UAVs to succeed a mission under hostile interference was modeled as non-zero game. Proportional fairness in mission success by each of the UAVs is considered as criteria for the GCS. The problem is formulated and solved as non-zero some game The considered game differs remarkably from the conventional jamming games considered in literature [16,20,24] because the structure of the rivals' strategies differ from from each other. In particular, the GCS's strategy is power allocation between the UAVs, while the interferer's strategy is a common power level assignment to jam the whole UAV's group. Moreover, in OFDM jamming game with throughput as transmitter's payoff [8], transmitter's equilibrium strategy is uniform power allocation for large total transmitting power, while, in the considered game, GCS's equilibrium strategy is uniform power allocation for small total transmitting power.

References

1. Arafa, A., Yang, J., Ulukus, S., Poor, H.V.: Age-minimal online policies for energy harvesting sensors with incremental battery recharges. In: Information Theory and Applications Workshop (ITA), pp. 1–10 (2018)
2. Baston, V., Garnaev, A.: A search game with a protector. Naval Res. Logist. **47**, 85–96 (2000)
3. Costa, M., Codreanu, M., Ephremides, A.: On the age of information in status update systems with packet management. IEEE Trans. Inf. Theory **62**, 1897–1910 (2016)
4. Fudenberg, D., Tirole, J.: Game Theory. MIT Press, Boston (1991)
5. Garnaev, A., Baykal-Gursoy, M., Poor, H.V.: Security games with unknown adversarial strategies. IEEE Trans. Cybern. **46**, 2291–2299 (2016)
6. Garnaev, A., Trappe, W.: Bargaining over the fair trade-off between secrecy and throughput in OFDM communications. IEEE Trans. Inf. Forensics Secur. **12**, 242–251 (2017)
7. Garnaev, A., Trappe, W.: The rival might be not smart: revising a CDMA jamming game. In: IEEE Wireless Communications and Networking Conference (WCNC) (2018)

8. Garnaev, A., Trappe, W., Petropulu, A.: Equilibrium strategies for an OFDM network that might be under a jamming attack. In: 51st Annual Conference on Information Sciences and Systems (CISS), pp. 1–6 (2017)

9. Hausken, K.: Information sharing among firms and cyber attacks. J. Account. Public Policy **26**, 639–688 (2007)

10. Huang, L., Modiano, E.: Optimizing age-of-information in a multi-class queueing system. In: IEEE International Symposium on Information Theory (ISIT), pp. 1681–1685 (2015)

11. Jia, H.: A stochastic derivation of the ratio form of contest success functions. Public Choice **135**, 125–130 (2008)

12. Jia, L., Yao, F., Sun, Y., Niu, Y., Zhu, Y.: Bayesian Stackelberg game for anatijamming transmission with incomplete information. IEEE Commun. Lett. **20**, 1991–1994 (2016)

13. Kam, C., Kompella, S., Nguyen, G., Wieselthier, J., Ephremides, A.: Information freshness and popularity in mobile caching. In: IEEE International Symposium on Information Theory (ISIT) (2018)

14. Kaul, S., Yates, R., Gruteser, M.: Real-time status: how often should one update? In: Proceedings of the IEEE INFOCOM, pp. 2731–2735 (2012)

15. Kaul, S., Yates, R., Gruteser, M.: Status updates through queues. In: Conference on Information Sciences and Systems (CISS), March 2012

16. Li, T., Song, T., Liang, Y.: Multiband transmission under jamming: a game theoretic perspective. In: Li, T., Song, T., Liang, Y. (eds.) Wireless Communications under Hostile Jamming: Security and Efficiency, pp. 155–187. Springer, Singapore (2018). https://doi.org/10.1007/978-981-13-0821-5_6

17. Nguyen, G., Kompella, S., Kam, C., Wieselthier, J., Ephremides, A.: Impact of hostile interference on information freshness: a game approach. In: 15th International Symposium on Modeling and Optimization in Mobile, Ad Hoc, and Wireless Networks (WiOpt) (2017)

18. Shi, H., Prasad, R.V., Onur, E., Niemegeers, I.G.M.M.: Fairness in wireless networks: issues, measures and challenges. IEEE Commun. Surv. Tutor. **16**, 5–24 (2014)

19. Skaperdas, S.: Contest success functions. Econ. Theor. **7**, 283–290 (1996)

20. Song, T., Stark, W.E., Li, T., Tugnait, J.K.: Optimal multiband transmission under hostile jamming. IEEE Trans. Commun. **64**, 4013–4027 (2016)

21. Tullock, G.: Efficient rent seeking. In: Buchanan, J., Tollison, R., Tullock, G. (eds.) Toward a Theory of Rent-Seeking Society, pp. 97–112. Texas A&M University Press (2001)

22. Xiao, L., Chen, T., Liu, J., Dai, H.: Anti-jamming transmission Stackelberg game with observation errors. IEEE Commun. Lett. **19**, 949–952 (2015)

23. Xiao, Y., Sun, Y.: A dynamic jamming game for real-time status updates. In: IEEE INFOCOM, Age of Information Workshop (2018)

24. Yang, D., Xue, G., Zhang, J., Richa, A., Fang, X.: Coping with a smart jammer in wireless networks: a Stackelberg game approach. IEEE Trans. Wirel. Commun. **12**, 4038–4047 (2013)

25. Yates, R.D., Ciblat, P., Yener, A., Wigger, M.: Age-optimal constrained cache updating. In: IEEE International Symposium on Information Theory (ISIT) (2017)

26. Yates, R.D., Najm, E., Soljanin, E., Zhong, J.: Timely updates over an erasure channel. In: IEEE International Symposium on Information Theory (ISIT) (2017)

5G and Beyond 5G Networks

Optimal Placement of User Plane Functions in 5G Networks

Irian Leyva-Pupo[✉], Cristina Cervelló-Pastor,
and Alejandro Llorens-Carrodeguas

Department of Network Engineering, Universitat Politècnica de Catalunya,
Barcelona, Spain
{irian.leyva,cristina,alejandro.llorens}@entel.upc.edu

Abstract. Because of developments in society and technology, new services and use cases have emerged, such as vehicle-to-everything communication and smart manufacturing. Some of these services have stringent requirements in terms of reliability, bandwidth, and network response time and to meet them, deploying network functions (NFs) closer to users is necessary. Doing so will lead to an increase in costs and the number of NFs. Under such circumstances, the use of optimization strategies for the placement of NFs is crucial to offer Quality of Service (QoS) in a cost-effective manner. In this vein, this paper addresses the User Plane Functions Placement (UPFP) problem in 5G networks. The UPFP is modeled as a Mixed-Integer Linear Programming (MILP) problem aimed at determining the optimal number and location of User Plane Functions (UPFs). Two optimization models are proposed that considered various parameters, such as latency, reliability and user mobility. To evaluate their performance, two services under the Ultra-Reliable and Low-Latency Communication (URLLC) category were selected. The acquired results showcase the effectiveness of our solutions.

Keywords: 5G · User Plane Functions Placement (UPFP) · MILP

1 Introduction

The Fifth Generation (5G) of mobile networks has been envisioned as a system capable of overcoming current network limitations as well as an enabler for the development of industry and society. Among the wide range of service scenarios expected of 5G networks, those that fall under the Ultra-Reliable and Low-Latency Communication (URLLC) category are the most challenging to fulfill because of their strict requirements in terms of reliability and latency.

To this end, many research studies have presented their primary target as an air interface, control and/or user planes design, handover (HO) procedures management, or network functions (NFs) placement. The present paper focuses on the last category, specifically, the placement of the User Plane Functions (UPFs). UPFs are the main NFs within the 5G user plane and play a similar role

© IFIP International Federation for Information Processing 2019
Published by Springer Nature Switzerland AG 2019
M. Di Felice et al. (Eds.): WWIC 2019, LNCS 11618, pp. 105–117, 2019.
https://doi.org/10.1007/978-3-030-30523-9_9

to that of Serving Gateways (SGWs) and Packet Gateways (PGWs) in Evolved Packet Core (EPC) networks, with the main difference being that UPFs only perform functions related to the user plane.

In 5G networks, services with high demands on latency and bandwidth require the movement of NFs such as gateways, toward the local or central office data centers (DCs) through a downward shift. This means that the number of gateway nodes (e.g., UPFs) must increase by a factor of 20 to 30 times the original amount [1]. A higher number of UPFs will not only result in an increase in network operator expenditures but also in UPF relocations. The latter occurs because of user mobility when a user attaches to a radio access node served by a UPF that differs from the one of its source access node.

Unnecessary relocations can severely impact users' Quality of Experience (QoE) by incurring additional delays and signaling during handover procedures, thereby leading to the necessity and importance of optimal UPF placement. This enables the stringent requirements of 5G networks to be more effectively coped with while simultaneously reducing capital and operational expenditures.

The remainder of this paper is organized as follows. Section 2 presents a brief overview of selected studies that are related to mobile gateway placement and reliability metrics. Section 3 introduces the 5G user plane reference architecture. Section 4 presents two Mixed-Integer Linear Programming (MILP) models to address the UPF Placement (UPFP) problem. Section 5 evaluates and compares these MILP models as well as present an extensive analysis of their results. Finally, Sect. 6 concludes the paper and suggests directions for future studies.

2   Related Work

In this section, selected studies related to the placement of mobile gateways and reliability metrics are reviewed.

Taleb and Ksentini [2] asserted the importance of considering gateway relocations in reducing costs as well as their impact on users overall QoE. The authors formulated SGW placement as a service area planning optimization problem aimed at reducing the costs of gateway relocations subject to SGW capacity restrictions. Similarly, in [3], the SGW placement problem was addressed from the perspective of SGW relocations; however, the main objective was not only to minimize relocations but also to minimize the load in SGWs. In [4], the authors proposed an algorithm to place virtual instances of PGWs with the aim of reducing costs while ensuring QoE. To this end, the load assigned to PGWs and their imbalance were optimized; nonetheless, they overlooked service latency requirements and the occurrence of PGW relocations. In [5], the placement of SGWs and PGWs was addressed by considering delay and relocation constraints. In this paper, various algorithms aimed at minimizing SGW relocations and the paths between users and PGWs were presented.

Much of the literature addressing the placement of mobile gateways has focused on specific parameters such as capacity, relocations and latency. However, none of these studies have addressed all of these metrics at once. Moreover, solutions regarding the use of reliability metrics in the placement of mobile gateways are missing, despite being utilized in a wide variety of studies related to the placement problem. In particular, those papers tackling the placement of Virtual Network Functions (VNFs) and Software Defined Networking (SDN) controllers [6–8] have relied on reliability considerations for their solutions.

Liu et al. [6] jointly addressed the placement of SDN controllers and satellite gateways in a 5G-satellite integrated network. Their main objective was to determine the most reliable locations for SDN controllers and satellite gateways to maximize the average reliability for a given number of controllers and latency constraints. Authors in [7] proposed the Resilient Controller Placement (RCP) which assigns the switches to m resilient levels of SDN controllers to enhance the resilience of the control plane. The RCP was aimed at minimizing the total incurred cost by considering the number of controllers and propagation latency, mainly. Likewise [7], Tanha et al. in [8], proposed assigning switches to r levels of controllers to improve resilience. Their main objective was to minimize the number of deployed controllers subject to resilience levels, latency and capacity requirements. Although their method guaranteed the existence of r controllers for each switch, they did not distinguish master from backup controllers because the master selection was outside their papers scope.

Similar to [7,8], our present study is based on the assignment of backup NFs to enhance network reliability. However, unlike [7,8], our network functions cannot be both main and backup simultaneously. Moreover, all of the aforementioned studies, related to the placement of gateways, take as a reference the LTE network architecture. In this paper, we propose a more revolutionary approach based on the recent standard of the 3GPP for 5G networks [9]. Furthermore, we analyze the UPFP problem by taking into account parameters such as reliability, latency and relocations. Thus, our paper makes the following **contributions**: 1. It addresses the UPFP problem in the 5G architecture standardized by the 3GPP. 2. It incorporates reliability metrics into the mobile gateways (i.e., UPFs) placement problem. 3. It proposes two MILP to determine the optimal locations of UPFs by considering relocations, latency and reliability metrics. 4. It conceives a strategy that allows for providing resilience against multiple failures while reducing the number of backup UPFs.

3   5G User Plane Reference Architecture

The first standard for the 5G system architecture was defined by the 3GPP in Technical Specifications (TS) 23.501 [9] and 23.502 [10]. This architecture is a (r)evolution of the current 4G network because many of its NFs are the result of the decomposition of some functions executed by nodes of EPC networks, whereas others are entirely new.

The 5G user plane is comprised of UPFs. These NFs can be distributed and deployed closer to the User Equipment (UE) to meet increasing traffic demands while serving low-latency applications hosted at the edge. UPFs are in charge of processing data plane packets between the (Radio) Access Network ((R)AN) and the Data Network (DN). Moreover, they provide access control, packet routing and forwarding, and Quality of Service (QoS) handling. The UPFs act as anchor points for intra/inter-radio access technology mobility as well as an external Protocol Data Unit (PDU) session point for interconnecting to the DN. To be able to perform these functions, they rely on the Session Management Functions (SMFs) located in the control plane. The SMFs select, manage and control the UPFs to establish PDU sessions. Figure 1 depicts the 5G user plane architecture and its interaction with the access and data networks and control plane.

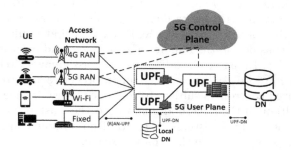

Fig. 1. 5G converged architecture [11].

4   Problem Formulation

Increasing traffic demands along with the stringent requirements of forthcoming services in terms of latency and reliability entail further network transformation. Specifically, low-latency requirements demand the placement of NFs (e.g., UPFs) closer to users at the network edge. Thus, the network response time as well as links congestion can be reduced. In addition, reliability requires the deployment of more NFs to provide higher resilience against failures. This situation implies an increase in the number of UPFs that must be deployed, which translates to increased costs and UPF relocations. Relocations not only degrade QoS but also increase operational costs because of the additional signaling exchanged among NFs to maintain or reestablish PDU sessions. In this context, novel optimization models for the UPFP that comprise latency, reliability and relocation metrics are mandatory for ensuring QoS while reducing deployment and operational costs.

In this section, two optimization models are presented to tackle the UPF placement. The main objective of these models is to determine the optimal placement for virtual instances of UPFs given a set of possible locations; thus, costs are reduced while service requirements of latency and reliability are satisfied. The set of locations may comprise Edge Nodes (ENs) and DCs facilities already deployed by network operators. Moreover, the network model and used notation are also introduced.

4.1 Network Model

The 5G network topology is represented as a graph $G(N; E)$, where N is the set of network nodes and E the links among them. The set of network nodes is formed by UPF candidate placements (N_c) and access nodes (N_r), which can be fixed and/or radio access technologies. Let L_{rc} denote the shortest distance among access nodes and UPF candidate placements, measured in terms of propagation delay, and L_{req} denote the maximum permissible latency between them. Furthermore, K_u represents the minimum number of backup UPFs to which the access nodes must be assigned to meet reliability requirements. The used notation is summarized in Tables 1 and 2.

Table 1. Sets and parameters

Notation	Description
N_r	Set of access nodes
N_c	Set of UPF candidate placements
d_r	Traffic demand at each access node
C_u	Capacity of each UPF
α	Percentage of the UPF capacity to be occupied
L_{rc}	Latencies between access nodes and UPF candidate placements
L_{req}	Latency requirement between access nodes and UPFs
K_u	Minimum number of backup UPFs to comply with reliability requirements
h_{ij}	Average frequency of handovers between access nodes i and j
F_c	Fixed cost of deploying a UPF at candidate node c
F_h	UPF relocation cost

4.2 Model 1: Cost-Aware User Plane Function Placement (CUPFP)

A minimum number of deployed NFs considerably reduce deployment and operational costs. Thus, the main objective of the CUPFP model is to determine the minimum number of UPFs to be deployed while satisfying the service requirements of latency and reliability. Accordingly, the CUPFP problem can be formulated as follows:

$$\text{Min} \sum_{\forall c \in N_c} F_c \cdot (x_c + y_c) \tag{1}$$

Table 2. Binary Variables

Notation	Description
x_c	1 if there is a main UPF installed at node c, $c \in N_c$
y_c	1 if there is a backup UPF installed at node c, $c \in N_c$
z_c	1 if backup UPF at node c, $c \in N_c$, shares its capacity
p_{rc}	1 if access node r, $r \in N_r$, has a main UPF installed at node c, $c \in N_c$
b_{rc}	1 if access node r, $r \in N_r$, has a backup UPF installed at node c, $c \in N_c$
$w_{rcc'}$	1 if access node r, $r \in N_r$, with main UPF at node c, $c \in N_c$, has a backup UPF at node c', $c' \in N_c$
a_{ijc}	1 if access node i or j, $i, j \in N_r$, is assigned to a main UPF installed at node c, $c \in N_c$
k_{ijc}	1 if access node i or j, $i, j \in N_r$, is assigned to a backup UPF installed at node c, $c \in N_c$

s.t.:

$$x_c + y_c \leq 1 \qquad\qquad \forall c \in N_c \qquad (2)$$

$$p_{rc} \leq x_c \qquad\qquad \forall r \in N_r, \forall c \in N_c \qquad (3)$$

$$b_{rc} \leq y_c \qquad\qquad \forall r \in N_r, \forall c \in N_c \qquad (4)$$

$$p_{rc} \geq x_c \qquad\qquad \forall r \in N_r, \forall c \in N_c: Loc_r = Loc_c \qquad (5)$$

$$\sum_{\forall c \in N_c} p_{rc} = 1 \qquad\qquad \forall r \in N_r \qquad (6)$$

$$\sum_{\forall c \in N_c} b_{rc} \geq K_u \qquad\qquad \forall r \in N_r \qquad (7)$$

$$z_c \leq y_c \qquad\qquad \forall c \in N_c \qquad (8)$$

$$w_{rcc'} = p_{rc} \wedge b_{rc'} \qquad\qquad \forall c, c' \in N_c, \forall r \in N_r \qquad (9)$$

$$\text{if } z_c = 1 \Rightarrow \sum_{\forall r \in N_r} d_r \cdot w_{rcc'} \leq C_u/K_u \qquad\qquad \forall c, c' \in N_c \qquad (10)$$

$$\text{if } z_c = 0 \Leftrightarrow \sum_{\forall c \in N_c} \sum_{\forall r \in N_r} d_r \cdot w_{rcc'} \leq C_u \qquad\qquad \forall c' \in N_c \qquad (11)$$

$$\sum_{\forall r \in N_r} d_r \cdot p_{rc} \leq \alpha \cdot C_u \qquad\qquad \forall c \in N_c \qquad (12)$$

$$L_{rc} \cdot (p_{rc} + b_{rc}) \leq L_{req} \qquad\qquad \forall r \in N_r, \forall c \in N_c \qquad (13)$$

$$x_c, y_c, p_{rc}, b_{rc}, w_{rcc'} \text{ binary} \qquad\qquad \forall r \in N_r, \ \forall c \in N_c \qquad (14)$$

The objective function, Eq. (1), is aimed at minimizing the deployment cost by taking into account the number of main and backup UPFs to be deployed and their location-dependent cost (F_c). The latter may include other costs, e.g., equipment and operation costs, according to network operator preferences. Equations (2) to (14) define the constraints of the optimization problem.

Inequality (2) ensures that at a specific candidate location just can be placed a main or backup UPF, but not both at the same time. The distinction between main and backup UPFs allows energy saving. As in normal network conditions (no-failure scenarios), the backup UPFs do not have any access nodes assigned; they can be instantiated only when failures occur. In addition, constraints (3) and (4) indicate that an access node cannot be assigned to a candidate location where there is not placed either a main or backup UPF. Moreover, Eq. (5) restricts the assignment of an access node to a specific UPF if this UPF has been placed at the same location. Specifically, if the access node location has a main UPF, then it must be assigned to it.

Constraint (6) ensures that the access nodes demands are served by exactly one main UPF at a given time. Note that the access nodes could have more than one main UPF assigned if their demands were split by service type or other criteria; however, considering their demands as a whole was preferred to simplify the problem formulation. Additionally, to guarantee the service reliability requirement, constraint (7) was defined. It ensures that the access nodes are assigned to at least the minimum number of backup UPFs (K_u) necessary to provide the required level of reliability. Thus, the user plane can resist against a maximum number of K_u UPF failures by mitigating service interruption.

Because not all UPFs will fail simultaneously, the access nodes that do not belong to the same main UPF could share the capacity of their assigned backup UPF. Therefore, a backup UPF could share its capacity as long as, in the case of K_u failures, its capacity is sufficient to serve the assigned access nodes of the K_u-failed main UPFs. Thus, the number of UPFs for deployment can be reduced by sharing the capacity of the backup UPFs. Equations (8)–(11) express system constraints on sharing backup capacity. Constraint (8) indicates that only the backup UPFs can share their capacity, whereas Eq. (9) expresses the relationship between a main and backup UPF of an access node. Because constraint (9) is nonlinear, it requires further transformation to be linearized. Thus, it can subsequently be replaced with the following expressions: $w_{rcc'} \leq p_{rc}$, $w_{rcc'} \leq b_{rc'}$ and $w_{rcc'} \geq p_{rc} + b_{rc'} - 1$.

Knowing beforehand which exact combination of UPFs will fail at a given time and the capacity occupied in the backup UPFs by their access nodes is almost impossible. To overcome this limitation, the following assumption was made: *if a backup UPF shares its capacity, the total demand of its access nodes that belong to the same main UPF cannot exceed the backup capacity divided by the number of failures to which the system must resist* (see Eq. (10)). Thus, in the case of K_u main UPF failures, the backup UPFs will be able to attempt all the demands of the affected access nodes. By contrast, if a backup does not share its capacity, then its total capacity cannot be exceeded (see Eq. (11)). Note that constraints (10) and (11) are nonlinear and they can be equivalently expressed in a linear form as follows:

$$\sum_{\forall r \in N_r} d_r \cdot w_{rcc'} \leq C_u/K_u + M_1 \cdot (1 - z_c) \qquad \forall c, c' \in N_c \qquad (15)$$

$$\sum_{\forall c \in N_c} \sum_{\forall r \in N_r} d_r \cdot w_{rcc'} \leq C_u + M_2 \cdot z_c \qquad \forall c' \in N_c \qquad (16)$$

$$\sum_{\forall c \in N_c} \sum_{\forall r \in N_r} d_r \cdot w_{rcc'} \leq C_u + \varepsilon + M_3 \cdot (1 - z_c) \qquad \forall c' \in N_c \qquad (17)$$

where M_1, M_2 and M_3 are sufficiently large constants and $\varepsilon > 0$ is a lower bound.

Constraint (12) ensures that the capacity of the main UPFs is not exceeded, where α is the maximum UPF capacity to be occupied by the access nodes to avoid slowing the UPFs performance. Additionally, expression (13) guarantees that an access node is not assigned to either a main or backup UPF if the latency requirement is not satisfied. Finally, Eq. (14) indicates that x_c, y_c, p_{rc}, b_{rc}, and $w_{rcc'}$ are binary variables.

4.3   Model 2: Mobility-Aware User Plane Function Placement (MUPFP)

Unlike the CUPFP model, which only considers deployment costs, the MUPFP is aimed at jointly optimizing the deployment and operation costs by considering the effects of user mobility on UPF relocations. Hence, the main objective of the MUPFP is not only to determine the optimal location for the UPFs to minimize the number of UPFs deployed but also the number of UPF relocations.

As previously stated, UPF relocations occur when a user moves between two access nodes that are served by different UPFs. Therefore, the occurrence of relocations in either the main or backup UPFs can be indicated using Eq. (18), where a_{ijc} and b_{ijc} are binary variables that express the relationship between two access nodes and their assignment to a UPF, either main or backup.

$$a_{ijc} = p_{ic} \oplus p_{jc}, \ k_{ijc} = b_{ic} \oplus b_{jc} \qquad \forall r \in N_r, \ \forall c \in N_c \qquad (18)$$

Thus, the MUPFP problem can be formulated as follows:

$$\text{Min} \sum_{\forall c \in N_c} F_c \cdot (x_c + y_c) + \sum_{\forall c \in N_c} \sum_{\forall i \in N_r} \sum_{\forall j \in N_r} F_h \cdot h_{ij} \cdot (a_{ijc} + k_{ijc}) \qquad (19)$$

s.t.: (2) to (14), (18)

In this formulation, the first term of the objective function is associated with the number of deployed UPFs. The second term is related to the cost of UPF reallocations (F_h). The number of UPF relocations is determined by the frequency of handovers (h_{ij}) between access nodes served by different UPFs. Thus, the objective function is aimed at optimizing costs by not only considering the costs caused by the number of deployed UPFs but also the costs associated with the occurrence of UPF relocations. This approach will increase the likelihood of having more access nodes served by the same UPF. Therefore, the number of UPFs and their relocations will be reduced. Note that constraint (18) introduces no linearity to our model and must be replaced with the following inequalities: $a_{ijc} \leq p_{ic}+p_{jc}$, $a_{ijc} \geq p_{ic}-p_{jc}$, $a_{ijc} \geq p_{jc}-p_{ic}$, $a_{ijc} \leq 2-p_{ic}-p_{jc}$, $k_{ijc} \leq b_{ic}+b_{jc}$, $k_{ijc} \geq b_{ic}-b_{jc}$, $k_{ijc} \geq b_{jc}-b_{ic}$ and $k_{ijc} \leq 2-b_{ic}-b_{jc}$.

The computational complexity of the CUPFP model, in terms of its number of variables and constraints, can be expressed as $O(|N_c|^2 \cdot |N_r|)$ whereas the MUPFP has $O(|N_c|^2 \cdot |N_r|+|N_r|^2 \cdot |N_c|)$ variables and $O(|N_c|^2 \cdot |N_r|)$ constraints. Thus the complexity of both models is asymptotically the same.

5 Performance Evaluation

To assess the performance of the proposed solutions, a test scenario was generated. The scenario represents a 5G network topology deployed in a city of $14\,km \times 16\,km$, see Fig. 2. Its access network is composed of 32 nodes (i.e., 22 fixed and 10 radio). The radio access nodes represent centralized Baseband Units (C-BBUs) with a maximum service radius of $3\,km$. For the placement of UPFs, 13 ENs with a maximum processing capacity of $2.5\,Tb/s$ were considered as candidate locations. To evaluate the performance of our solutions, two services from the URLLC category were selected, i.e., mIoT and vehicle-to-infrastructure cooperative sensing. Their demands were generated using the information provided in Table 3 and considering one active PDU session per user; specifically, a total demand of $2.67\,Tb/s$ in the (R)AN was considered.

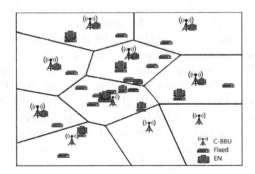

Fig. 2. 5G access network topology.

To compare the performance of our solutions with selected relevant studies, the RCP [7] and the unextended version of the Resilient Capacitated Controller

Table 3. Use cases requirements [11,12]

Service	Latency	Data Rate per user	Density	Reliability
mIoT	≤ 1 ms	≤ 1 Mbps	$10^4\,users/km^2$	99.999%
Cooperative sensing	≤ 1 ms	≤ 5 Mbps	$\leq 100\,users/km^2$	99.999%

Placement Problem (RCCPP) [8] were used as references. We selected the RCP and RCCPP because of their similarities to our models. Their main purpose are to minimize the number of controllers subject to latency, resilience and capacity constraints. To apply these models to the UPFP problem, the controllers were considered UPFs and the switches as access nodes. Additionally, for the RCP implementation a UPF failure probability of 10^{-4} was assumed whereas, in the RCCPP, the intercontroller latency constraint was relaxed. For the implementation of the models, the Python-based package Pyomo was selected along with Gurobi as its underlying solver.

5.1   Analysis of the Results

All the models (i.e., CUPFP, MUPFP, RCCPP and RCP) were evaluated for different values of UPF capacity by considering one level of backup ($K_u = 1$). Their optimal solutions were determined with zero optimality gap and analyzed in terms of the number of UPFs necessary to cover the services demand, load distributions, worst case delays and UPF relocations (see Fig. 3).

Number of Required UPFs: The total number of UPFs required by all the models is shown in Fig. 3a. Additionally, the number of main UPFs obtained by the proposed models and RCP is also represented. At first glance, in all the solutions, it can be observed that the number of required UPFs decreases as the capacity increases. Moreover, the total number of UPFs of the proposed models was always lower than or equal to that of the reference models. This difference is more notable for small values of capacity where the number of UPFs is higher.

For all the values of capacity, the CUPFP and MUPFP models always obtained similar results, either in terms of total or main UPFs. Moreover, their numbers of main UPFs were always lower than the total. Therefore, the proposed solutions are more cost-effective in terms of the numbers of UPFs and resources consumption than the RCCPP and RCP models. Thus, the total numbers of UPFs can be considerably reduced by sharing the backups capacity. Specifically, by placing one backup UPF the reliability requirement of all access nodes was satisfied. Moreover, the distinction between main and backup UPFs allows energy saving because the backup UPFs can be instantiated only when failures occur.

Load Distribution: For our solutions and the RCP, the load distribution was measured only in the main UPFs, whereas in the RCCPP, all the UPFs were included. In Fig. 3b, our proposed solutions can clearly be observed to outperform the reference models for all values of capacity analyzed, with the exception

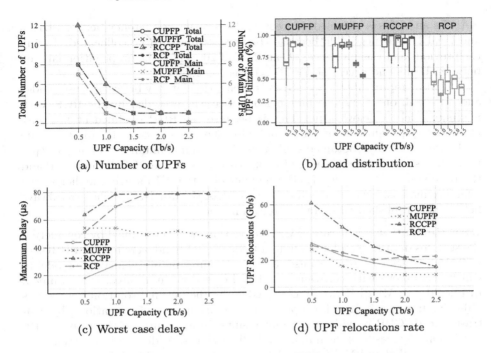

Fig. 3. Performance comparison against UPF capacity variation

of $C_u = 0.5\,\mathrm{Tb/s}$. Their maximum imbalance obtained was always below 20% except for $C_u = 0.5\,\mathrm{Tb/s}$ where the imbalance in the CUPFP was around 60%. By contrast, the RCCPP and RCP lowest imbalance was always above 25%, and for $C_u = 2.5\,\mathrm{Tb/s}$, the imbalance nearly reached 100% in the RCCPP.

Moreover, our models provided a UPF average utilization between 50 and 90% whereas this metric was always above 90% for the RCCPP and below 50% for the RCP what can lead to overload and underutilized UPFs, respectively. These satisfactory outcomes are because of the utilization of the α factor in Eq. (12), which restricts the capacity to be occupied in the main UPFs, thereby allowing for an enhanced distribution of load. This factor was determined in function of the total demand in the (R)AN and the expected number of UPFs for each value of capacity. In addition, the load distributions obtained with the CUPFP and MUPFP models were quite even, although CUPFP outperforms MUPFP for capacities values higher than 1 Tb/s.

Maximum Delay: The maximum propagation delay between UPFs and access nodes was calculated in terms of the Euclidean distance divided by the speed of light $2 \times 10^8\,\mathrm{m/s}$, assuming optical fiber as the underlying transport. To meet the latency requirement of 1 ms, the overall latency (Round-Trip-Time (RTT)) in the (R)AN, should not exceed 0.5 ms [13]. Therefore, the propagation and processing delays in the segment (R)AN-DN cannot excess 0.5 ms. Considering that SGWs and PGWs have a processing time of 100 μs [14], a total processing time of 300 μs in UPFs and DNs is assumed. Moreover, the propagation latency between UPFs and local DNs is negligible because they are assumed to be collocated. Taking the previous analysis into account, an RTT of 200 μs for the propagation latency between UPFs and access nodes (L_{req}) was considered.

Figure 3c represents the worst-case propagation latency between access nodes and UPFs, in one way. The best performance was provided by the RCP, with maximum delays below 30 μs. This is because the RCP is aimed at not only minimizing the number of UPFs but also the routing cost. In addition, the CUPFP and RCCPP obtained similar results with maximum delays up to 78 μs. Notably, a substantial difference did not exist between the RCCPP and RCP and the proposed solutions, despite the number of active UPFs being higher in the reference models. Furthermore, in all the models, the worst-case delay was always below the established threshold ($\leq$100 μs in one way).

UPF Relocations: The rate of UPF relocations was determined by considering the services data rate and a maximum frequency of handovers between BBUs of [350, 550] HO/s, according to user density. For user mobility, a simple model in which users move with constant speed and direction, in an area, was assumed. In Fig. 3d, the MUPFP can be observed to be the optimal solution because its objective function is aimed at optimizing the occurrence of relocations; by contrast, the RCCPP provides the worst results. In all solutions, the rate of UPF relocations decreases as the number of UPFs reduces. Additionally, a comparison between CUPFP and MUPFP models revealed a remarkable difference in terms of relocations, despite the models having the same number of active UPFs. This result demonstrates the importance of considering user mobility patterns during the placement. Furthermore, this consideration guarantees enhanced QoE without incurring additional costs, measured in terms of the number of deployed UPFs.

6   Conclusion

In this paper, we proposed two MILP models to address the placement of UPFs in 5G networks. The proposed solutions are aimed at not only minimizing the number of UPFs but also their relocations while satisfying the service requirements of latency and reliability. The obtained results showcase the effectiveness of the proposed approaches. Specifically, the number of UPFs to be deployed can be considerably reduced by sharing the capacity of backup UPFs, and UPF relocations can be diminished by considering user mobility and differentiating the main UPFs from the backups.

In future works, we will consider the design of heuristic solutions for the UPFP as well as their evaluation in different settings. Additionally, dynamic optimization of nodes assignment and UPFs placement to adapt to variations in traffic and user locations will be addressed. Furthermore, we intend to solve the placement problem of 5G UPFs by considering the existence of several network slices to optimize resource utilization when services with different requirements coexist.

Acknowledgment. This work has been supported by the Ministerio de Economía y Competitividad of the Spanish Government under the project TEC2016-76795-C6-1-R and through a predoctoral FPI scholarship.

References

1. Huawei Technologies Co.: 5G network architecture a high-level perspective (2016). https://www.huawei.com/minisite/hwmbbf16/insights/5G-Nework-Architecture-Whitepaper-en.pdf
2. Taleb, T., Ksentini, A.: Gateway relocation avoidance-aware network function placement in carrier cloud. In: Proceedings of the 16th ACM International Conference on Modeling, Analysis & Simulation of Wireless and Mobile Systems, pp. 341–346. ACM (2013)
3. Ksentini, A., et al.: On using SDN in 5G: the controller placement problem. In: Global Communications Conference (GLOBECOM), pp. 1–6. IEEE (2016)
4. Bagaa, M., Taleb, T., Ksentini, A.: Service-aware network function placement for efficient traffic handling in carrier cloud. In: 2014 IEEE Wireless Communications and Networking Conference (WCNC), pp. 2402–2407, April 2014
5. Taleb, T., Bagaa, M., Ksentini, A.: User mobility-aware virtual network function placement for virtual 5G network infrastructure. In: 2015 IEEE International Conference on Communications (ICC), pp. 3879–3884. IEEE, June 2015
6. Liu, J., Shi, Y., Zhao, L., Cao, Y., Sun, W., Kato, N.: Joint placement of controllers and gateways in SDN-Enabled 5G-Satellite Integrated Network. IEEE J. Sel. Areas Commun. **36**(2), 221–232 (2018)
7. Tanha, M., Sajjadi, D., Pan, J.: Enduring node failures through resilient controller placement for software defined networks. In: 2016 IEEE Global Communications Conference (GLOBECOM), pp. 1–7. IEEE (2016)
8. Tanha, M., Sajjadi, D., Ruby, R., Pan, J.: Capacity-aware and delay-guaranteed resilient controller placement for software-defined WANs. IEEE Trans. Network Serv. Manag. **15**, 991–1005 (2018)
9. 3GPP: TS 23.501- System Architecture for the 5G System; Stage 2. http://www.3gpp.org/ftp/Specs/archive/23_series/23.501/23501-f00.zip
10. 3GPP: TS 23.502- Procedures for the 5G System; Stage 2. http://www.3gpp.org/ftp/Specs/archive/23_series/23.502/23502-f10.zip
11. 5G Americas: 5G Network Transformation. Technical report, 5G Americas (2017). http://www.5gamericas.org/files/3815/1310/3919/5G_Network_Transformation_Final.pdf
12. NGMN Alliance: Perspectives on Vertical Industries and Implications for 5G. Technical report, NGMN Alliance (2016), https://www.ngmn.org/fileadmin/user_upload/160922_NGMN_-_Perspectives_on_Vertical_Industries_and_Implications_for_5G_final.pdf
13. Parvez, I., Rahmati, A., Guvenc, I., Sarwat, A.I., Dai, H.: A survey on low latency towards 5G: RAN, core network and caching solutions. IEEE Commun. Surv. Tutorials **20**(4), 3098–3130 (2018)
14. Tawbeh, A., Safa, H., Dhaini, A.R.: A hybrid SDN/NFV architecture for future LTE networks. In: 2017 IEEE International Conference on Communications (ICC), pp. 1–6. IEEE (2017)

Evaluating Multi-connectivity in 5G NR Systems with Mixture of Unicast and Multicast Traffic

Roman Kovalchukov[1], Dmitri Moltchanov[1], Alexander Pyattaev[2], and Aleksandr Ometov[1(✉)]

[1] Tampere University, Korkeakoulunkatu 10, 33720 Tampere, Finland
aleksandr.ometov@tuni.fi
[2] Peoples' Friendship University of Russia (RUDN University),
6 Miklukho-Maklaya Street, Moscow 117198, Russian Federation

Abstract. The future 5G New Radio (NR) systems are expected to support both multicast and unicast traffic. However, these traffic types require principally different NR system parameters. Particularly, the area covered by a single antenna configuration needs to be maximized when serving multicast traffic to efficiently use system resources. This prevents the system from using the maximum allowed number of antenna elements decreasing the inter-site distance between NR base stations. In this paper, we formulate a model of NR system with multi-connectivity capability serving a mixture of unicast and multicast traffic types. We show that multi-connectivity enables a trade-off between new and ongoing session drop probabilities for both unicast and multicast traffic types. Furthermore, supporting just two simultaneously active links allows to exploit most of the gains and the value of adding additional links is negligible. We also show that the service specifics implicitly prioritize multicast sessions over unicast ones. If one needs to achieve a balance between unicast and multicast session drop probabilities, explicit prioritization mechanism is needed at NR base stations.

Keywords: New Radio · 5G cellular systems · Multicasting · Multi-connectivity · Session drop probabilities · Resource utilization

1 Introduction

The Third Generation Partnership Project (3GPP) is currently in the process of specifying a new 5th generation (5G) radio interface widely known as 5G NR [1]. The first phase of the system is expected to be the "ready" in 2020, and the standartization is pacing its' way fast [2]. Industry and academia show great interest in 5G NR technology providing the initial performance evaluation not only

Work of the last author is supported by Nokia Foundation under a personal grant. The publication has been prepared with the support of the "RUDN University Program 5–100".

© IFIP International Federation for Information Processing 2019
Published by Springer Nature Switzerland AG 2019
M. Di Felice et al. (Eds.): WWIC 2019, LNCS 11618, pp. 118–128, 2019.
https://doi.org/10.1007/978-3-030-30523-9_10

by simulations but also with testbeds in the field and laboratory environments [3–5]. 5G NR is generally aiming at bringing high rates and reducing latencies to the air interface at the same time [6], thus, enabling an entirely new range of bandwidth-hungry real-time applications such as HD streaming, augmented- and virtual reality [7], etc.

The use of millimeter wave (mmWave) band for NR operation brings specific challenges to system designers. These include unique propagation properties, dynamic human-body blockage environment with the mobility of users and blockers, beam steering with large antenna arrays, the mobility of users [8–10], etc. Accordingly, performance analysis of unicast traffic support in NR systems has received considerable attention over the last few years. The authors in [11] quantify the effect of antenna pattern directivity and human-body blockage on mean interference and signal-to-interference (SIR) ratio in NR systems. Corresponding Laplace transforms of these metrics have been reported in [12]. Three-dimensional deployments have been considered in [13]. The engineering studies focused on assessing the effects of mitigating blockage techniques, such as multi-connectivity and guard capacity, recently started to appear [14,15].

Most of the studies performed so far concentrated solely on the unicast type of traffic. However, similarly to other radio access technologies NR should also support multicast sessions [16]. Unfortunately, only little is known regarding the support of multicast service in 5G NR systems. In [17], the authors propose a dynamic grouping scheme for mobile users having the same multicast session based on their proximity. The associated algorithm is based on consecutive testing of different antenna half-power beamwidths (HPBW) maximizing the sum rate of the system. A similar approach is proposed in [18]. In addition to the use of dynamic HPBW, the optimization framework developed in [19] accounts for non-equal power-sharing between beams.

The only study, where the mixture of unicast and multicast traffic is addressed is due to Samuilov et al. [20]. Among other conclusions, the authors demonstrated that there exist a specific parameters for base station (BS) and user equipment (UE) inducing BR BS coverage R_M with session drop probabilities (p_M, p_U) for a given arrival rates of multicast and unicast sessions (λ_M, λ_U). Thus, there is a principal trade-off between system characteristics required for unicast and multicast traffic affecting the inter-site distance (ISD) between NR BS: while unicast traffic requires small HPBW to extend ISD and decrease deployment cost, multicast traffic needs higher HPBW to form larger multicast groups and thus decrease the load imposed on NR BS.

One of the consequences of increased ISD in NR deployment is potential session drops caused by human-body blockage phenomenon or insufficient resources available at the NR BS to support a session changing its state from non-blocked to blocked [15,21]. To alleviate these effects, 3GPP has recently proposed so-called multi-connectivity operation (also known as macro-diversity), where UE is allowed to simultaneously support connections to multiple NR BSs and switch between them in case of outage events [22].

In this paper, we investigate the effect of recently standardized 3GPP multi-connectivity operation on performance metrics of a mixture of unicast and multicast traffic in the cellular deployment of NR systems. Based on the developed system level modeling framework we analyze user- and system-centric performance metrics provided to multicast and unicast sessions in the presence of multi-connectivity capabilities.

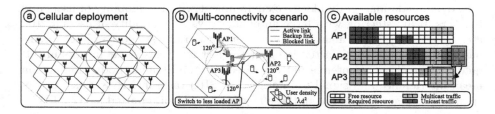

Fig. 1. An illustration of the considered NR cellular deployment.

The paper is organized as follows. In Sect. 2, the system model is described. We introduce out system level modeling framework in Sect. 3. Numerical results are presented in Sect. 4. The last section concludes the paper.

2   System Model

The system model is introduced in this section by specifying the corresponding components including deployment, antenna, propagation, blockage, traffic, connectivity, and service models. Finally, we specify the metrics of interest.

Deployment, Traffic, and Blockage Models. We consider a standard NR cellular deployment illustrated in Fig. 1(a). The height of all NR BSs is assumed to be h_A. The ISD is assumed to be D.

In the considered deployment, moving pedestrians, represented by cylinders with constant height and base radius, h_B and r_B, respectively, may block the line-of-sight (LoS) path between BS and UE, see Fig. 1(b). Pedestrians, also acting as blockers, are assumed to move according to random direction model (RDM) with constant speed v_B, and run the length of τ_B s [23]. Using the property of RDM model, at each instant of time blockers organize a Poisson point process (PPP) in $\Re^2$. The density of blockers is assumed to be λ_B blockers/m^2. According to [24], the blockage of human-body in NR bands result in additional degradation of 15–40 dB. In this study, we assume 20 dB losses.

The session arrival rate is assumed to be λ session/m^2. With probability p_M, the session is assumed to be of a multicast type. A session is classified as multicast with complementary probability $1 - p_M$. Unicast and multicast sessions are characterized by constant rate requirements of T_U and T_M Mbps, respectively. The corresponding session durations are exponentially distributed with parameters μ_U and μ_M.

Propagation and Antenna Models. In this work, we use 3GPP urban micro (UMi) street canyon propagation model [25] providing the following path loss at the three-dimensional distance x between NR BS and UE

$$L(x) = \begin{cases} 52.4 + 21.0 \log x + 20 \log f_c, & \text{LoS blocked}, \\ 32.4 + 21.0 \log x + 20 \log f_c, & \text{LoS non-blocked}, \end{cases} \tag{1}$$

where f_c is the carrier frequency measured in GHz.

The selected model specifies three zones around BS. Up to the distance R_B, UE is never in outage conditions even when LoS path is blocked. In the interval (R_B, R_O), UE is in outage only when the LoS is blocked. Finally, R_O defines the distance when UE is in outage even when LoS is not blocked.

Linear antenna array is assumed to be utilized at BSs an UEs. The gain at transmit and receive sides is computed as [26]

$$G = \frac{1}{\theta_{3db}^+ - \theta_{3db}^-} \int_{\theta_{3db}^-}^{\theta_{3db}^+} \frac{\sin(K\pi \cos(\theta)/2)}{\sin(\pi \cos(\theta)/2)} d\theta, \tag{2}$$

where K is a number of elements in a linear array.

Connectivity and Service Models. We assume that the UE has the 3GPP multi-connectivity functionality [22], where each node maintains the links to M neighboring BSs. M is referred to as "degree of multi-connectivity". According to the multi-connectivity operation, the UE can switch to one of the available BSs in case current link becomes unavailable.

Upon arrival, a unicast session is assumed to establish M active connections with M nearest NR BSs based on time-averaged SNR metric. A connection with the nearest BS is first tried. Depending on the distance between BS and UE the required rate T_U is translated into the bandwidth requirements B_U using the set of NR modulation and coding schemes (MCS, [27]). If there is an insufficient amount of resources at this BS, BS with the next nearest distance is used. If none of those BSs have a sufficient amount of resources, a unicast session is dropped. Upon blockage event, SNR drops by 20 dB and session changes its resource requirements. If there are no resources available to support these new bandwidth requirements, BS with the nearest distance is tried next. If there are no BSs out of M available that may support these new bandwidth requirements, a session is dropped during service.

The connectivity process of multicast sessions is similar to described above for unicast sessions. The principal difference is in the resource allocation at BSs. In particular, upon arrival of the multicast session, the nearest BS tests whether there is an ongoing multicast service and, if yes, what kind of MCS it uses. If there is an ongoing multicast service, a new session is accepted to the system whenever the MCS order is higher than the one used for ongoing multicast sessions. If the MCS order is lower, the BS tests whether it can support multicast service at this lower MCS. If the conclusion is positive, session is accepted to the system and the current MCS of the multicast service is lowered. Otherwise, other $M - 1$

is descending order of distances are tested using the same procedure. Finally, if there is no ongoing multicast service, the session acceptance logic is similar to unicast sessions. At the blockage time instant, the procedure described above is tested first for the currently active BS and then for the remaining $M - 1$ BSs. If none of those may support an ongoing session in blockage state, a multicast session is dropped.

Metrics of Interest. In the considered system model, we are interested in new and ongoing multicast, $p_{N,M}$ and $p_{O,M}$, and unicast, $p_{N,U}$ and $p_{O,U}$, session drop probabilities. The new session drop probability is defined as the probability that at the moment of new session arrival there are no resources to accept the session for service. Ongoing session drop probability is defined as the probability that a session accepted for service is then dropped at the moment of blockage due to insufficient resources available. As a system-centric performance metric, we concentrate on system resource utilization averaged over all NR BSs.

3   Performance Evaluation Framework

To characterize the system performance, we have developed a system level simulation framework (SLS) is based on discrete-event simulation (DES) with multithread optimization in Java.

To achieve reliable results, we have executed the simulations for 10^6 s of the simulated system time. Since all stochastic processes in our system are stationary, the system of interest eventually converges to the steady-state. The beginning of the steady-state is detected using the exponentially-weighted moving average (EWMA) technique with the weighting parameter 0.1 [28]. The average duration of the transient period has been found to be 134 s.

During the simulation run, the data is collected during the steady-state period only. On top of sampling the system-state every 10 s, the batch means strategy is used to exclude residual correlation in the statistical data. According to it, batches of 10^3 observations were collected first. The means of these batches are considered as independent identically distributed (iid) observations. The resulting iid samples were processed using conventional statistical methods. Due to the large sample sizes, in what follows, only point estimates are demonstrated. The reason is that the interval estimates do not differ by more than ± 0.01 from the point estimates under the level of significance $\alpha = 0.1$.

4   Selected Numerical Results

In this section, we numerically assess the performance gains provided by multi-connectivity operation at BSs serving mixtures of unicast and multicast traffic. The default input system parameters used in this section are provided in Table 1.

First, we consider the new session drop probability for multicast and unicast sessions with different degrees of multi-connectivity as a function of the fraction

Table 1. Main parameters for numerical assessment.

System parameter	Value
User density, λ	0.5 users/m^2
User velocity, v_B	4 m/s
BS height, h_A	4 m
UE height, h_U	1.5 m
Blocker height, h_B	1.7 m
Blocker radius, r_B	0.3 m
Multi-connectivity degree, M	$(1, 2, 3)$
Number of NR BSs, N	3
Transmit power, P_T	0.2 W
Planar antenna elements at BS, K_A	32
Planar antenna elements at UE, K_U	4
Carrier frequency, f_c	28 GHz
Bandwidth at each NR BS, B	1 GHz
LoS blockage loss, L_B	20 dB
Mean session time, $1/\mu$	20 s
Session initiation probability, p_A	3.14×10^{-4}
Session rate, R	100 Mbps

of multicast sessions, p_M, illustrated in Fig. 2. As one may observe, the presence of multi-connectivity has a profound negative effect on the new session drop probabilities for both types of traffic. Analyzing the presented data further, we may observe that the new session drop probabilities of both type of traffic decrease as the fraction of multicast sessions increases. This behavior is logical for the unicast sessions as their fraction decreases as p_M increases. In cases, of the multicast session, this effect is explained by the nature of the service process. Indeed, as multicast sessions do not always require a new set of resources upon their arrival. If there is at least one multicast session in the system, they may change the amount of resources required for service. Thus, when p_M is not negligible, each NR BSs almost always have an active multicast session in the system drastically decreasing the multicast session drop probability.

Consider now the effect of multi-connectivity on ongoing session drop probability illustrated in Fig. 3 for a range of values of a fraction of multicast sessions, p_M. As one may observe, there is a noticeable positive effect of multi-connectivity on both considered types of traffic. Quantitatively, it is essential to note that the gains of the system with $M = 3$ compared to $M = 2$ is much milder than that of $M = 2$ compared to no multi-connectivity at all, $M = 1$. This is essential observation as maintaining simultaneously active links is expensive from the control overhead point of view [22].

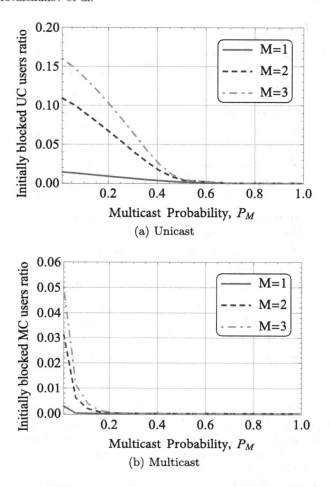

Fig. 2. New session drop probabilities for unicast and multicast traffic.

Analyzing the data corresponding to multicast service, illustrated in Figs. 2(b) and 3(b), one may notice that much sharper decays characterize the new and ongoing session drop probabilities compared to unicast traffic. As the service process of this traffic is drastically different the interplay between the unicast and multicast type of traffic in NR systems is of particular interest. Notably, for non-negligible values of p_M this type of traffic has implicit priority over unicast sessions. This conclusion is supported by the absolute values of new and ongoing session drop probabilities in Figs. 2(b) and 3(b). Thus, NR system may need some explicit mechanism to prioritize unicast traffic.

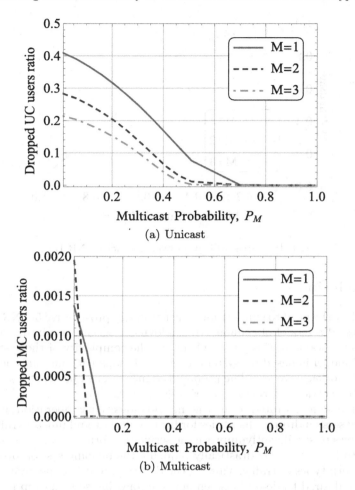

Fig. 3. Ongoing session drop probabilities for unicast and multicast traffic.

Finally, we assess the system-centric metric of interest – resource utilization averaged across NR BSs, illustrated in Fig. 4. As one may observe, the system with multi-connectivity operation enabled, $M = 2$ or $M = 3$, is characterized by much better performance compared to the system with $M = 1$ in overloaded regime corresponding to small values of p_M. When the fraction of multicast sessions increases, the systems switch to the underloaded regime, where the performance of systems with different degrees of multi-connectivity coincide.

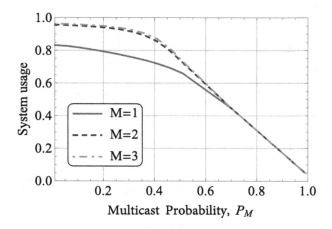

Fig. 4. Resource utilization averaged across NR BSs.

5   Conclusion

Motivated by the need to support multicast traffic in prospective 5G NR systems, we formulated a model of cellular NR deployment serving a mixture of unicast and multicast traffic in this paper. Owing to the complexity of the systems, the developed model is based on system level simulations with an analytical model of the LoS blockage process. The proposed framework can be used to assess user- and system-centric performance metrics of interest.

We have demonstrated that the multi-connectivity operation negatively affects new session drop probabilities for both multicast and unicast traffic. However, it allows to significantly improve the service performance of sessions already accepted to the system by drastically reducing the ongoing session drop probability for both types of traffic. Varying the degree of multi-connectivity one may achieve the desired trade-off between new and ongoing session drop probability. Quantitatively, the significant impact on both user- and system-centric performance metrics is produced by supporting just two simultaneously active links, so-called dual connectivity operation. The gains of adding additional links are much milder.

Finally, we would like to note that the specifics of the service process of multicast traffic profoundly affects unicast traffic performance. In particular, if the fraction of multicast session is non-negligible, there is resource capturing effect, when multicast sessions exclusively occupy a fraction of resources. Thus, if one needs to achieve a balance between unicast and multicast new and ongoing session drop probabilities, explicit prioritization mechanism is needed.

References

1. Parkvall, S., Dahlman, E., Furuskar, A., Frenne, M.: NR: the new 5G radio access technology. IEEE Commun. Stand. Mag. **1**(4), 24–30 (2017)

2. 3GPP, Multiplexing and Channel Coding, 3rd Generation Partnership Project (3GPP). TS 38.212, v15.4.0, Release 15, December 2018
3. Qualcomm: mmWave 5G NR prototype demo video, May 2018. https://www.qualcomm.com/videos/mmwave-5g-nr-prototype-demo-video
4. Halvarsson, B., et al.: 5G NR coverage, performance and beam management demonstrated in an outdoor urban environment at 28 GHz. In: Proceedings of IEEE 5G World Forum (5GWF), pp. 416–421 (2018)
5. Morant, M., Trinidad, A., Tangdiongga, E., Koonen, T., Llorente, R.: Experimental demonstration of mm-Wave 5G NR Photonic Beamforming Based on ORRs and Multicore Fiber. IEEE Trans. Microw. Theory Tech. **67**(7), 2928–2935 (2019)
6. Ghosh, A.: 5G New Radio (NR): physical layer overview and performance. In: Proceedings of IEEE Communication Theory Workshop, pp. 1–38 (2018)
7. Prasad, A., Benjebbour, A., Bulakci, O., Pedersen, K.I., Pratas, N.K., Mezzavilla, M.: Agile radio resource management techniques for 5G new radio. IEEE Commun. Mag. **55**(6), 62–63 (2017)
8. Moltchanov, D., Ometov, A.: On the fraction of LoS blockage time in mmWave systems with mobile users and blockers. In: Chowdhury, K.R., Di Felice, M., Matta, I., Sheng, B. (eds.) WWIC 2018. LNCS, vol. 10866, pp. 183–192. Springer, Cham (2018). https://doi.org/10.1007/978-3-030-02931-9_15
9. Zeman, K., Stusek, M., Masek, P., Hosek, J.: Improved NLOS propagation models for wireless communication in mmWave bands. In: Proceedings of the of 8th International Conference on Localization and GNSS (ICL-GNSS), pp. 1–6. IEEE (2018)
10. Moltchanov, D., Ometov, A., Andreev, S., Koucheryavy, Y.: Upper bound on capacity of 5G mmWave cellular with multi-connectivity capabilities. Electron. Lett. **54**(11), 724–726 (2018)
11. Petrov, V., Moltchanov, D., Koucheryavy, Y.: On the efficiency of spatial channel reuse in ultra-dense THz networks. In: Proceedings of IEEE Globecom, December 2015
12. Singh, S., Kulkarni, M.N., Ghosh, A., Andrews, J.G.: Tractable model for rate in self-backhauled millimeter wave cellular networks. IEEE J. Sel. Areas Commun. **33**(10), 2196–2211 (2015)
13. Kovalchukov, R.: Evaluating SIR in 3D millimeter-wave deployments: direct modeling and feasible approximations. IEEE Trans. Wireless Commun. **18**(2), 879–896 (2019)
14. Petrov, V., et al.: Achieving end-to-end reliability of mission-critical traffic in softwarized 5G networks. IEEE J. Sel. Areas Commun. **36**(3), 485–501 (2018)
15. Kovalchukov, R., et al.: Improved session continuity in 5G NR with joint use of multi-connectivity and guard bandwidth. In: Proceedings of Global Communications Conference (GLOBECOM), pp. 1–7. IEEE (2018)
16. Biason, A., Zorzi, M.: Multicast via point to multipoint transmissions in directional 5G mmWave communications. IEEE Commun. Mag. **57**(2), 88–94 (2019)
17. Park, H., Park, S., Song, T., Pack, S.: An incremental multicast grouping scheme for mmWave networks with directional antennas. IEEE Commun. Lett. **17**(3), 616–619 (2013)
18. Feng, W., Li, Y., Niu, Y., Su, L., Jin, D.: Multicast spatial reuse scheduling over millimeter-wave networks. In: Proceedings of 13th International Wireless Communications and Mobile Computing Conference (IWCMC), pp. 317–322. IEEE (2017)
19. Sundaresan, K., Ramachandran, K., Rangarajan, S.: Optimal beam scheduling for multicasting in wireless networks. In: Proceedings of the 15th Annual International Conference on Mobile Computing and Networking, pp. 205–216. ACM (2009)

20. Samuvlov, A., Moltchanov, D., Krupko, A., Kovalchukov, R., Moskaleva, F., Gaidamaka, Y.: Performance analysis of mixture of unicast and multicast sessions in 5G NR systems. In: Proceedings of 10th International Congress on Ultra Modern Telecommunications and Control Systems and Workshops (ICUMT), pp. 1–7. IEEE (2018)
21. Moltchanov, D., et al.: Improving session continuity with bandwidth reservation in mmWave communications. IEEE Wirel. Commun. Lett. **8**(1), 105–108 (2019)
22. 3GPP, NR; Multi-connectivity; Overall description (Release 15), 3GPP TS 37.340 V15.2.0, June 2018
23. Nain, P., Towsley, D., Liu, B., Liu, Z.: Properties of random direction models. In: Proceedings of 24th Annual Joint Conference of the IEEE Computer and Communications Societies, vol. 3, pp. 1897–1907. IEEE (2005)
24. Haneda, K., et al.: 5G 3GPP-like channel models for outdoor urban microcellular and macrocellular environments. In: Proceedings of IEEE Vehicular Technology Conference (VTC 2016-Spring), May 2016
25. 3GPP, Study on channel model for frequencies from 0.5 to 100 GHz (Release 15), 3GPP TR 38.901 V15.0.0, June 2018
26. Balanis, C.A.: Antenna Theory: Analysis and Design. Wiley, New York (2016)
27. 3GPP, NR; Physical channels and modulation (Release 15), 3GPP TR 38.211, December 2017
28. Perros, H.: Computer Simulation Techniques. The definitive introduction. North Carolina State University (2009)

Performance of mmWave-Based Mesh Networks in Indoor Environments with Dynamic Blockage

Rustam Pirmagomedov[1,2](✉), Dmitri Moltchanov[2], Viktor Ustinov[3],
Md Nazmus Saqib[2], and Sergey Andreev[2]

[1] Peoples' Friendship University of Russia (RUDN University),
6 Miklukho-Maklaya St, Moscow 117198, Russian Federation
prya.spb@gmail.com
[2] Tampere University, Korkeakoulunkatu 1, 33720 Tampere, Finland
[3] St. Petersburg State University of Telecommunication,
Bolshevikov 22/1, St. Petersburg 190000, Russian Federation

Abstract. Due to growing throughput demands dictated by innovative media applications (e.g., 360° video streaming, augmented and virtual reality), millimeter-wave (mmWave) wireless access is considered to be a promising technology enabler for the emerging mobile networks. One of the crucial usages for such systems is indoor public protection and disaster relief (PPDR) missions, which may greatly benefit from higher mmWave bandwidths. In this paper, we assess the performance of on-demand mmWave mesh topologies in indoor environments. The evaluation was conducted by utilizing our system-level simulation framework based on a realistic floor layout under dynamic blockage conditions, 3GPP propagation model, mobile nodes, and multi-connectivity operation. Our numerical results revealed that the use of multi-connectivity capabilities in indoor deployments allows for generally improved connectivity performance whereas the associated per-node throughput growth is marginal. The latter is due to the blockage-rich environment, which is typical for indoor layouts as it distinguishes these from outdoor cases. Furthermore, the number of simultaneously supported links at each node that is required to enhance the system performance is greater than two, thus imposing considerable control overheads.

Keywords: Milliliter-wave mesh · 5G NR · PPDR · Emergency response · Indoor environment

1 Introduction

Due to the growing capacity requirements on the air interface as demanded by innovative media applications, such as 360° HD streaming, augmented and virtual reality (AR/VR), millimeter-wave (mmWave) wireless access is considered as a promising technology for future mobile networks.

The publication has been prepared with the support of the "RUDN University Program 5-100". This work was also supported by the project TAKE-5: The 5th Evolution Take of Wireless Communication Networks, funded by Business Finland.

© IFIP International Federation for Information Processing 2019
Published by Springer Nature Switzerland AG 2019
M. Di Felice et al. (Eds.): WWIC 2019, LNCS 11618, pp. 129–140, 2019.
https://doi.org/10.1007/978-3-030-30523-9_11

In addition to their undisputed benefits, mmWave networks bring new challenges to systems designers, which include high propagation losses, sensitivity to blockage by obstacles, and beamsteering functionality for highly directive transmission [1]. Particularly, free space propagation loss at 60 GHz is 28 decibels higher than that at 2.4 GHz [2]. For these reasons, mmWave links are highly directional, and they use steerable antenna arrays with sufficient gain to compensate for these extreme losses. Moreover, due to shorter wavelength (approximately 5 mm at 60 GHz), even small objects may block the mmWave link [3]. Finally, mmWave connections are highly affected by atmospheric and molecular absorption [4]. Altogether these three factors significantly affect the reliability of mmWave communication.

In addition to conventional setups, such as cellular systems where 3GPP is currently at the completion phase of the New Radio (NR) standardization, the extreme throughputs make mmWave communications technology appealing for extending the conventional mobile access by implementing wireless mesh networking. The mmWave mesh topologies may improve coverage of mmWave access points by utilizing multi-hop links and at the same time enhance communications reliability with multi-connectivity operation [5]. One of the crucial use cases in this context is public protection and disaster relief (PPDR) missions, which may greatly benefit from using 360° HD streaming and AR/VR applications enabled by bandwidth-rich mmWave communications technology.

Performance of mmWave systems with multi-connectivity capabilities in outdoor environments has been investigated thoroughly. An upper bound for the capacity of multi-connectivity mmWave systems has been obtained in [6]. This bound has been refined in [7,8]. Recently, engineering studies addressing multi-connectivity aspects of mmWave networks have started to emerge [9,10]. These works reveal that multi-connectivity operation improves both outage probability and system throughput non-incrementally. These results have been extended to mmWave mesh deployments in the outdoor use cases in [11–13], where the multi-connectivity operation has also been shown to considerably improve the network connectivity and throughput.

Compared to outdoor environments, indoor mmWave mesh deployments bring additional challenges that are primarily caused by an extremely complex propagation process. The use of mmWave meshes in dynamic PPDR use cases, such as fire suppression missions where the environment may change dynamically, adds another level of complexity. Notably, link blockage in such indoor scenarios is induced by the interior of buildings (e.g., partitions, walls) as well as mobile objects (e.g., people, moving equipment). Taking into account the potential mobility of nodes, indoor mmWave mesh deployments are expected to be highly dynamic, with continuously changing connectivity patterns between the mesh nodes. In these conditions, multi-connectivity can be considered as an efficient enabler for both maintaining network connectivity and improving its throughput.

In this paper, we evaluate the performance of mmWave mesh systems in a realistic indoor environment characterized by the mobility of nodes, dynamic blockers, 3GPP-compatible propagation model, and multi-connectivity operation.

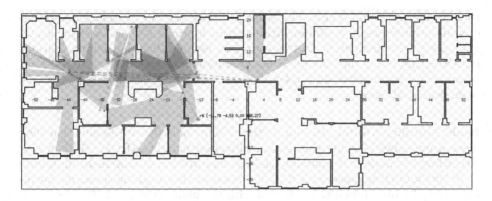

Fig. 1. Nodes on the layout during simulation 2D view.

Particularly, we consider our PPDR scenario as an illustrative use case for investigating network connectivity and throughput characteristics. Our main findings are:

- the use of multi-connectivity operation drastically improves mmWave mesh connectivity in indoor deployments but its effect on the per-node throughput is minor;
- to augment connectivity and throughput in dense indoor mmWave mesh topologies, the number of simultaneously supported links needs to be greater than two, thus implying considerable control signaling overheads.

The rest of this text is organized as follows. In Sect. 2, we introduce the system model and its components. Our system-level simulation framework and data collection/analysis procedures are described in Sect. 3. We report our results in Sect. 4. Conclusions are provided in the last section.

2   System Model

In this section, we introduce our system model by first outlining the scenario of interest and briefly specifying its sub-modules including mobility, propagation, beamforming, and dynamic blockage models. Finally, we introduce the connectivity process and define the metrics on interest.

Illustrative Scenario. We address a fire suppression mission as a representative example for the evaluation of mmWave mesh network performance in a realistic single-floor indoor deployment, see Fig. 1. Specifically, we consider a team of firefighters operating on the floor of an office building. The team utilizes assisting media applications enabled by the mmWave mesh. These acquire their information streams from the firefighters' on-body video cameras and transmit them to the command center. The latter processes the video streams and develops an optimized team operation strategy, which provides digital assistance and guidance to the firefighters. In this setup, we assume that the communications infrastructure inside the building is not operational. Connectivity with the command center is provided via a relay node (access point) installed by the rescue team near a window.

Node Mobility Model. To capture the mobility of nodes, we assume that they move around by following the random direction mobility (RDM, [14]) model. Accordingly, a node first randomly chooses its direction of movement uniformly in $(0, 2\pi)$ and then proceeds in this direction at the constant speed v_B for an exponentially distributed time interval with the parameter $\gamma = 1/E[\tau]$, where τ is the mean movement duration. The process is restarted at each stopping point. If during such movement an obstacle is encountered, the node chooses a new direction.

Propagation Model. The received signal power at a mesh node is given by

$$P_R(x) = P_T G_T G_R - PL, \tag{1}$$

where P_T is the transmit power, G_T and G_R are the antenna gains at the transmitter and the receiver sides, respectively, which depend on the antenna array (these parameters can be obtained from the beamforming model introduced in the following subsection), PL is the path loss. Following 3GPP TR 38.901, the mmWave path loss in dB for the line-of-sight (LoS) links is given by

$$PL_{InH-LOS} = 32.4 + 17.3 \lg(d_{3D}) + 20 \lg(f_c), \tag{2}$$

where f_c is the center frequency, d_{3D} is the three-dimensional distance between the radio interfaces of two communicating nodes.

For the non-LoS (NLoS) links, the path loss is determined as

$$PL_{InH-NLOS} = \max(PL_{InH-LOS}, PL'_{InH-NLOS}), \tag{3}$$

where

$$PL'_{InH-NLOS} = 38.3 lg(d_{3D}) + 17.3 + 24.9 \lg(f_c). \tag{4}$$

Beamforming Model. We assume linear antenna arrays at both the transmitter and the receiver sides [15]. Half-power beamwidth (HPBW) of the array, α, is defined as [16]

$$\alpha = 2|\theta_m - \theta_{3db}|, \tag{5}$$

where θ_{3db} is the 3-dB point and $\theta_m = \arccos(-\beta/\pi)$ is the array maximum, while β is the array direction angle. Letting $\beta = 0$, the upper and lower 3-dB points are

$$\theta_{3db}^{\pm} = \arccos[-\beta \pm 2.782/(N\pi)], \tag{6}$$

where N is the number of antenna elements.

Finally, the mean antenna gain over HPBW is expressed as [16]

$$G = \frac{1}{\theta_{3db}^+ - \theta_{3db}^-} \int_{\theta_{3db}^-}^{\theta_{3db}^+} \frac{\sin(N\pi \cos(\theta)/2)}{\sin(\pi \cos(\theta)/2)} d\theta. \tag{7}$$

Dynamic Blockage Model. In this paper, we consider three types of blockage: (i) blockage by inherent indoor constructions, e.g., walls, furniture; (ii) self-blockage; and (iii) dynamic blockage by environmental objects. The former option is captured by the considered propagation model introduced in the previous subsection. Self-blockage refers to particular positioning of a node, such that it may no longer beamform its antenna towards the intended recipient.

We also follow a dynamic spatially-temporal blockage model. Accordingly, blockers appear at a randomly chosen position that is uniformly distributed over the area of the floor according to a homogeneous temporal Poisson process with the intensity λ. Each blocker is assumed to exist for an exponentially distributed period of time with the mean $1/\mu$. Observe that this stochastic process is inherently of M/M/∞ type, and the number of active blockers is provided by the Poisson distribution with the parameter λ/μ. Given the radius of a blocker, r_B, the fraction of the floor covered by this type of blockers can be obtained by using integral geometry formulations as follows [17]

$$p_C = (1 - f_{C,1})^{\lambda/\mu}, \, p_{C,1} = \frac{2\pi S_B}{2\pi(S_A + S_B) + L_A L_B}, \tag{8}$$

where S_A is the floor area and $S_B = \pi r_B^2$ is the blocker radius.

Connectivity and Metrics of Interest. To improve system performance, we assume that a single node supports 3GPP multi-connectivity operation as described in Rel.-15 NR specifications (see TS 37.340) [5]. Accordingly, a node supports multiple connections to its adjacent systems simultaneously, and may dynamically switch between them in case where its current connection is unavailable. In our study, the number of simultaneously supported connections, known as the degree of multi-connectivity, is assumed to be M. It should be noted that depending on the locations of the nodes forming the mesh, the actual number of connections at any given instant of time can be less than M.

In our study, we address connectivity and throughput related performance indicators. These are: (i) the fraction of time when at least one node is disconnected from the mesh network, (ii) the mean number of disconnected nodes at an arbitrary instant of time, and (iii) the mean per-node throughput.

3 Simulation Framework

3.1 Simulator Design

For the numerical evaluation of the mmWave mesh system performance, we develop a custom simulator based on the Stage simulator code [18,19].

The primary part of this tool is a 3D model of an office floor, see Fig. 2. This model allows to assess whether there is a LoS condition between two points in the coordinate plane. The simulation process starts with the coordinate simulation of the node mobility and dynamic blockage. At each iteration, the tool checks the LoS condition between all of the nodes of the mesh. When verifying it, the antenna directivity is also taken into account. The results are stored in the SQL database.

The second phase utilizes the results obtained during the first phase for evaluating the parameters of interests. It starts with the calculation of path losses between all the nodes by using the system model described in Sect. 2. If the signal strength between the two nodes (at the receiver side) is lower than a preset threshold, the simulator assumes that there is no direct connection between these nodes. If there is a connection between them, the tool calculates the throughput by using the Shannon–Hartley theorem for all pairs of nodes in the mesh wherever a direct connection is available. This part abstracts the physical layer of the network. In the next step, the simulator considers radio channels between the nodes, including the medium access control procedures. This delivers a channel topology graph. The third step mimics addressing and routing within the mesh topology as delivered by the second step.

The developed framework is flexible for further extensions. The modifications (e.g., implementation of alternative protocols or applications) can be pursued by applying modified SQL scripts on the coordinate simulation traces stored in the SQL database, without launching a new simulation.

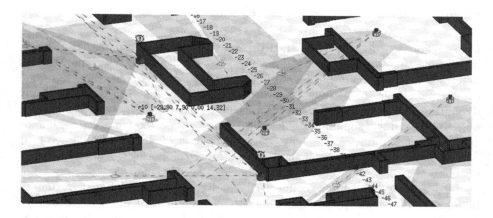

Fig. 2. Three-dimensional view of mesh nodes in simulated layout.

3.2   Data Collection and Analysis

A simulation campaign has been carried out to obtain the metrics of interest by relying on the following procedure. For each considered set of input parameters (termed a round), simulations were set to run for 1200 s of the system time, with

Table 1. Simulation parameters.

Parameter	Value
Operating frequency, f_c	28 GHz
Antenna array	16×16 el. (planar array)
Channel model	3GPP InH
Transmit power	1 W
Receiver sensitivity	-91 dBm
Fraction of floor covered by blockers, p_C	0.15
Number of fire crew members	$\{8, 10, 12, 14, 16\}$
Velocity of crew members	1 m/s
Mobility of crew members	RDM model
Number of simultaneously supported links	$\{2, 3, 4, \infty\}$
Number of iterations per simulation round	4800

a 0.25 change of the system time at each iteration of simulations. The chosen duration of a simulation round approximately corresponds to the time required for checking the floor of the considered size by the rescue team (e.g., firefighters).

Statistical data has only been collected during the steady-state period. The starting point of the steady-state period was detected by utilizing the exponentially-weighted moving average (EWMA) statistics with the weighting parameter set to 0.05 and by employing the procedure from [20].

To remove the residual correlations in the statistical data, we used the batch means strategy. Accordingly, the entire steady-state period duration has been subdivided into 1000 data blocks. The metrics of interest computed for these periods were treated as independent to form statistical samples. The output values for the metrics of interest have been estimated by processing the respective samples.

4   Numerical Results

In this section, we report our numerical results for the mmWave mesh performance in indoor environments. The default system parameters are summarized in Table 1.

Indoor deployments of mmWave systems are characterized by much higher complexity as compared to widely considered outdoor scenarios. Hence, to develop intuition about the system under investigation we start our analysis by assessing the time-dependent behavior of connectivity and throughput processes for three randomly selected mesh nodes as illustrated in Fig. 3. Observing the connectivity performance shown in Fig. 3(a), where 0 indicates the connectivity periods and 1 implies the absence of an active connection, one may conclude that connectivity intervals are rather long as compared to outages. The outage intervals are considerably short but their periodicity is relatively high. This behavior

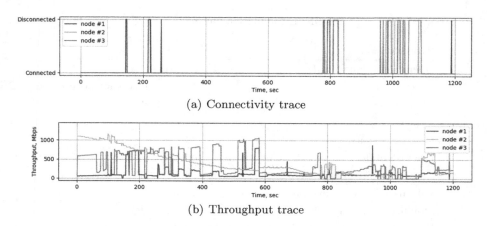

(a) Connectivity trace

(b) Throughput trace

Fig. 3. Time-dependent behavior of connectivity and throughput.

is a consequence of the realistic indoor deployment and mobility models, where layout features and dynamic blockage result in many short-lived outage events.

The associated throughput of the nodes is illustrated in Fig. 3(b), where the averaging interval was set to 1 s. As one may observe, the throughput may drastically deviate during the connectivity intervals. For some nodes, these fluctuations are rather smooth but one may also notice many sharp peaks in the perceived throughput. Note that the mobility of nodes primarily results in smooth deviations while quick jumps are associated with the blockage process (floor layout geometry and dynamic blockage events).

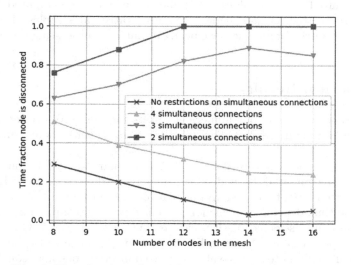

Fig. 4. Time fraction when at least one node is disconnected.

After observing the time-dependent behavior of the system, we proceed by analyzing the stationary state metrics. We start with the time fraction when at least one node is disconnected from the network; it is illustrated in Fig. 4 as a function of the number of nodes in the mesh network and the number of simultaneously supported links, M. Note that this parameter can be considered as an integral measure of the mesh network connectivity, which characterizes the fraction of time when at least one node does not have access to the gateway. One may observe that as the number of nodes increases, and depending on the degree of multi-connectivity, the analyzed value demonstrate fundamentally different behavior.

For $M = 2$ and $M = 3$, the time fraction when at least one node is disconnected increases as the number of nodes in a mesh grows. The rationale behind this behavior is straightforward: for a larger node count the probability that at least one node finds itself in unfavorable position becomes higher, and multi-connectivity may be insufficient to overcome this. However, as the degree of multi-connectivity grows further, the effects of diversity start to dominate when the number of nodes increases. Therefore, we may conclude that multi-connectivity operation in mmWave systems may drastically improve mesh connectivity for indoor deployments. However, the number of simultaneously supported links might be rather high, thus resulting in significant control overheads.

We can now characterize the mesh network connectivity quantitatively in the stationary state. Figure 5 reports the mean number of disconnected nodes as a function of the total number of nodes and the degree of multi-connectivity. Similarly to Fig. 4, we may observe that the degrees of multi-connectivity of $M = 2$ and $M = 3$ do not permit the network to scale appropriately as the mean number of disconnected nodes starts to grow. However, increasing M further to 4 allows this value to remain well below one. One may also notice that if we do not limit the number of simultaneously supported links, the mean number of nodes actually decreases as the number of disconnected nodes in the mesh network grows.

Finally, Fig. 6 studies the mean per-node throughput as a function of the number of nodes in the mesh and the degree of multi-connectivity. As one may notice, this parameter exhibits qualitatively similar behavior for all the values of M. Comparing the mean throughput results corresponding to $M = \infty$ and $M = 2$, one of the key observations here is that the system operates in blockage-limited conditions for the realistic values of M. Indeed, when imposing no restrictions on the degree of multi-connectivity, the per-node throughput is $3 - 4$ times higher as compared to the case of $M = 2$. It is also important to note that for higher degrees of multi-connectivity the system approaches this regime rather slowly, e.g., the mean per-node throughput obtained with $M = 4$ is still approximately half of that for $M = \infty$. This behavior is different from the one reported for outdoor scenarios in, e.g., [7,8], where both capacity and outage probabilities grow exponentially with M.

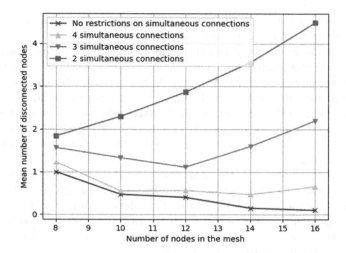

Fig. 5. Mean number of disconnected nodes.

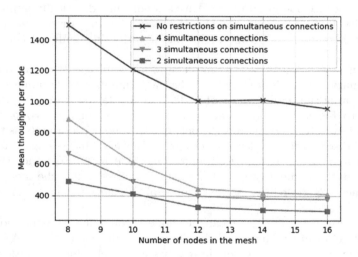

Fig. 6. Mean per-node throughput in mesh network.

5   Conclusion

Motivated by the need for on-demand and high throughput mesh networking in indoor PPDR use cases, we investigated the capabilities of mmWave technology to support these types of applications. Our developed model employed system-level simulations of the mesh system with node mobility, 3GPP-like indoor propagation, dynamical link blockage, and multi-connectivity operation, all for a realistic indoor layout. In this study, the metrics of interest were related to network connectivity and throughput.

Our simulation campaign revealed that the connectivity of individual nodes in indoor environments is characterized by frequent short-lived outage events and causes sharp fluctuations in node throughput even in the presence of multi-connectivity capabilities. Hence, multi-connectivity operation may significantly improve the overall network performance in terms of the fraction of time when at least one node is disconnected as well as the mean number of disconnected nodes. However, the associated increase in per-node performance is less noticeable, which implies that indoor mmWave mesh deployments primarily operate in a blockage-rich environment. This is different from outdoor deployments, where multi-connectivity improves both the connectivity and throughput performance exponentially [7, 8].

References

1. Al-samman, A.M., Azmi, M.H., Rahman, T.A.: A survey of millimeter wave (mmwave) communications for 5G: channel measurement below and above 6 GHz. In: Saeed, F., Gazem, N., Mohammed, F., Busalim, A. (eds.) IRICT 2018. AISC, vol. 843, pp. 451–463. Springer, Cham (2019). https://doi.org/10.1007/978-3-319-99007-1_43
2. Singh, S., Mudumbai, R., Madhow, U.: Interference analysis for highly directional 60-GHz mesh networks: the case for rethinking medium access control. IEEE/ACM Trans. Netw. (TON) **19**(5), 1513–1527 (2011)
3. Cheffena, M.: Industrial wireless communications over the millimeter wave spectrum: opportunities and challenges. IEEE Commun. Mag. **54**(9), 66–72 (2016)
4. Humpleman, R., Watson, P.: Investigation of attenuation by rainfall at 60 GHz. In: Proceedings of the Institution of Electrical Engineers, vol. 125, pp. 85–91. IET (1978)
5. 3GPP: NR; Multi-connectivity; Overall description (Release 15), 3GPP TS 37.340 V15.2.0, June 2018
6. Moltchanov, D., Ometov, A., Andreev, S., Koucheryavy, Y.: Upper bound on capacity of 5G mmWave cellular with multi-connectivity capabilities. Electron. Lett. **54**(11), 724–726 (2018)
7. Gapeyenko, M., et al.: On the degree of multi-connectivity in 5G millimeter-wave cellular urban deployments. IEEE Trans. Veh. Technol. **68**(2), 1973–1978 (2019)
8. Gerasimenko, M., Moltchanov, D., Gapeyenko, M., Andreev, S., Koucheryavy, Y.: Capacity of multi-connectivity mmWave systems with dynamic blockage and directional antennas. IEEE Trans. Veh. Technol. **68**(4), 3534–3549 (2019)
9. Petrov, V., et al.: Dynamic multi-connectivity performance in ultra-dense urban mmWave deployments. IEEE J. Sel. Areas Commun. **35**(9), 2038–2055 (2017)
10. Polese, M., Giordani, M., Mezzavilla, M., Rangan, S., Zorzi, M.: Improved handover through dual connectivity in 5G mmWave mobile networks. IEEE J. Sel. Areas Commun. **35**(9), 2069–2084 (2017)
11. Niu, Y., Li, Y., Jin, D., Su, L., Vasilakos, A.V.: A survey of millimeter wave communications (mmWave) for 5G: opportunities and challenges. Wirel. Netw. **21**(8), 2657–2676 (2015)
12. Thornburg, A., Bai, T., Heath Jr., R.W.: Performance analysis of outdoor mmWave ad hoc networks. IEEE Trans. Signal Process. **64**(15), 4065–4079 (2016)

13. Qiao, J., Shen, X.S., Mark, J.W., Shen, Q., He, Y., Lei, L.: Enabling device-to-device communications in millimeter-wave 5G cellular networks. IEEE Commun. Mag. **53**(1), 209–215 (2015)
14. Nain, P., Towsley, D., Liu, B., Liu, Z.: Properties of random direction models. In: Proceedings of 24th Annual Joint Conference of the IEEE Computer and Communications Societies, vol. 3, pp. 1897–1907. IEEE (2005)
15. Petrov, V., Komarov, M., Moltchanov, D., Jornet, J.M., Koucheryavy, Y.: Interference and SINR in millimeter wave and terahertz communication systems with blocking and directional antennas. IEEE Trans. Wirel. Commun. **16**(3), 1791–1808 (2017)
16. Balanis, C.A.: Antenna Theory: Analysis and Design. Wiley, Hoboken (2016)
17. Petrov, V., Moltchanov, D., Kustarev, P., Jornet, J.M., Koucheryavy, Y.: On the use of integral geometry for interference modeling and analysis in wireless networks. IEEE Commun. Lett. **20**(12), 2530–2533 (2016)
18. Vaughan, R.: Massively multi-robot simulation in stage. Swarm Intell. **2**(2–4), 189–208 (2008)
19. Gerkey, B., Vaughan, R.T., Howard, A.: The player/stage project: tools for multi-robot and distributed sensor systems. In: Proceedings of the 11th International Conference on Advanced Robotics, vol. 1, pp. 317–323 (2003)
20. Perros, H.: Computer simulation techniques. The definitive introduction. North Carolina State University (2009)

Opportunistic D2D-Aided Uplink Communications in 5G and Beyond Networks

Baldomero Coll-Perales[1(✉)], Loreto Pescosolido[2], Andrea Passarella[2], Javier Gozalvez[1], and Marco Conti[2]

[1] UWICORE Laboratory, Universidad Miguel Hernádez de Elche, Elche, Spain
{bcoll,j.gozalvez}@umh.es
[2] IIT Institute, Italian National Research Council (CNR), Pisa, Italy
{loreto.pescosolido,andrea.passarella,marco.conti}@iit.cnr.it

Abstract. 5G and Beyond 5G networks are calling for advanced networking schemes that can efficiently contribute to deal with the foreseen increase of the mobile data traffic, which inherently brings along an increase of the energy consumed by mobile nodes to support it. The non-real-time nature of an important share of that traffic makes it possible to use opportunistic networking mechanisms in cellular networks that can exploit the traffic's delay-tolerance to find efficient transmission conditions. In this context, this paper proposes an scheduling and mode selection scheme that integrates opportunistic Device-to-Device (D2D) networking mechanisms in cellular networks to reduce the energy consumption for non-real-time traffic. The proposed scheme utilizes a probabilistic model that exploits context information available in cellular networks to obtain an a-priori estimate of the energy cost for transmitting the different fragments of a content using any of the following modes: single-hop traditional, opportunistic cellular and opportunistic D2D-aided cellular. Based on these estimates, the proposed scheme selects the communication mode for each fragment, and schedules the time instant at which the transmission should take place. Our performance evaluation shows that the proposed scheme results in up to 90% energy consumption reduction, compared to traditional single-hop cellular communications, and performs closely to an optimal scheme which assumes full knowledge of network conditions and nodes' trajectories.

Keywords: 5G · D2D · Energy efficiency · Opportunistic networking

1 Introduction

5G and Beyond 5G networks will be challenged, in terms of both spectrum use and energy consumption, by the increasing mobile data traffic demand. The integration of Device-to-Device (D2D) communications in the design of cellular networks [1] has been proposed as a powerful means to cope with this unprecedented traffic demand, and is expected to play a key role in 5G networks and beyond [2]. 5G and beyond 5G networks will require advanced networking mechanisms to adapt data transfers to the variable spatial-temporal characteristics

© IFIP International Federation for Information Processing 2019
Published by Springer Nature Switzerland AG 2019
M. Di Felice et al. (Eds.): WWIC 2019, LNCS 11618, pp. 141–153, 2019.
https://doi.org/10.1007/978-3-030-30523-9_12

of the traffic demands [2,3]. This includes opportunistic networking mechanisms that empower mobile devices to become more active members of the network with the ability, for instance, to autonomously establish communication links under favorable conditions. Traditionally, opportunistic networking has focused on self-organized/ad-hoc mobile networks that lack end-to-end connections [3]. In these scenarios, the devices are allowed to temporarily store the information, and eventually forward it to another device, which is more likely to be within the communication range of the destination, when a connection opportunity arises. In cellular networks, the end-to-end connectivity is not an issue thanks to the increasing densification of the infrastructure. Hence, devices will have a direct cellular connection to the infrastructure almost everywhere. In this context, opportunistic networking can be used for dynamically selecting, at each point in time, the best communication mode among the available ones. In particular, this work considers the following communication modes: (i) *Single-Hop (SH) traditional:* direct cellular transmission between the UE (user equipment) and the BS; (ii) *opportunistic cellular:* direct but *deferred* transmission between the UE and the BS which seeks to take advantage of better channel quality in the near future; (iii) *opportunistic D2D-aided cellular:* eventual D2D transmission from the source node to an intermediate UE (or relay), which forwards the data to the BS. The decision on the communication mode to use can be based on latency, reliability or throughput metrics, to name a few. This paper focuses on selecting the communication mode that minimizes the energy consumption while guaranteeing the traffic QoS.

The integration of D2D-aided communications and opportunistic networking concepts can be exploited with the aim to increase the energy efficiency of non-real-time data transmissions. Indeed, according to recent estimates [4], non-real-time services (e.g. social networking, cloud services, data metering, mobile video, etc.) will represent an important share of the forthcoming mobile data traffic. And, for this type of services, the amount of data in the uplink direction is expected to increase considerably. The potential benefits of opportunistic D2D-aided uplink mechanisms are especially relevant in the context of this type of services.

The idea of integrating D2D communications in the architecture of a cellular network dates back to the work of Lin and Hsu [5], where a Multi-hop Cellular Network (MCN) architecture was proposed. In the last decade, researchers have been working on the integration of D2D in wideband multicarrier-based cellular networks (i.e., 4G, 5G, and beyond). The initial studies focused on local (proximity) services (see, e.g., [6]) whereas, subsequently, the research on D2D data offloading techniques (e.g. [7]) has widened the scope of integrating D2D and opportunistic networking concepts. Indeed, the combination of D2D and opportunistic networking can induce a significant performance improvement in obtaining/uploading contents from/to some remote server. In some recent theoretical and experimental studies, we have shown that considerable benefits can be obtained, in terms of energy consumption and cellular spectral efficiency, from the integration of D2D and opportunistic networking in cellular networks in the uplink ([3,8,9]) and in the downlink ([10–12]). However, these studies target a different problem than the one studied in this work, namely data offloading, or

have focused on deriving and identifying optimum locations at which the D2D
and cellular transmissions should take place to minimize the energy consumption.

Giving these previous promising findings, this work proposes and evaluates
a mechanism that integrates opportunistic D2D-aided transmissions in cellular networks. In particular, this work develops a novel probabilistic model, and
apply it to decide, at a source mobile node, through which communication mode
(i.e. SH traditional, opportunistic cellular or opportunistic D2D-aided cellular)
data should be transferred to the BS in order to minimize the transmission
energy consumption. Using context information available in cellular networks
(e.g. spatial density and distribution of nodes within the cell, nominal channel
gains between each pair of locations in the physical area of interest, etc.), which
we assume to be periodically broadcast by the BS, the devised model estimates
the energy cost for each of the communication modes along the time available
to complete the data transfer. The proposed mode selection scheme also considers that the data can be fragmented into chunks or fragments that can be
uploaded at separate time instants within the available time. For each of these
fragments, the proposed scheme selects a communication mode, and schedules
the time instant at which the transmission should take place in order to minimize the overall energy consumption. Finally, the proposed scheme executes the
selected communication modes at the scheduled time instants considering the
real network conditions (e.g. location of potential relays).

The obtained results show that the proposed scheme, that integrates opportunistic D2D networking in cellular network, results in up to 90% energy consumption reduction compared to traditional SH cellular communications, and
performs closely to an ideal optimal scheme (used for upper-bound benchmark-
ing) that assumes full knowledge of the network state and all nodes' trajectories
to select the most efficient communication mode.

2   Opportunistic D2D-Aided Scheduling and Transmission

Without loss of generality, we focus on a mobile node having to transmit to the
BS a content of size D_c bits. The application QoS sets a time limit T_{max} to upload
the content. Time is organized in Control Intervals (CI) of duration T_{CI}. The
duration of a control interval is considered to be smaller than the time limit, i.e.
$T_{CI} << T_{max}$. For instance, T_{max} can be in the order of tens of seconds, or even
several minutes, whereas T_{CI} is in the order of 1 s. We consider that the content
size is larger than some maximum data that can be transmitted by a user in a
CI. Therefore, the content to be transmitted is divided into fragments or chunks.
Within each control interval CI, each transmitter can be allocated an amount of
radio resources so that it can transmit D_{CI} bits ($D_{CI} < D_c$). In this context, the
content to be uploaded is divided into $N_c = \lceil D_c/D_{CI} \rceil$ fragments. Each source
node s has $N_{CI} = T_{max}/T_{CI}$ control intervals to complete the transmission of the
N_c fragments. In the considered scenario $N_c \leq N_{CI}$ and each node can transmit
at most one fragment in a control interval.

Considering the scenario setup described above, this work proposes a scheme
that seeks identifying the subset of N_c control intervals where fragments should

be uploaded in order to minimize the overall energy consumption. For these identified control intervals, the proposed scheme also decides what communication mode to use (i.e. SH traditional, opportunistic cellular or opportunistic D2D-aided cellular) for the transmission of the fragment. The proposed scheme is carried out in two phases that are described below: mode selection & scheduling phase, and execution phase.

2.1 Mode Selection and Scheduling Phase

First, the mode selection & scheduling phase is executed at the source node when the content to be uploaded is generated. The source node uses a probabilistic model to estimate the energy cost of performing opportunistic cellular and opportunistic D2D-aided cellular transmissions in each of the available N_{CI} control intervals[1]. Then, and building on these estimates, the mode selection & scheduling phase selects the transmission mode and the control interval at which the source node will transmit each fragment of the content. To calculate the cost estimates, the proposed scheme uses context information that can be made available in the cellular network, and a trajectory prediction of the source node. More specifically, contextual information refers to (i) a map of nominal channel gains between each pair of locations (x, y) in the region, indicated with $g_{\mathrm{D2D}}(x, y)$, where x and y represent the location of the transmitter and receiver of a D2D transmission, respectively, and a map of the nominal channel gains between any location x and the BS, indicated with $g_{\mathrm{cell}}(x, x_b)$, where x_b is the location of the BS[2]; (ii) information about the urban structure of the region (streets, buildings, etc.); (iii) statistical information about the nodes' density and distribution within the cell.

In the following, we indicate with $E_{\mathrm{cell}}(x, x_b)$ the energy cost of transmitting a fragment from a node (be it a source or a relay) located at x, to the BS through a cellular link, and with $E_{\mathrm{D2D}}(x, y)$ the energy cost of transmitting a fragment from a source located at x to a relay located at y. These energy costs are deterministic functions of the respective nominal channel gains $g_{\mathrm{cell}}(x, x_b)$ and $g_{\mathrm{D2D}}(x, y)$, and of the cellular and D2D technologies (see Sect. 3). We represent the (discrete-time) trajectory, of a source node s as $x_s(t_k) = x_s(t_0) + v_s k T_{\mathrm{CI}}$, where $t_k \triangleq k T_{\mathrm{CI}}$, and both the location (x_s) and speed (v_s) vectors belong to $\mathbb{R}^2$. At this stage, we assume that the source node knows its own trajectory, which is not constrained to a specific model. We leave the evaluation considering source nodes' trajectory uncertainty to our future work. Finally, we indicate with

---

[1] It should be noted that the opportunistic cellular mode includes the SH traditional mode if the transmission between the UE and the BS is not deferred.

[2] The nominal channel gains depend on the geometry of the system, and not on the instantaneous channel conditions that are subject to time varying effects such as shadowing, fast fading and frequency selectivity (these effect are taken into account by adding a suitable link margin, see Sect. 3). We assume that the nominal channel gains maps $g_{\mathrm{cell}}(x, x_b)$ and $g_{\mathrm{D2D}}(x, y)$ are computed offline, or acquired through measurements sent periodically by the devices and suitably processed, over a very large time scale, by the network operator.

$\hat{E}_{\text{cell}}^{(s,k)}$ the expected energy cost associated to the direct cellular transmission of a fragment from source node s to the BS in the k-th control interval, and with $\hat{E}_{\text{D2D-aided}*}^{(s,k)}$ the expected energy cost for the D2D-aided transmission in the k-th control interval. $\hat{E}_{\text{D2D-aided}*}^{(s,k)}$ includes the cost of both transmissions, from source to relay and from relay to BS, and considers that the source node selects, among the available potential relays (i.e. neighboring nodes of the source node), the relay that minimizes the energy consumption of the overall opportunistic D2D-aided transmission.

Estimation of the Energy Cost of Opportunistic Single Hop Cellular Transmissions - The expected energy cost for the direct cellular transmission at time instant t_k, i.e. $\hat{E}_{\text{cell}}^{(s,k)}$, is computed in this work considering the location of the source node and nominal channel gain $g_{\text{cell}}(x, x_b)$ at this location. Based on $g_{\text{cell}}(x, x_b)$ and link margin (see Sect. 3), it can be computed the transmit power and hence the energy cost for a cellular transmission from the source node s to the BS at time instant t_k as

$$\hat{E}_{\text{cell}}^{(s,k)} = E_{\text{cell}}(x_s(t_k), x_b), \tag{1}$$

where we recall that the right-hand-side is a deterministic function of the channel gain map $g_{\text{cell}}(x, x_b)$.

Estimation of the Energy Cost of Opportunistic D2D-Aided Transmissions - The estimation of the energy cost $\hat{E}_{\text{D2D-aided}*}^{(s,k)}$ needs to take into account that the future location of the relays is unknown at the time the mode selection & scheduling phase is performed (i.e., at time $t = t_0$). To this end, we have derived a probabilistic model for computing such cost. For space limit reasons, we omit the details of the derivations (which will be included in a future work). Instead, in this Subsection, we provide an outline of the steps we followed, and the main result given by the estimation of the cost associated to a D2D-aided transmission in Eq. (3).

- First, based on the density and distribution of nodes within the cell, the source node's trajectory prediction, and the nominal channel gain maps, it is possible to compute the cumulative distribution function (CDF) of the energy cost (which includes the cost of both D2D and cellular transmissions) assuming there will be a relay *at an unknown location*.
- Then, *conditioned on the number J of relays* that will be available at a given time instant t_k (at unknown and statistically independent locations), it is possible to obtain the CDF of the minimum energy cost that would be incurred by the opportunistic D2D-aided cellular transmission (achieved by using the "best" relay). This is conditioned to the number of relays that will be available.
- Finally, using the information about the density and distribution of the nodes within the cell, it is possible to compute the probability mass function of the

number of relays that will be available. Removing the conditioning on the J available relays from the CDF of the minimum energy cost, it is possible to obtain the CDF of the minimum cost associated to each instant t_k considering a source node s and, ultimately, its expected value. This expected value is used as an estimate of the energy cost for performing a D2D-aided fragment transmission at the k-th control interval, see Eq. (3).

More technical details are provided in the following. We indicate with $C_s(t_k)$ the nominal D2D coverage region of a source node s at given time instant t_k. This coverage region is defined as a disk of radius R_{D2D} centered at $x_s(t_k)$, deprived of unreachable spaces for D2D transmissions like, for instance, locations inside buildings. $C_s(t_k)$ is represented as a tessellation of square tiles of equal surface (e.g. $1\,\mathrm{m}^2$). Let $1, ..., Q$ be an arbitrary labeling of the tiles available at $C_s(t_k)$, and $x_i(t_k), \forall i \in \{1, \ldots, Q\}$, be the center of the tiles at time instant t_k. Following the previous notation, the total energy cost that would be incurred by opportunistic D2D-aided cellular for transmitting a *fragment* from a source node s located (in the k-th control interval) at $x_s(t_k)$, and using a relay r located at the center of tile i of the coverage region in the k-th control interval, i.e., at $x_i(t_k)$, can be computed as

$$E_{\mathrm{D2D\text{-}aided}}\left(x_s(t_k), x_i(t_k)\right) = E_{\mathrm{D2D}}\left(x_s(t_k), x_i(t_k)\right) + E_{\mathrm{cell}}\left(x_i(t_k), x_b\right). \quad (2)$$

The quantities $E_{\mathrm{D2D\text{-}aided}}\left(x_s(t_k), x_i(t_k)\right)$, computed for each tile $i \in \{1, \ldots, Q\}$, allow to establish a ranking of the locations (i.e., the tiles) in which it would be more preferable to have a relay. For a given position q in the ranking, we indicate with $i(q)$ the labeling index of the tile at position q in the ranking. Conversely, for a given tile i, we indicate with $q(i)$ the position of the tile i in the ranking. All possible values of the energy cost that would be incurred by the opportunistic D2D-aided cellular transmission at t_k can be expressed as $e_1(t_k), \ldots, e_Q(t_k)$, where the numbering order follows the energy cost-based ranking order, i.e., $e_1(t_k) \leq e_1(t_k) \leq \ldots \leq e_Q(t_k)$. We label the streets in the entire cell with the numbers in the set $\Psi \triangleq \{1, \ldots, N_\Psi\}$ and indicate with λ_ψ the (linear) density of nodes present on street $\psi \in \Psi$. For each time instant t_k, we consider the subset $\Psi_k^{(s)} \triangleq \left\{\psi_1^{(s,k)}, \ldots, \psi_{N^{(s,k)}}^{(s,k)}\right\} \subset \Psi$ of the $N^{(s,k)}$ streets whose median axis is at least partially within the coverage region $C_s(t_k)$, and we also indicate with $l_n^{(s,k)}$ the length of the portion of street $\psi_n^{(s,k)}, \forall n \in \{1, \ldots, N^{(s,k)}\}$, covered by $C_s(t_k)$.

Following the derivation steps outlined above, it is possible to obtain the following expression for the expected energy cost of the opportunistic D2D-aided transmission, which we use as the desired estimation:

$$\hat{E}_{\mathrm{D2D\text{-}aided}*}^{(s,k)} \triangleq \mathbb{E}_{E_{\mathrm{D2D\text{-}aided}*}^{(s,k)}}(e) = \sum_{q=1}^{Q}\left(e_q^{(s,k)}\sum_{j=0}^{\infty}\left(p_{J^{(s,k)}}(j)\, p_{E*}\left(e_q^{(s,k)} \mid j\right)\right)\right), \quad (3)$$

where $p_{J^{(s,k)}}(j) = \frac{1}{j!}\left(\sum_{n=1}^{N^{(s,k)}}\lambda_{\psi_n^{(s,k)}} l_n^{(s,k)}\right)\exp\left(\sum_{n=1}^{N^{(s,k)}}\lambda_{\psi_n^{(s,k)}} l_n^{(s,k)}\right).$

Control Interval and Transmission Mode Selection - Considering the k-th control interval, we indicate the minimum among the expected energy cost associated to a direct opportunistic cellular transmission and the expected energy cost associated to an opportunistic D2D-aided one as

$$\hat{E}(s,k) = \min\left(\hat{E}_{\text{cell}}^{(s,k)}, \hat{E}_{\text{D2D-aided*}}^{(s,k)}\right). \tag{4}$$

The N_{CI} control intervals can be ranked, in ascending order, according to their energy cost $\hat{E}(s,k) \; \forall k \in \{0,\ldots,N_{\text{CI}}-1\}$. The source node's strategy for the transfer of the content (i.e. of the N_c fragments) can be scheduled by selecting the N_c control intervals with the minimum expected energy cost. Clearly, the communication mode that will be used at the scheduled control interval k is the one which minimizes the expected energy cost in (4).

2.2 Execution Phase

The execution phase is in charge of implementing the communication modes selected in Sect. 2.1 at the scheduled control intervals, considering the real network conditions (i.e., the location of potential relays). In the control intervals for which a direct transmission was scheduled, the source node s transmits directly the fragment to the BS. In the control intervals for which an opportunistic D2D-aided cellular transmission was scheduled, the source node selects a relay among its neighbors. More specifically, it selects the relay with the lowest overall cost, i.e., including the source-to-relay D2D transmission cost and the relay-to-BS transmission cost. At execution time t_k it is possible to identify this relay. During the mode selection & scheduling phase, the source node s had determined the cost of the opportunistic D2D-aided transmission for each tile within the D2D coverage region $C_s(t_k)$. This allows to establish a ranking of the locations (i.e. the tiles) in which it would be more desirable to have the relay. Note that, in Sect. 2.1, it was necessary to consider all the tiles since the source had no knowledge of where the potential relays would be located in the future. Then, in the execution phase, the source node selects as relay the neighbor that is located on the tile with the highest ranking (i.e., the lowest energy cost) among those tiles which have a neighbor on them. In case the source node finds no relays, it directly transmits the fragment to the BS.

3 Performance Evaluation

We have evaluated, using a Matlab-based simulator, the performance of the proposed scheme in a "Manhattan" grid scenario of 6×6 blocks. The widths of streets and buildings are set to 10 m and 90 m, respectively. The average height of the buildings is 20 m, and they have on average 4 floors. The BS is located at a height of 25 m on top of a building at the center of the scenario. A map-based channel model for urban macro-cell scenarios [13], which takes into account all the layout of the scenario and buildings described above, is used to compute the nominal channel gains for the cellular transmissions. The propagation losses for the D2D transmissions are modeled following the METIS Project's D1.4 on channel models [14]. This D2D model distinguishes between line-of-sight (LOS) and Non-LOS (NLOS) conditions. The mobility traces of the nodes in the scenario are obtained using the SUMO (Simulation of Urban MObility) simulator [15]. The nodes' speed is set to 1.5 m/s. At streets crossings, the nodes can turn right or left, or continue straight with equal probability. Different densities of nodes in the scenario are considered. Out of all the available nodes, the source nodes are selected randomly.

The evaluation has been conducted considering that the cellular and D2D technologies use the LTE spectrum band (a.k.a. in-band D2D) at 2.3 GHz. The control interval T_{CI} is set to 1 s. The considered traffic load guarantees that the cellular system can provide the required radio resources (i.e. Physical Resource Blocks) to the D2D and cellular links to transmit D_{CI} bits in a CI[3]. In our simulations, the traffic uploading requests follow a Poisson distribution with a rate $\lambda_{\mathrm{req}} = 1/10$. We considered contents with a size of $D_c = 24$ Mbits, made of $N_c = 6$ fragments of $D_{CI} = 4$ Mbits each. We considered $T_{\max}$ values in the set $\{10, 20, 30\}$ s.

The computation of the energy consumption of D2D and cellular transmissions takes into account both the nominal channel gain and random channel effects, including shadowing and multi-path fading, that are included through a suitable link margin (different for D2D and cellular transmissions). Following [11], we compute the energy consumed to transmit a single fragment (i.e. D_{CI} bits) as

$$E_{\mathrm{CI}} = n_u \tau_{\mathrm{PRB}} M \cdot (1/g) \mathcal{N}_0 B_{\mathrm{PRB}} \left(2^{(D_{\mathrm{CI}}/(n_u \tau_{\mathrm{PRB}} B_{\mathrm{PRB}}))} - 1 \right), \tag{5}$$

where g is the nominal channel gain. n_u is the number of PRBs used to transmit the D_{CI} bits in a control interval (assumed to be fixed). B_{PRB} and τ_{PRB} are the bandwidth and duration of a single PRB, that are equal to 180 KHz and 0.5 ms for LTE. $\mathcal{N}_0$ is the thermal noise power spectral density, and M is a suitable link margin calculated for the scenario under study[4].

For comparison purposes, besides the proposed scheme, the following schemes have been also evaluated under the conditions described above:

(i) Single-Hop (SH) traditional: In the SH traditional scheme, the source node does not implement any opportunistic networking scheme. Therefore, it uses the first N_c control intervals to upload the content to the BS.

---

[3] For example, considering an LTE system, each PRB carries a number of bits in the range from 16 to 720 (based on [16]). Assuming that a PRB carries 400 bits, there would be needed 10.000 PRBs to transmit a content fragment of size D_{CI} bits. In the considered control interval of 1 s, there are approximately $\{50.000, 100.000, 200.000, 500.000\}$ PRBs for a LTE system of $\{5, 10, 20, 50\}$ MHz bandwidth. In our simulations, we used a system bandwidth of 10 MHz.

[4] For the purposes of this work, we have computed, through offline simulations, suitable link margins for both cellular and D2D transmissions, obtaining values of 10 dB for D2D transmissions, and 4 dB for cellular transmissions.

(ii) Opportunistic cellular-only: For a fair comparison with the proposed scheme, the source nodes implementing the opportunistic cellular-only scheme uses the probabilistic model presented in Sect. 2.1 to select the N_c control intervals to complete the upload. Contrary to the proposed scheme, however, it only considers the costs associated to direct cellular transmissions.

(iii) Optimal scheme: The optimal scheme assumes the source nodes have full knowledge about the network conditions and other nodes' trajectory. Therefore, it can select the modes to use (either opportunistic cellular or opportunistic D2D-aided cellular) for each of the N_c control intervals that minimize the energy consumption. The implementation of this scheme is unfeasible in real networks and is utilized in this work to identify what would be the upper-bound of the proposed scheme.

For a fair comparison, the selected source nodes implement the four schemes under evaluation at the same position and time instant. The results reported in the next sub-sections are obtained over several simulation runs to guarantee the statistical accuracy of the results.

3.1 Mode Selection Accuracy

It is important to investigate how the proposed scheme adapts to the context conditions of the scenario to select the communication mode, and more specifically, to the node density. In Fig. 1, we report the average percentage share of the selected communication modes for the transmission of a fragment among opportunistic SH cellular and opportunistic D2D-aided cellular. We considered different values for the number of nodes present in the scenario, and three different values for the maximum time limit within which the transfer of the content needs to be completed. For example, when there are 100 nodes in the scenario, the opportunistic D2D-aided cellular mode is scheduled 54.2% of the times[5]. This percentage increases to 99% when the number of nodes in the scenario is 1500 nodes. The opportunistic D2D-aided communication mode is selected more frequently when the density of nodes in the scenario increases. This is the case because the proposed scheme takes this context information as an input for the estimation of the energy cost of the opportunistic D2D-aided transmissions. Practically speaking, the energy cost that the model estimates for the opportunistic D2D-aided transmissions reduces when it is more likely to find relays within the source node's D2D coverage region. This favors that one of the potential relays is under "good" conditions to the BS.

Regarding the effect of T_{max}, a larger value of this parameter allows the source nodes to delay the start of the transmission to search for more efficient

---

[5] It has to be pointed out that for a scenario of the considered size, 100 nodes is a quite low number. For instance, in scenarios with the size considered in this study, the simulation guidelines reported in [17] suggest considering 1500 nodes for the test case "dense urban scenario societies". However, we believe that testing worst-case scenarios is also interesting to gain insights into the effectiveness and limits of the proposed scheme.

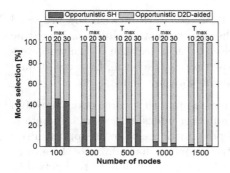
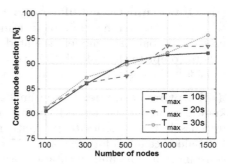

Fig. 1. Selected communication mode share

Fig. 2. Correct mode selection [%]

communication conditions. This allows to find more favorable conditions for both the opportunistic SH transmissions and the opportunistic D2D-aided ones. Therefore, the results reported in Fig. 1 show similar trends of the mode selection share as a function of $T_{\max}$. As we will see in the next subsection, however, $T_{\max}$ has an effect on the performance in terms of energy savings.

In Fig. 2, we show the accuracy of the proposed scheme in selecting the correct communication mode at the scheduled control interval. A correct selection is represented by the occurrence that a selection based on the actual conditions found at execution time would have provided the same choice performed by the proposed scheme in the mode selection & scheduling phase. A non-correct decision may arise since the proposed scheme selects the communication mode based on the probabilistic model, without knowing exactly the conditions the source node will find at execution time (i.e., the position of the potential relays) in the considered control interval. The results show that the accuracy of the proposed scheme in selecting the correct communication mode is above 80% for the scenarios under study, even under a very low node density.

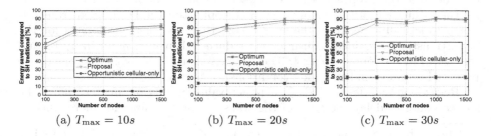

(a) $T_{\max} = 10s$ (b) $T_{\max} = 20s$ (c) $T_{\max} = 30s$

Fig. 3. Energy consumption compared to traditional single-hop.

3.2 Energy Consumption Reduction

This section analyzes the reduction in average energy consumption achieved by the proposed scheme compared to the benchmark 'opportunistic cellular-only' and 'optimum' schemes described above. The performance of the 'SH traditional' scheme is used as a reference. The results reported in Fig. 3 show average energy reduction percentage with respect to 'SH traditional'. The plots in Fig. 3 also display the 95% confidence intervals obtained with our set of simulations.

The results reported for 'opportunistic cellular-only' show that the sole use of opportunistic networking in cellular networks already helps reducing the energy consumption compared to 'SH traditional' communications. For example, when T_{max} is set to 10 s (Fig. 3a), the 'opportunistic cellular-only' scheme reduces the energy consumption by 7% compared to 'SH traditional'. The benefits of integrating opportunistic networking in cellular networks increase with the available T_{max} since this allows the source nodes to search for more efficient communication conditions. In fact, the results reported in Fig. 3c show that the 'opportunistic cellular-only' scheme reduces the energy consumption by more than 20% compared to 'SH traditional' in the scenario in which T_{max} is set to 30 s. However, the scheme proposed in this work that, besides opportunistic cellular, also integrates D2D and opportunistic networking can achieve significant additional energy benefits. For instance, when T_{max} is set to 10 s (Fig. 3a), the proposed scheme reduces the energy consumption by 55% (in the worst case of 100 nodes) and up to 80% (with 1500 nodes) compared to 'SH traditional'. Since the proposed scheme also exploits opportunistic networking, it benefits from larger values of T_{max}. In particular, Fig. 3c shows that with the proposed scheme the energy consumption is reduced by 65% (in the worst case of 100 nodes) and close to 90% (with 1000 or 1500 nodes) compared to 'SH traditional', in the scenario in which T_{max} is set to 30 s. The main reason for the reported energy reductions is that, in a urban scenario, as the one considered, NLOS links with the BS are quite frequent. If the source node is under NLOS with the BS, the effect of the combined exploitation of delay tolerance and the possibility to use an intermediate relay is to significantly increase the possibility to find a condition in which the final cellular transmission to the BS is under LOS, which requires a much lower transmit power. Regarding the performance trend with increasing node density, the energy reduction levels of the proposed scheme increase compared to 'SH traditional'. This is the case because with the increasing node density it is more likely to find a relay in a favorable position (and this is incorporated in the statistical model used to perform the mode selection & scheduling). Finally, it is interesting to observe that the gap with the performance of the 'optimal' scheme is quite small. The 'optimal' scheme only reduces by 10% or less the energy consumption compared to the proposed scheme under the worst-case node density, and the gap reduces with an increasing node density, with a ~3% gap at 300 and 500 nodes, and a ~1% gap at 1000 and 1500 nodes. It is important to remember that the 'optimum' scheme assumes the source nodes are able to predict, error-free, what is the best communication mode to use at each control interval (either opportunistic cellular or opportunistic D2D-aided) and its actual associated energy cost.

Therefore, the source nodes implementing the 'optimum' scheme can select communication modes and the control intervals that minimize the total energy consumption. The proposed scheme, that is designed for practical implementations, exploits instead context information available in cellular networks to make a probabilistic estimate of the energy costs, but can still achieve a performance quite close to the 'optimum' scheme.

4   Conclusions

This study has investigated the potential of integrating D2D and opportunistic networking in cellular networks to reduce the energy consumption in the uplink. We have proposed a probabilistic model that derives the communication mode and the time instant at which transmissions should take place in order to minimize the energy consumption. The proposed scheme exploits both opportunistic direct and D2D-aided transmissions across the time window allowed by a delay-tolerant application. The proposed scheme also divides contents into fragments and performs independent strategies for each fragment. To this aim, the proposed scheme uses context information available in cellular networks including density and distribution of nodes within the cell, statistical information about the channel gain, and the trajectory of the source node. The conducted evaluation has shown that the proposed scheme allows to select the correct transmission mode for each fragment (which minimizes the energy cost for the transmission), with very high accuracy (always above 80%). In terms of energy consumption reduction, the performance gains achieved by the proposed scheme are quite significant. The results show that the proposed scheme can significantly reduce the energy consumption (by up to 90% under the considered conditions) compared to a single-hop traditional scheme. In future works, we will expand the proposed technique by considering uncertainties in the source nodes' trajectory prediction and using a nesting mechanism which provides more freedom to the relays to decide how to upload the received data to the BS.

Acknowledgements. This work has been partially funded by the Spanish Ministry of Science, Innovation and Universities, AEI, and FEDER funds (TEC2017-88612-R), the UMH ('Ayudas a la Investigación e Innovación de la UMH 2018'), and by the European Commission under the H2020 REPLICATE (691735), SoBigData (654024) and AUTOWARE (723909) projects.

References

1. Asadi, A., Wang, Q., Mancuso, V.: A survey on device-to-device communication in cellular networks. IEEE Comm. Surv. Tutorials **16**(4), 1801–1819 (2014)
2. NetWorld 2020: Strategic research and innovation agenda. pervasive mobile virtual services, Technical report (2016)
3. Coll-Perales, B., Gozalves, J., Mestre, J.L.: 5G and beyond: smart devices as part of the network fabric. IEEE Netw. Mag. (Early Access). https://doi.org/10.1109/MNET.2019.1800136

4. Cisco visual networking index: Global mobile data traffic forecast update, 2016–2021, Cisco's White Paper, February 2017
5. Lin, Y.-D., Hsu, Y.-C.: Multihop cellular: a new architecture for wireless communications. In: Proceedings INFOCOM (2000)
6. Doppler, K., Rinne, M., Wijting, C., Ribeiro, C., Hugl, K.: Device-to-device communication as an underlay to LTE-advanced networks. IEEE Commun. Mag. **47**(12), 42–49 (2009)
7. Rebecchi, F., Dias de Amorim, M., Conan, V., Passarella, A., Bruno, R., Conti, M.: Data offloading techniques in cellular networks: a survey. IEEE Commun. Surv. Tutorials **17**(2), 580–603 (2015)
8. Coll-Perales, B., Gozalvez, J., Friderikos, V.: Context-aware opportunistic networking in multi-hop cellular networks. Ad Hoc Netw. **37**, 418–434 (2016)
9. Coll-Perales, B., Gozalvez, J., Friderikos, V.: Energy-efficient opportunistic forwarding in multi-hop cellular networks using device-to-device communications. Trans. Emerg. Telecommun. Technol. **27**(2), 249–265 (2016)
10. Pescosolido, L., Conti, M., Passarella, A.: Performance analysis of a device-to-device offloading scheme for vehicular networks. In: Proceedings WoWMoM 2018 (2018)
11. Pescosolido, L., Conti, M., Passarella, A.: On the impact of the physical layer model on the performance of D2D-offloading in vehicular environments. Ad Hoc Netw. **81**, 197–210 (2018)
12. Pescosolido, L., Conti, M., Passarella, A.: D2D data offloading in vehicular environments with optimal delivery time selection. Comput. Commun. **146**, 63–84 (2019). arXiv:1901.01744
13. Monserrat, J.F., Inca, S., Calabuig, J., Martín-Sacristán, D.: Map-based channel model for urban macrocell propagation scenarios. Int. J. Antennas Propag. **2015**, 1–5 (2015)
14. ICT METIS Project Deliverable 1.4: METIS Channel Models, Technical report (2015)
15. Krajzewicz, D., Erdmann, J.: Recent development and applications of SUMO-simulation of urban mobility. Int. J. Adv. Syst. Meas. **5**, 128–138 (2012)
16. 3GPP TS 36.213 v15.3.0: Evolved Universal Terrestrial Radio Access (E-UTRA); Physical layer procedures, September 2018
17. ICT METIS Project Deliverable 6.1: Simulation guidelines, Technical report (2013)

Forwarding and Congestion Control

ECN-Enhanced CoDel AQM

Dhulfiqar A. Alwahab[✉] and Sándor Laki[✉]

Faculty of Informatics, ELTE Eötvös Loránd University, Budapest, Hungary
{aalwahab,lakis}@inf.elte.hu

Abstract. Novel interactive applications require small end-to-end latency for providing end users with good Quality of Experience. To prevent the bufferbloat problem causing increased delay, various AQM solutions have recently emerged. One of the most widely adopted method is called CoDel that detects the increased delay by maintaining the per packet sojourn times and compering them to a desired target delay. Accordingly, congestion situation is indicated when the sojourn time exceeds the target delay. CoDel applies a drop-based feedback to notify the responsive sources about congestion only when the deviation from the target delay is permanent. Dropping packets is then compensated by packet re-transmissions in case of TCP which worsens utilization. In this paper, we propose an ECN-enhanced CoDel that distinguishes between low and high levels of congestion, and ECN-marks or drops the packets, respectively. The performance of the proposed method is analyzed in thorough NS-3 simulations with variable number of flows. The proposed ECN-marking reduces the number of packets re-transmissions and provides similarly good characteristics including convergence time and fairness to the original drop-based CoDel.

Keywords: ECN · DCE · AQM · CoDel · Congestion · Bufferbloat

1 Introduction

End-to-end delay became one of the key issues that attract network researchers and developers since most of the novel applications require fast and reliable Internet service. The end to end delay is affected by many additive factors: transmission, propagation, processing and queuing delays. Processing delay is mostly negligible, while transmission and propagation delays are determined by the physical properties of network paths. Only queuing delay can be managed to reduce the overall end to end delay in heterogeneous networks. The traditional congestion control mechanism of TCP by its nature tries to fill the queue till it notices a packet loss to slow down the sending rate, this mechanism introduces what is known as saw-tooth behavior. Using large buffers to store the packet in routers causes high latency because of increased queuing delay. This may lead to the bufferbloat problem that reduces the network performance by increasing the end-to-end delay specifically; when real time applications such as panoramic real-time video, online games, remote control, etc., or when sharing the same bottleneck link with packet from other nodes or applications. To improve overall

© IFIP International Federation for Information Processing 2019
Published by Springer Nature Switzerland AG 2019
M. Di Felice et al. (Eds.): WWIC 2019, LNCS 11618, pp. 157–169, 2019.
https://doi.org/10.1007/978-3-030-30523-9_13

utilization and handle these applications' sensitivity to throughput fluctuations, fast transmission and fast recovery are used as built-in techniques in TCP to minimize the impact of loss [1]. Bufferbloat problem can be addressed by two approaches: (1) by using end-to-end congestion control; (2) by involving Active Queue Management in the network devices.

Active Queue Management (AQM) had been considered as the best way to deal with the bufferbloat problem. The aims of any AQM algorithm are: absorb packet bursts; prevent packets to spend long time in the queue; deal with aggressive or misbehaving flows, as well as support Explicit Congestion Notification (ECN) [2]. The problem of formal AQM mechanism, like (Tail drop or Random Early Detection (RED)), lies in parameters setting on their algorithms where the parameters needed to be tuned depending on the actual traffic and network condition [3]. The parametrization issue urges researchers to directing their researches toward parameter-less or auto-tuning AQM mechanisms like Controlled Delay Active Queue Management (CoDel) or Proportional Integral Controller Enhanced (PIE). Another problem that limits all the traditional AQM mechanism is that they designed to operate only at layer three [4]. ECN [1] has been introduced as mean for notifying the end node about congestion by marking packets in the ECN-enabled routers based on the decision of the applied AQM mechanism instead of dropping them. This technique may enhance the overall performance of an AQM algorithm [5]. One of the biggest problem with TCP-based communication is that sources only reduce their sending rate after they noticed a packet loss. Retransmission of packets is consuming resources and increasing delay, eventually leading to worst network utilization.

In this paper, we introduce a conservative ECN marking scheme for CoDel that at low congestion level uses ECN-marking while at high and permanent congestion situations applies the original drop-based strategy of CoDel. The key benefits of the proposed method include: (1) It does not affect the good properties of CoDel; (2) It significantly reduces the number of packet retransmissions caused by drops; (3) The implementation is incremental and does not require the deep modification of the original CoDel.

The rest of this paper is organized as follows. In Sect. 2 we summarized the most related research work. Section 3 deals with the technique used to combine ECN with CoDel in more real-way. Next, in Sect. 4 we present simulation results done using NS-3 that prove our design. Finally, we present our conclusion in the last Section.

2 Related Work

The literature on AQM is vast, a lot of research papers for AQM has been proposed. In this section we will review a few researches that are most related to our work. Authors in [6] propose CoDel-Lifo as a new AQM algorithm to reduce the loss rate in multipath TCP congestion control mechanism, CoDel-Lifo differs from other AQM by treat the most recent packets with higher priority. Also, they compare coDel-lifo with CoDel, and Drop-Tail queue algorithms to show that

CoDel-lifo precedes in reduction the number of packets drop, goodput improvement and keep Round Trip Time (RTT) low. CoDel-lifo improves the performance of the network by depending on end nodes (TCP) and router (AQM). Authors in [3] shows its possible to adapt the setting of CoDel and Fq-CoDel to preserve low queuing delay and high link utilization. The experiments were presented over an emulated test bed and a satellite network in a capacity-limited network. Results show that the modification improves the download time and reduces the latency. In [4] a new class of AQM has been introduced called Active Sense Queue Management (ASQM). A comparison between the proposed mechanism and the traditional AQM (CoDel and PiE) was also presented. Results show the ability of ASQM to manage buffer bloat by decreasing queuing delay more than the traditional AQM. The authors in [7] analyze in theoretical and empirical way to address this question: is there a universal packet scheduling algorithm? After answered this question, they proved theoretically that least slack time first (LSTF) can be a universal solution, and empirically can closely reply to a wide range of scheduling algorithms. Then, they mentioned how to use LSTF with AQM in term of emulation (CoDel and ECN) on the edge nodes. without modifying the network's core. In [8], the benefits of using ECN with AQM, to avoid congestion, were discussed. These benefits can be summarized: (1) improve throughput up to 2% in some type of network. (2) Reduce head-of-line blocking by reduce the number of drop in the router (AQM). (3) Reduce probability of recovery time objective Retransmission Timeout (RTO) expiry by decrease the probability of loss. (4) improve the performance of latency-critical application by decoupling congestion control from loss. (5) Make incipient congestion visible. (6) opportunity for new transport mechanism. In [9], A PID controller with ECN based on neural network is presented, result of this work shows a better performance in compare to RED and typical PID AQM on the queue stability and mean time delay.

3 CoDel and ECN Marking

CoDel allows the sojourn time to be higher than target delay time for one interval, indicating permanent congestion, before it starts dropping packets. In practice this interval parameter is an order of magnitude larger than the target delay and ideally proportional to the observed RTT in the given system. After permanent congestion is detected, CoDel starts dropping packets from the head of the queue and applies a control rule to determine the next drop time. The time of the next drop is decreased gradually to control the TCP behavior in the network. One can see that CoDel's behavior only depends on the congestion level. When the congestion level is high, the sojourn time goes above a threshold value (target delay). When the sojourn time remains above the target for a duration more than one interval, CoDel starts dropping packets from the buffer. After another interval time, if the sojourn time goes back below the target delay, it stops the dropping process. Otherwise, CoDel enters the next drop state for a time interval equal to (interval $\sqrt{(Number\_of\_Drop)}$). On the other hand, it has been shown in [10,11] that CoDel cannot always control the queue delay, while may decrease the bottleneck-link utilization. Additionally, it cannot tune itself for network conditions and objectives without the adaptation of its parameters [3].

Explicit Congestion Notification (ECN) enables routers to manage the amount of cross traffic on the time scale of one RTT by marking the IP packets with a Congestion Experienced (CE) flag. When this flag is received by the TCP end-point, an ECN Echo (ECE) is sent back to the source. The source reacts to ECE flags similarly to packet drops with a much faster feedback loop, reducing its sending rate.

Figure 1(a) [4] overviews the original CoDel algorithm, where m is the interval time value in default (100 ms), τ is the target value (default 5 ms), Spi is the sojourn time of packets to be dequeued. $t1$ is first packet dequeue time in each m long interval, $t2$ is $t1 + m$, and Tpi is the packet's dequeue time when the packet is removed from the queue. In [12], the interval has been chosen with regard to RTT to give endpoint time to react for the congestion, the default value (100 ms) is recommended since this value works well across a range of RTT from 10ms to 100 ms (or even more). The role of the interval is to ensure that CoDel algorithm is up to date and it reacts to delay experience in the last epoch of the length interval [13]. When sojourn time of the packet goes higher than τ (5 ms), the original CoDel waits an interval (m) to check the sojourn time of the next packet. During this interval m, packets are forwarded or dropped. In the early appearance of congestion, before CoDel enter the drop state (in the first interval (m, usually 100 ms), the packet is still forwarded in spite of crossing the target delay by the packet's sojourn time. It is expected that TCP sources, by its nature, will continually increase the traffic rate because they did not know about the congestion appearance (no packets loss) at that moment.

According to our proposal, ECN will take place here, in the first interval (m) when the sojourn time first exceeds the target value. To avoid the effect of short temporal bursts experienced in the first interval period before entering packet dropping phase, we introduce a parameter C and mark a packet with probability P if the sojourn time goes above the threshold $C\tau$ (C times the target delay, indicating the beginning of a permanent congestion) Note that we tried several C and P values and found that $C = 1.5$ and $P = 0.3$ can significantly reduce the number of re-transmissions while provide similar flow fairness as original CoDel. The role of ECN markings are to inform the receivers that sojourn time significantly pass the target value in these packets. The receiver then notifies the source of this packet about the congestion appearance through the acknowledgment, resulting in a reduced sending window at the source. Figure 1(b) summarizes the ECN-enhanced CoDel algorithm. If the packets arrived to the AQM router and the queue is full, packet will be drop automatically, in the ECN-enhanced CoDel real packet drops can rarely experienced. In the remaining part of this paper, we will show that this slight modification can reduce the number of unnecessary re-transmissions while reducing the observed average sojourn times by multiple factors.

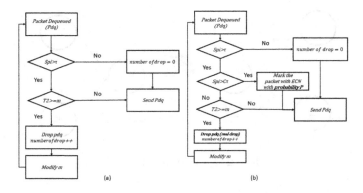

Fig. 1. CoDel (a) and ECN-enhanced CoDel (b) algorithms.

4   Simulation Results

The experiment of ECN-enhanced CoDel has been implemented in NS-3 Network Simulator,using respectively the IP and TCP stacks of Direct Code Extension (DCE). DCE is a framework that offers many advantages, among them are; enable executing network protocols and unmodified applications (i.e TCP) on the traditional library founded in the Linux kernel (libos); and its compatibility with NS-3 network simulator allowing fully reproducible experiments where, in this case, NS-3 is only responsible for network topology and packets issue (forwarding, marking or dropping). Based on these two-main advantages of DCE, our modification only affected the CoDel queue discipline model of NS-3, letting the TCP protocol react to ECN notification as it is implemented in the kernel [14]. We assume that in this way more realistic results can be achieved. The topology (dumbbell topology) of the network is shows in Fig. 2 that has been chosen because it is used in a variety of TCP performance comparison papers [15]. Accordingly, two-pairs of end-nodes are connected through two network devices (routers), and the link between the routers forms the bottleneck link of 50 Mbps in our case. In this way, there will be degradation in the goodput and packet will be enqueued even when there is only one flow. The ECN-enhanced CoDel has been tested under different number of TCP flows (2, 5 and 10 flows) and the results have been compared to the original CoDel.

First we compare the performance of ECN-enhanced CoDel with the normal one, using only two TCP flows. Source 1 starts application at time 0 s till the end of the simulation, and the application in Source 2 starts in the interval 3–40 s, randomly.

Figure 3 compares the number of re-transmitted packets for the ECN-enhanced and the original CoDel. In the original CoDel, the saw-tooth of TCP behavior is obvious in the figure, resulting in periodic re-transmission peaks. Whereas the ECN-enhanced CoDel reduces the re-transmissions in the network by informing the source node to reduce the sending rate earlier, using the previously described ECN mechanism.

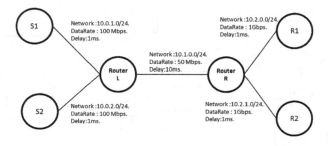

Fig. 2. Network topology.

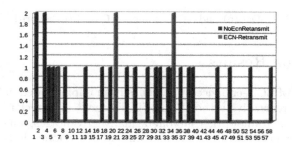

Fig. 3. Number of packets re-transmissions over time (2-TCP flows).

In case of normal CoDel, 32 segments had been lost whereas 10 segments in case of ECN-enhanced CoDel. Figure 4 shows the throughput of each flow in the network between the two nodes using the same application and port numbers. ECN-enhanced CoDel (with parameter $C = 1.5$ and $P = 0.3$) and original CoDel show similar performance but the fairness between the two TCP flows is slightly better for the original CoDel.

Figure 5 depicts the queue-length (byte) in this network within the two TCP flows. ECN-enhanced CoDel shows better result in the usage of buffer by keeping the buffer size low during most of the simulation time, compared to normal CoDel. Figure 6 displays the sojourn time for both variants in nanoseconds. One can observe that the modified CoDel could achieve more stability in the queue during the simulation time.

To test how ECN-enhanced CoDel works in more realistic scenarios, we increased the number of applications to 5 and 10. Each flow represents an application (with pre-specified port number) with different starting and ending time in the simulation. Table 1 details the operation time, source and destination nodes and port number of each application. Figure 7 shows the throughput

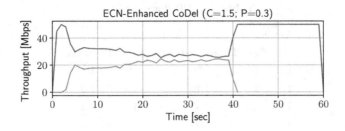

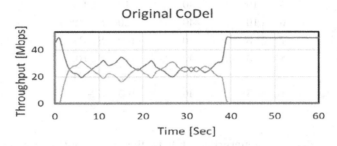

Fig. 4. Throughput of CoDel with/wo ECN (2-TCP flows)

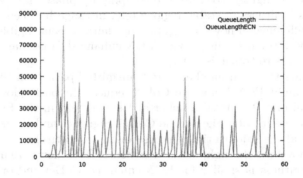

Fig. 5. Queue length in bytes over time (2-TCP Flows).

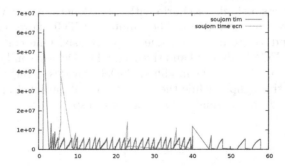

Fig. 6. Sojourn time in ns over time (2-TCP Flows).

Table 1. TCP flows details

No.	StartTime	EndTime	Port	Between
Application				
1	1	70	9	S1-R1
2	3	40	10	S2-R2
3	2	55	19	S1-R1
4	6	55	20	S2-R2
5	10	40	17	S1-R1
6	10	40	60	S2-R2
7	3	40	100	S1-R1
8	3	40	101	S2-R2
9	3	40	102	S1-R1
10	3	40	103	S2-R2

values of 5 applications generating TCP traffic at the bottleneck link for both ECN-enhanced and normal CoDel, respectively. One can observer that ECN-enhanced CoDel is slightly slower in the rumping up phase of TCP and results in slightly better fairness in stable regions (e.g. in range between 40 and 55 s). However, the difference in flow throughput and fairness is negligible, we can say that from the performance point of view ECN-enhanced CoDel can reach similar properties with less re-transmissions.

Figure 8 shows the total number of re-transmitted packets in the scenario of 5 flows. Accordingly, ECN-Enhanced CoDel reduces the packet loss in compare with the normal one. The total number of lost segment in the ECN-enhanced CoDel is 22 whereas its 99 in the normal CoDel. Figures 9 and 10 show the queue length (byte) and the sojourn time (nanosecond), respectively.

Figure 11 shows the throughput curves when 10 TCP flows are in the system. The observed fairness is similar for ECN-enhanced CoDel and original CoDel while the number of real packet drops is 1 and 441 for ECN-enhanced and original CoDel respectively.

Figure 12 depicts a similar scenario with a bottleneck of 500 Mbps (10 times more than in previous scenarios). The number of TCP flows is 10 while the parameters C and P are also the same as previously. One can note that the characteristics of ECN-Enhanced and the original CoDel are similar and in stable ranges (e.g. from 10 s to 40 s) the modified CoDel provides slightly better fairness and more stable throughput while the number of real packet drops is 1 and 183 for ECN-Enhanced and original CoDel variants, resp.

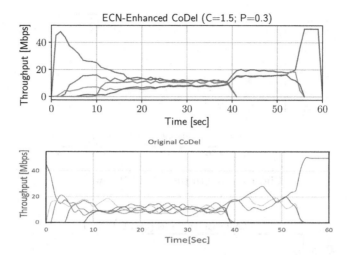

Fig. 7. Throughput with ECN-enhanced/Original CoDel (5-TCP flows)

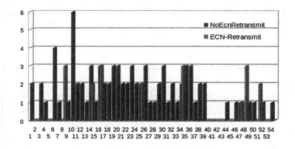

Fig. 8. Packets re-transmission process (5-TCP flows).

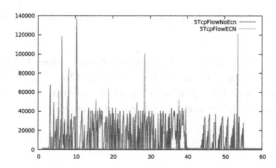

Fig. 9. Queue length (5-TCP flows).

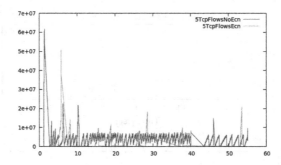

Fig. 10. Sojourn time (5-TCP flows).

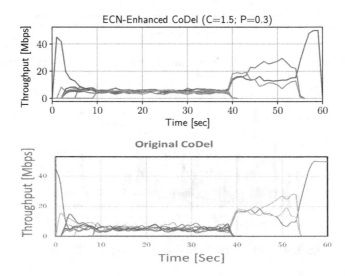

Fig. 11. Throughput with ECN-enhanced/Original CoDel (10-TCP flows)

Figure 13 summarizes the total number of segments loss for all the scenarios. HS is for high speed where links set to 1 Gbit/s. One can observe that ECN-enhanced CoDel reduces the number of packets re-transmission and resources consumption by lowering the number of packets drops.

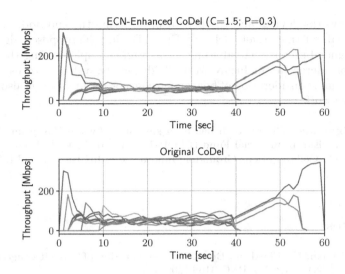

Fig. 12. Throughput with ECN-enhanced/Original CoDel (10-TCP flows) and a 500 Mbps bottleneck

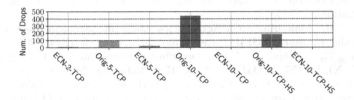

Fig. 13. Packet drop statistics for all scenarios.

5 Conclusions

In this work, we propose a slight modification of CoDel called ECN-enhanced CoDel that exploits the benefits of ECN marking to notify TCP sources faster without segment loss about congestion than traditional CoDel. The key benefit of the proposed method are: (1) It does not affect the good properties of CoDel; (2) It significantly reduces the number of packet re-transmissions caused by bufferbloat drops; (3) It reduces the observed sojourn times; (4) The implementation is incremental and does not require the deep modification of the original CoDel.

The performance of the proposed method has been investigated in simulations under various traffic mixes. In some scenarios TCP flows with ECN-enhanced CoDel show a slightly slower ramping up behaviour that seems to be affected by the introduced C parameter. This work proposes the concept of combining the advantage of using AQM (CoDel) for measuring the packets waiting time inside the inter-networks devices and the benefit of notifying the end-nodes devices in the network about the packets delay by ECN. Testing the proposed algorithm in a more expanded scenario (Real scenario) as well as implementing the test-bed for it are considered in our future work. Additionally, a deeper investigation of this problem and consideration of flow queue concept (FQ-CoDel) is also included in our future work.

Acknowledgments. The research has been supported by the European Union, co-financed by the European Social Fund (EFOP-3.6.2-16-2017-00013, Thematic Fundamental Research Collaborations Grounding Innovation in Informatics and Infocommunications).

References

1. Ramakrishnan, K., Floyd, S., Black, D.: The addition of explicit congestion notification (ECN) to IP. No. RFC 3168 (2001)
2. White, G. Pan, R.: A PIE-based AQM for DOCSIS cable modems. Internet-Draft draft-ietf-aqm-docsis-pie-02, Internet Engineering Task Force (2016)
3. Kulatunga, C. et al.: Tackling Bufferbloat in capacity-limited networks. In: 2015 European Conference on Networks and Communications (EuCNC), pp. 381–385. IEEE (2015)
4. Havey, D.M., Almeroth, K.C.: Active sense queue management (asqm). In: IFIP Networking Conference (IFIP Networking), 2015, pp. 1–9. IEEE (2015)
5. Hamann, T., Walrand, J.: A new fair window algorithm for ECN capable TCP (new-ECN). In: INFOCOM, vol. 3, pp. 1528–1536, March 2000
6. Felix, B. et al.: A New Queue Discipline for Reducing Bufferbloat Effects in HetNet Concurrent Multipath Transfer. arXiv preprint arXiv:1609.09314 (2016)
7. Mittal, R. et al.: Universal packet scheduling. In: Proceedings of the 14th ACM Workshop on Hot Topics in Networks, p. 24. ACM (2015)
8. Fairhurst, G., Welzl, M.: The Benefits of using Explicit Congestion Notification (ECN). No. RFC 8087 (2017)
9. Zhou, C., Zhang, L., Chen, Q.: An adaptive PID controller for AQM with ECN marks based on neural networks. In: 7th Asian Control Conference, 2009, ASCC 2009, pp. 779–783. IEEE (2009)
10. Järvinen, I., Kojo, M.: Evaluating CoDel, PIE, and HRED AQM techniques with load transients. In: 2014 IEEE 39th Conference on Local Computer Networks (LCN), pp. 159–167. IEEE (2014)
11. Schwardmann, J., Wagner, D., Kühlewind, M.: Evaluation of ARED, CoDel and PIE. In: Kermarrec, Y. (ed.) EUNICE 2014. LNCS, vol. 8846, pp. 185–191. Springer, Cham (2014). https://doi.org/10.1007/978-3-319-13488-8_17
12. Nichols, K., Jacobson, V.: A Modern AQM is just one piece of the solution to bufferbloat. ACM Queue Netw. **10**(5) (2012)
13. Hoeiland-Joergensen, T., McKenney, O., Taht, D., Gettys, J., Dumazet, E.: The Flow Queue CoDel Packet Scheduler and Active Queue Management Algorithm. No. RFC 8290 (2018)

14. Tazaki, H. et al.: Direct code execution: revisiting library OS architecture for reproducible network experiments. In: Proceedings of the ninth ACM Conference on Emerging Networking Experiments and Technologies, pp. 217–228. ACM (2013)
15. Alwahab, D.A., Laki, S.: A simulation-based survey of active queue management algorithms. In: Proceedings of the 6th International Conference on Communications and Broadband Networking, pp. 71–77. ACM (2018)

On the Significance of Layer-3 Traffic Forwarding

Salim Mohamed[1]([⊠]), Saptarshi Das[1], Subir Biswas[1], and Osama Mohammed[2]

[1] Electrical and Computer Engineering, Michigan State University,
East Lansing, USA
mohame26@msu.edu, {dassapta,sbiswas}@egr.msu.edu
[2] Service Delivery and Management, Innovaway, Napoli, Italy
osama.mohammed@it.ibm.com

Abstract. Designing performance-enhanced and large-scale overlay networks over the conventional IP substrate encounters different implementation obstacles put in place by Internet Service Providers (ISPs). These include lack of proper privileges and restrictive routing policies that prevent the overlay services from being deployed easily. The evolution of Software Defined Networks (SDNs), however, helps to address these concerns by simplifying the mechanism for overlay router design. In this paper, we have included an analysis of 18,906 delay traces from a network of 138 hosts. Our main aim was to demonstrate the rich existence of IP overlay paths that can be leveraged to significantly enhance Internet routing performance. We try to make the case for using layer-3 forwarding minimum delay overlay paths by demonstrating superior performance in this approach compared to existing overlay designs which work mostly at the TCP and application layers. In particular, the study was conducted to benefit applications that are sensitive to end-to-end delay and throughput. This paper presents a specific analysis of end-to-end delay in order to enhance TCP performance. The current work aims at increasing throughput and reducing file transfer time via overlay while maintaining simplicity and preserving all TCP characteristics. The results of this study show that the use of the shortest delay paths between physically disjoint node pairs can benefit TCP throughput and minimize file transfer time by orders of magnitude. The ultimate objective behind this study is to develop a reliable and scalable over-lay design for file transfers that require high transmission rates.

Keywords: Overlay routing · Delay characteristics · TCP performance

1 Introduction

Background: Traditional Internet connections are established via a set of underlying routing protocols at the IP substrate. On a consistent basis, overlay routing can provide better end-to-end performance such as faster download times, lesser stream re-buffering [8] or higher throughput for end-users. Overlay routing achieves this via exploring non-congested paths that are not necessarily discovered by best-effort Internet routing protocols. This flexibility helps to

© IFIP International Federation for Information Processing 2019
Published by Springer Nature Switzerland AG 2019
M. Di Felice et al. (Eds.): WWIC 2019, LNCS 11618, pp. 170–181, 2019.
https://doi.org/10.1007/978-3-030-30523-9_14

direct traffic away from congested segments of the network and subsequently improves performance. Overlay paths can be chosen based on different parameters including lower delay, drop rate, or higher bandwidth along the path. The main goal of this work is to improve layer-3 TCP performance using minimum delay overlay routing.

The following key questions have being investigated in our analysis. For a given physical network topology, are there overlay paths that can provide lower delay compared to the best-effort paths offered by the current Internet protocols? How stable such paths are? What is the additional resource burden for such overlay paths that are generally longer than the best-effort paths? What improvement can be achieved by choosing such overlay paths? By answering these questions, our approach has achieved significant TCP throughput gain and file transfer delay reduction when comparing some underlay to overlay paths.

Methodology: Here, we describe the used platform, performed experiments and our designed procedure for conducting measurements. Platform: Networking testbeds such as Planetlab and Emulab are distinct. Planetlab, for instance, connects global clusters, from which a user can subscribe to a set of nodes in a slice. Our measurements are conducted using 140 nodes distributed according across the globe: North America 63.57%, South America 4.29%, Australia 3%, Asia 17.86% and Europe 12.86%. Experiments: Traceroute and Ping were used to conduct $18,906$ and $19,460$ end-to-end measurements respectively in a network of $n = 140$ nodes. Traceroute performed short-spaced measurements, i.e., $[5 \rightarrow 10]$ min interval. Ping sends bulk of packets of four distinct sizes, i.e., $0.05, 0.1, 0.25$ and 0.5 megabytes. These loads were scheduled in same order 4 times, i.e., a result of 16 experiments. Having a diverse measurements interval as suggested in [1], provides more confidence in capturing possible routing changes. Probing daemon: Throughout measurement period, all experiments followed exact probing abstraction illustrated as follows: The probing complexity is $O(m)$, where m is the average number of allowed probers in a subset of nodes, i.e., group. In our case, we allowed one probing per group g_i where $i \in [1 \rightarrow m]$. Generally, maximum probing time t_i among all groups is an experiment running time. The probing time is considered at our server-side to represent the difference between a request time and response time from a daemon. Each daemon iterates into two loops: The first, is to probe all $n - 1$ nodes, and the second loop is for re-probing unresponsive nodes once again. The actual group time is: $t_i = \sum_{k=1}^{|g_i|} \lambda_i(k) + \beta_i(k)$ as $\lambda_i(k)$ and $\beta_i(k)$ are probing loops times. These times can be determined as: $\lambda_i(k) = \sum_{j=1}^{n-1} \bar{\tau}$ and similarly $\beta_i(k) = \eta \sum_{j=1}^{\theta_i(k)} \bar{\tau}$, where $\theta_i(k)$ is number of nodes failed to be probed in first loop, $\bar{\tau}$ is average probing time in network and $\eta = 1$ is an average count of re-probing in our case. Our probing scheme used a server-based synchronization for each daemon, and afterward each daemon sends back its conducted measurements to our server. To minimize the effect of imperfect measurements occur when a large number of daemons probe a particular node simultaneously, we forced each daemon to probe at a time few randomly-selected destinations until covering all nodes. The possible consequence without such a procedure would be that the observed delays to any destination can be influenced by our probing packets. Despite such randomness, we defined for successful measurement, a probability of success as described below. Probability of success: To reduce the influence of probing packets on the actual routing, such probability concerns for $n - m$ nodes, there is no node to be targeted simultaneously by all m probers. Determining such a probability as a function of m is identical to many existing problems such as birthday-paradox and withdraw with replacement. Solutions of different variations are in [4,5]. Her, we just compute the probability of success as a function of the number of groups used in probing. The probability of success, i.e., no collision in probing as in [4] is:

$$\Pr(\text{success}) = \prod_{i=1}^{m-1} \left(1 - \frac{i}{n-m}\right)$$

Recall, n and m are the numbers of nodes and groups respectively. Practically, m represents the number of active probers that can probe the network within a particular time. Therefore, m must be chosen carefully to satisfy desired success probability. Due to tedious computation when solving for an exact solution for m that satisfies a given demand for success, we can approximate the probability of success if $m \ll n$ by:

$$\Pr(\text{success}) = \exp\left\{-\frac{m^2}{2(n-m)}\right\}$$

Solving for success demand equals 70% leads to $m = \frac{1}{2}\sqrt{(2.8534n + 0.50887)} - 0.35667$. For our network $n = 140$, we find $m \approx 10$. Clearly, achieving 100% of success reduces m to one as expected, i.e., the probability of success vanishes as the number of concurrent probers increases.

Contributions: The main contributions of this paper are as follows: First, we experimentally demonstrate that in many situations, there exists a rich topology of overlay paths that can provide lower round-trip-time (RTT) comparing to the best-effort underlay paths. Second, we characterize these overlay paths in terms of their benefit, temporal stability and the link consumption, i.e., time-to-live (TTL). Finally, we demonstrate that such lower-delay overlay paths can eventually be leveraged to improve application layer performance. We demonstrate the latter using FTP as a target application while the transfer time and throughput were considered as performance metrics at the application layer. Packets in the segmented TCP approach suffer from additional delay at the application stack of every overlay node, and that requires a robust store-forward buffering design [13] in order to minimize the re-transmission times. Furthermore, buffers are required to be coupled with back-pressure schemes to avoid flooding the slowest hop at higher rates. On the other hand, this paper proposed a slightly different approach to eliminate the previous and cost. The implemented IP-layer forwarding preserves all the current properties of the end-to-end TCP protocols except redirecting traffic through other paths that experience the minimum delay among all possible.

2   Related Research

This work can be depicted as an experimental prototype to [3] for content delivery applications. The dominant Internet traffic is served over the connection-oriented transport protocol TCP [6]. Our approach, however, is not dedicated to TCP applications, but we analyzed its performance using TCP as a possible worst-case scenario for the following reasons. TCP's feedback control always starts with a small congestion window that impacts the number of packets in flight. Further, the three-way handshaking signals add new additional round trip times to path latency [6]. Thus, overlay paths must remain constant over long periods of time and must change only when the QoS suffers degradation. In our study, the seven examined overlay paths were reused over a period of 5-hour by a rate of 50 times per hour.

Based on the argument mentioned above, our approach is applicable for live and high-quality video streaming such as Netflix, Voice-over-IP like Skype. The VoIP design in [2] can be viewed as an application of our approach. The authors in [2] provide no details about their overlay structure that improves call quality by 45% to be close from an oracle-based solution, i.e., all metrics for all paths are known. The whitepaper [5] on Akamai's overlay and the study in [6] are further instances of the use of overlay schemes to reduce the content retrieve-time in Data Centers Networks (DCNs) which can be a possible use-case for the overlay design outlined in our study. Most of the literature on cloud services using overlay as demonstrated in [5–8] and [9] do not specify their internal overlay design which we have done in the current study.

The study in [3] proposes a combined bandwidth and delay aware routing scheme for enhancing internet QoS. Their emulated SDN controller takes bandwidth and latency measurements from a separate monitoring entity and pre-calculates appropriate routes for each pair of nodes in advance. Our study, in contrast, performs an experimental overlay topology that can serve high-rate content delivery applications using the single metric of delay calculated using active probing measurements. Interestingly, our design also has achieved higher throughput and delay reductions over the set of examined overlay routes and by a large magnitude. On average, in the semi-heterogeneous topology discussed in [3], the results show that there was 22% of bandwidth increase and [4 → 15] RTT reduction.

3   Results and Analysis

This section summarizes our results and analysis as follows: Subsect. 3.1 shows the real time achieved TCP performance. This gain has been achieved after implementing the proposed overlay on seven long-distance overlay paths that forward 5-megabytes content between their end-nodes. In Subsect. 3.2, we provide an abstract characterization for the existence of possible minimum delay overlay paths between all available source-destination pairs, and further evaluate the stability of this characterization across the network. Subsection 3.3 discusses the variation of the delay reduction between sources. For overlay networks that compete for small end-to-end delay, there is always a trade-off between the desired delay reduction and the burden of utilizing links extensively. Subsection 3.4 explores the total link consumption via both the underlying substrate and the obtained overlay paths. In Subsect. 3.5, however, we show the trade-off between the link consumption and the end-to-end delay. Subsection 3.6 illustrates the distribution of the RTT reduction at the node granularity.

3.1   Overlay and TCP Performance

The real-time implementation of the proposed single session and minimum end-to-end delay overlay routing was an essential stage in providing some insight about its importance and usability. Following the previous analysis, seven overlay pairs have been selected and configured to transfer the 5-megabyte file in between. We argue that although this number is small due to restrictions imposed at the IP layer by Planetlab and the no-flexibility using [1], our achieved performance via these paths can be considered as a generalization when using the same design. The comparison in Fig. 1 shows variation in the TCP throughput using the best effort IP routing and the proposed overlay design for the random set of overlay paths with different delay benefits. Regarding the TCP throughput, there is a considerable improvement for p_1, an increase of a magnitude for p_2, p_3, p_4 and p_6 while maintaining slightly the same underlay throughput for p_5 and p_7. The reason behind maintaining the same underlay throughput for p_5 and p_7 is that the overlays of these two paths originally provide small delay reductions, and so was the throughput improvement. The main reasons behind this leading performance of some paths are as follows: First, since the achieved throughput is inversely proportional to RTT, these minimum delay paths experienced less delay so that for any given TCP congestion window the throughput is maximized. From Fig. 1, the time required to transfer the 5-megabyte file as a second measure for TCP performance shows similar behavior to the corresponding

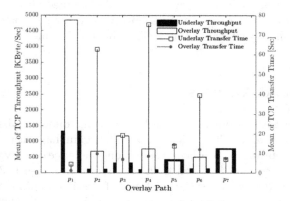

Fig. 1. TCP performance

throughput. In general, the transfer time has been reduced significantly except for p_5 and p_7 that provide minor delay reductions. This simple design overcomes the multi-segment and the multi-path forwarding by not requiring extensive packet buffering and reordering at the receiver end. Second, our design also has no packet encapsulation at the application layer.

3.2   Existence and Stability of Better Overlay Paths

Ideally, overlay paths are expected to be clustered around smaller RTTs when compared with the underlay RTTs that can be seen distributed across the entire delay range. Therefore, the overlay delay distribution curve should be clearly shifted to the left of the underlay distribution along the entire range, and its peaks raised up as much as possible at the smallest delay values of the range. In contrast, the two curves are expected to be aligned on each other as the RTT increases. Figure 2 confirms this description by showing the behavior of this distribution over the 24-hour measurement period. By considering the most commonly observed round-trip-times and excluding all delays of the one-hop overlay paths, the plot shows that there is only 2.8% of underlay paths out of 18, 906 with 40 ms end-to-end delay. The overlay routing, however, reduces the end-to-end delay to about 25 ms for 2.6% of the paths and raises the number of paths that experience 40 ms to 4% instead. Overlay paths competing for shorter delays exist up to the 500 ms mark after which overlay routing starts yielding to underlay as their pdfs are perfectly aligned.

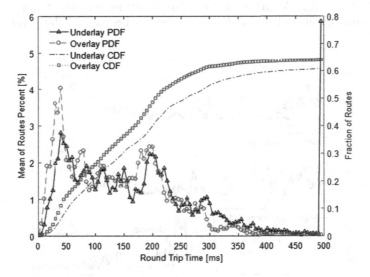

Fig. 2. Underlay and overlay RTT distributions

The range between $[10 \rightarrow 500]$ ms is commonly observed and solved by the proposed overlay, as the percent of overlay paths collapses outside this range. In this analysis, we only considered overlay paths whose end-to-end delays are less than 500 ms, and that is why the CDF curves do not approach one. The CDFs also show that for 250 ms delay, 49% and 40% are an overlay and underlay paths, respectively. We found that two hops overlay paths, however, can provide distinct delay reduction for 35% of the 18,906 end-to-end connections, i.e., more than the current IP routing can perform.

3.3   RTT Variations in Benefit

Overlay controllers should be able to enforce routing decisions based on benefit change. We decided to partition the entire overlay design into four routing sets. The set S_1 represents overlay paths that can reduce the physical end-to-end delay by more than 100 ms. S_2 accommodates paths for delay reduction within the range $[10 \rightarrow 100]$ ms. Failures indicate either one of two different scenarios. The first scenario is that a physical path has no better overlay alternative, while the second one is that for a physical failure that cannot be resolved even by the overlay routing. These two scenarios are represented by the sets S_3 and S_4 respectively. Figure 3 above shows the variation of this reduction between different nodes. Overlay benefit is indicated by the degree, to which the overlay distribution is shifted to the left of the underlay. It is evident that higher overlay benefit is achieved for nodes where the overlay or underlay distributions are toward the higher RTT values. This range of RTT reduction is further analyzed in Subsect. 3.5. We argue that our large-scale measurements represent this range reasonably enough for wide area networks because of the heterogeneous

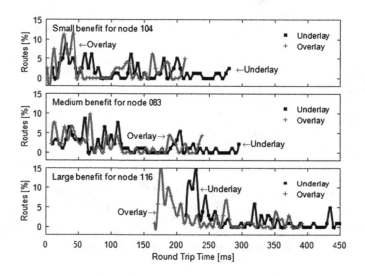

Fig. 3. Variations of RTT benefit

resources in Planetlab, and the underlying routing will start to be minimum beyond this range. By looking at the relationship between S_2 and S_3, we can infer the following. As $|i_{s_2}| - |i_{s_3}|$ increases, the overlay benefit increases, and therefore, compared to what we described in Subsect. 3.2, the RTT distribution will be further shifted left for the nodes with large overlay benefit. Nodes with small benefit from overlay will have almost two identical RTT curves. The analyzed traceroute experiments have shown identical behavior between the benefit curves, and Fig. 3 shows only random nodes from the first experiment.

3.4 Burden of Link Consumption

There is always a trade-off between minimizing the end-to-end delay and the number of links, i.e., network resources, used to achieve this objective. To understand such behavior, Fig. 4 shows the averaged link consumption for both the underlay and the overlay topologies. The underlay link consumption is be approximated by $\mu = 16.5$ and $\sigma = 4.7$ while overlay corresponds to $\mu = 33.7$ and $\sigma = 14$, where μ and σ are the mean and standard deviation of link distributions respectively. Surprisingly, from this result, there still exist overlay pairs that communicate under minimized end-to-end delay, while maintaining the common range of the underlay link consumption that is below 30 links. The jump at 30 links for the underlying consumption represents both underlay paths of 30 links and all failed paths.

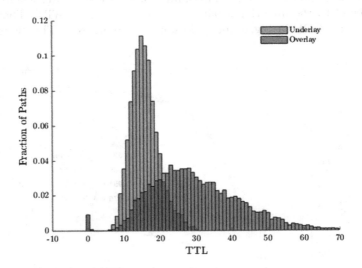

Fig. 4. Underlay and overlay TTL distributions

There is also strong stability in the underlay distribution over 24 h compared to the over-lay distribution since the link consumption over 24 h does not deviate much from their means that are represented vertically on the two curves. This indicates that any delay aware overlay routing can more greedy but sensitive to delay changes than the traditional IP protocols, and that is because of its global view about the network delay.

3.5   Link Consumption and RTT Benefit

Section 3.4 defined the amount of overlap between the link consumptions of both the underlay and overlay paths. In here, however, we relate the previous link characteristic to the end-to-end delay reduction. For a given end-to-end path p, we refer by $\delta_{rtt}(p)$ to the delay difference in RTT between the underlay and the overlay paths $r : i \rightarrow j$. That is $\delta_{rtt}(p) = \underline{d}(p) - \overline{d}(p)$, where $\underline{d}(p))$ is the underlay and $\overline{d}(p)$ is the overlay RTT. Based on this definition, $\delta_{rtt} \geq 0$ with equality if the overlay path is just one hop, i.e., the same as the underlying path. Therefore, when $\delta_{rtt}(p) > 0$, that means the overlay path is at least two hops in length: $\delta_{hop}(p) = \overline{h}(p) - \underline{h}(p) \geq 2$ hops. The $\overline{h}(p)$ represents the length in hops of the overlay path while $\underline{h}(p)$ represents the underlay path and is always equal to one. Similarly, at the link granularity, the introduced $\delta_{link}(p)$ on the other hand, can be either positive or negative. When $\delta_{link}(p) = 0$ it does not necessarily imply that for the given connection its overlay and underlay paths are identical, simply because an overlay path of at least two hops can use in total the same number of links used by the corresponding underlying one hop path. In this analysis, we only considered the overlay paths that are not in any of following underlay-overlay combinations: failure-recovery, failure-failure or recovery-failure, where the last one is related to the underlying paths that have minimum RTT. That is why the cumulative CDF in Fig. 5 above does not approach one. This figure shows

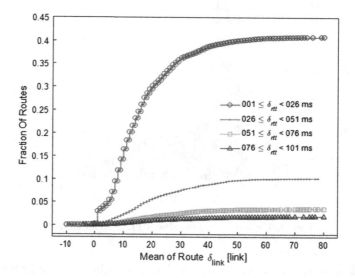

Fig. 5. Delay benefit vs. link consumption

a constrained $\delta_{link}(p)$ by a desired delay reduction, i.e., $\delta_{rtt}(p)$. From Fig. 5, we can conclude that the $[1 \to 25]$ ms is the range, on which we can maximize the performance of the overlay routing at the smallest link consumption.

Ideally, as the configuration of the overlay hops consumes less number of hops, the expected link consumption should not be high. Our analysis also has looked at the relationship between the three metrics: delay reduction, link and hop consumption across the entire network. The result in Fig. 6 shows that throughout the entire measurement period on average, the overlay topology uses two hops of an average link consumption within $[10 \to 15]$ links in order to achieve an average delay reduction of 30 ms.

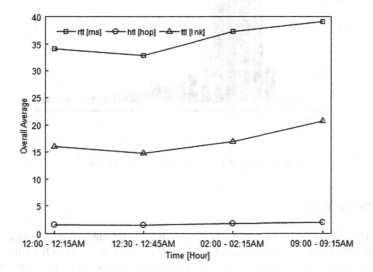

Fig. 6. Link and hop consumption vs. Delay

3.6   Node RTT Benefit

The previous Sect. 3.5 discussed δ_{rtt} only at the path granularity. The expectation at the node granularity is that the aggregated $\delta_{rtt}(n_i)$ for nodes that act as sources will show a peak at the most shared reduction between them. Since we have only considered the overlay set S_2, this lump will reside somewhere in the range $[1 \to 100]$. In a network of N nodes, and for a node i in particular, we define the average delay reduction per node as:

$$\delta_{rtt}(n_i) = \frac{1}{N-1} \sum_{j \neq i} \delta rtt(p : n_i \to n_j)$$

Fig. 7 depicts the complete picture of $\delta_{rtt}(n_i)$ of the first traceroute experiment peaked at 25 ms. This means that the averaged delay reduction range, at which all sources are functioning, is $[22 \to 27]$. This, of course, does not mean that the overall benefit from implementing an overlay will be only within that range, but on average, this is the trend at the source granularity.

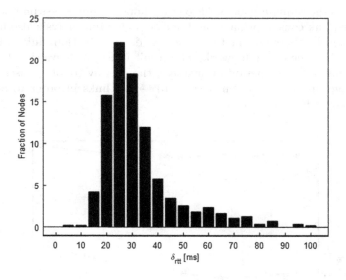

Fig. 7. Distribution of node delay benefit

4   Conclusion

This study analyzed the behavior of single session overlay routes that minimize the end-to-end delay for all possible TCP pairs in the network. Our analysis has been derived for the most observed and common range to reduce the delay of $[1 \rightarrow 100]$ ms. The study has confirmed the existence of a considerable number of overlay routes that can minimize the underlay round-trip times by the mentioned reduction range for the majority of nodes. The advantage of this overlay design varies from node to node, based on their topological positions. The study summarizes the trade-off between minimizing the end-to-end delay and the consumption of the network resources by showing the lack of delay reduction using fewer links than the underlying paradigm. In the future, we will investigate the difference in reduction between this minimum delay overlay routing and another overlay design that will optimize the overall network delay, while being less greedy in consuming network resources.

References

1. Freire, C., Quereilhac, A., Turletti, T., Dabbous, W.: Automated Deploy-ment and Customization of Routing Overlays on PlanetLab, TRIDENTCOM (2012)
2. Jiang, J., et al.: VIA: improving internet telephony call quality using predictive relay selection. In: Proceedings of ACM SIGCOMM (2016)

3. U-chupala, P., et al.: Application oriented bandwidth and latency aware routing with OpenFlow network. In: Proceedings of The 6th IEEE International Conference on Cloud Computing Technology and Science (CloudCom) (2014)
4. Lee, S., Banerjee, S., Sharma, P., Yalagandula, P., Basu, S.: Bandwidth-aware routing in overlay networks. In: Proceedings of IEEE-INFOCOM (2008)
5. Habib, S., Bokhari, F.S., Khan, S.U.: Routing techniques in data center networks. In: Khan, S.U., Zomaya, A.Y. (eds.) Handbook on Data Centers, pp. 507–532. Springer, New York (2015). https://doi.org/10.1007/978-1-4939-2092-1_16
6. Sitaraman, R., Kasbekar, M., Lichtenstein, W., Jain, M.: Overlay Networks: An Akamai Perspective. Advanced Content Delivery, Streaming and Cloud Services. John Wiley & Sons, New Jersey (2014)
7. Cheng, F., Sitaraman, R., Torres, M.: End-user mapping: next generation request routing for content delivery. In: Proceedings of ACM SIGCOMM (2015)
8. Maggs, B., Sitaraman, R.: Algorithmic nuggets in content delivery. In Proceedings of ACM SIGCOMM Computer Communication (2015)
9. Liu, Y., Gu, Y., Zhang, H., Gong, W., Towsley, D.: Application level relay for high-bandwidth data transport, GridNets (2004)

Delivering Multicast Content Through Secure D2D Communications in the Internet of Things

Chiara Suraci$^{(\boxtimes)}$, Sara Pizzi, Antonio Iera, Antonella Molinaro, and Giuseppe Araniti

DIIES, University "Mediterranea" of Reggio Calabria, Via Graziella, Loc. Feo di Vito, 89100 Reggio Calabria, Italy {chiara.suraci,sara.pizzi,antonio.iera,antonella.molinaro, giuseppe.araniti}@unirc.it

Abstract. Device-to-device (D2D) communications and cellular solutions represent key technologies for the development of a future infrastructure in which fifth-generation (5G) systems and the Internet of Things (IoT) will converge. A tricky issue to be carefully investigated in D2D communications is the prevention of threats to privacy and security caused by malicious devices. Thus, security mechanisms must be implemented in order to assure a reliable data exchange among involved devices. In this paper, we propose MtMS-sD2D (Machine-type Multicast Service with secure D2D), an architecture for the delivery of multicast traffic in an IoT scenario that takes advantage from D2D communications made reliable by means of a security mechanism. Furthermore, we discuss the procedures that must be followed to efficiently deliver multicast traffic. Finally, we provide some preliminary yet insightful simulation results.

Keywords: 5G · IoT · D2D · MtMS · Security

1 Introduction

Device-to-device (D2D) communication appears as a promising paradigm to support the interconnection of heterogeneous objects foreseen by the Internet of Things (IoT) [1]. An IoT system can be seen as a collection of smart devices that interact (by means of different processing and communication architectures, technologies, and design methodologies) on a collaborative basis to fulfill a common goal. The amount of interconnected devices is expected to grow heavily in the near future not only due to the increase in possible use cases, but also to the decrease in device costs and to the widespread use of technologies augmenting device capabilities at minimal costs. Thus, IoT is considered one of the key enabling technologies for the next-to-come fifth-generation (5G) cellular networks [2].

© IFIP International Federation for Information Processing 2019
Published by Springer Nature Switzerland AG 2019
M. Di Felice et al. (Eds.): WWIC 2019, LNCS 11618, pp. 182–193, 2019.
https://doi.org/10.1007/978-3-030-30523-9_15

As a consequence, a severe traffic overload problem will have to be faced in cellular networks. D2D communications represent a promising method for data offloading, spectrum efficiency enhancement, network resource utilization improvement, user's throughput improvement, and battery lifetime extension, thanks to its capability of leveraging the proximity between the devices involved in the direct communication. In literature, many works deal with the D2D technology. In [3], a taxonomy for D2D communications, based on the spectrum utilization, is presented.

The wide scale of IoT inherently magnifies the risk of security threats of the current Internet. In addition, despite the obvious advantages of D2D communications, their intrinsic nature causes also additional problems due to the fact that connections happen directly between devices in proximity. Thus, careful investigations are required on solutions finalized to mitigate the risk of threats to privacy and security caused by malicious devices when exploiting D2D communications. Evidently, any malicious behavior by devices may cause serious consequence and lead to deteriorated user experience.

Actually, an always increasing number of autonomously operated, low-cost devices (i.e. sensors, actuators, drones) requires to be connected with each other by exploiting wireless networks no longer exclusively dedicated to human communications. Not by chance, the support of a new type of traffic known as machine-type communications (MTC) has become one of the key objective of 5G networks. This new communication paradigm could benefit from group-oriented (e.g., multicast) services to achieve a reduction in energy consumption and delay. In particular, multicasting can be an effective means for simultaneously sending data to a group of IoT devices through point-to-multipoint communications [4].

Multimedia Broadcast Multicast Services (MBMS) is the architecture that the 3rd Generation Partnership Project (3GPP) has standardized to manage the delivery of multicast and broadcast services over cellular networks. The main nodes of this architecture are: the *broadcast multicast-service center (BM-SC)*, which is responsible for the initialization of the MBMS session and for some security functions, such as the management of the authorizations for the MBMS subscribers; the *MBMS-gateway (MBMS-GW)*, which is in charge of forwarding the MBMS packets to the BSs involved in the delivery service; the *multicell/multicast coordination entity (MCE)*, which has to manage the admission control and the radio resource allocation to every BS.

All these nodes need to be enhanced in order to enable multicasting also over future 5G networks. MBMS also specifies the procedures to follow in order to sustain a multicast session. The legacy MBMS is highly suitable to support multimedia applications, but many changes have to be applied to the standardized architecture and procedures in order to manage future MTC multicast traffic more properly. In this regard, in [5], the Machine-type Multicast Service (MtMS) is proposed to define the architecture and the most adequate transmission procedures to the management of the MTC multicast traffic.

With reference to this research area, this paper introduces a network architecture, MtMS-sD2D (MtMS with secure D2D), specifically designed for the highly reliable delivery of multicast traffic to a set of machines in IoT scenarios, which leverages D2D communications coupled to a secure mechanism based on the Diffie-Hellman key exchange (DHKE) protocol. Furthermore, it discusses the designed procedures introduced to efficiently transmit multicast data toward a set of MTC devices.

The remainder of the paper is organized as follows. In Sect. 2, the security mechanism implemented in the D2D communication is presented. Section 3 and Sect. 4 describe, respectively, the reference network architecture and the transmission procedures of the proposed MtMS-sD2D protocol. Obtained results are shown in Sect. 4. Conclusive remarks are given in the last section.

2   Securing D2D Communications

In [2], among the listed 5G requirements, improved security mechanisms are recommended that can work effectively in the presence of a likely huge increase in the amount of data transmitted over cellular networks. In the IoT landscape, machines often communicate sensitive data over the unsecure wireless channel; thus security and privacy requirements have to be satisfied to guarantee both data and devices protection. Among security requirements, data confidentiality and integrity, authentication, and authorization are highly relevant to the IoT scenario. As for privacy requirements, it is important to protect personal devices information [6].

This work considers an IoT scenario, wherein the MTC multicast traffic is managed through an enhanced version of the MtMS presented in [5], named *MtMS with secure D2D (MtMS-sD2D)*. D2D communications are established between devices directly served by the BS and those terminals excluded from the multicast transmission, because of their adverse channel conditions. A secure protocol is implemented over D2D communication in order to protect the transmitted data.

A secure data sharing strategy for D2D communication is presented in [7]. This protocol satisfies many security requirements, such as non-repudiation, authentication, authorization, confidentiality, and integrity. It uses some security mechanisms, such as encryption, HMAC, and signature to manage the messages exchanged between the two peers involved in direct communication. To this aim, the encryption of transmitted data is performed by using a symmetric (i.e., private-key) encryption algorithm; this means that the same key is used to encrypt and to decrypt data. The private key is generated through an enhanced version of the *Diffie-Hellman key exchange (DHKE)* protocol, in which the public keys exchange is intermediated by the trusted third party, represented by the BS. The effectiveness of the DHKE algorithm relies on the challenge of computing logarithms over a finite field *GF(q)* with a prime number q of elements.

As in [7], we exploit the DHKE protocol in order to secure data transmission on D2D communications. In the following, the basics of the DHKE protocol will be given.

Let

$$Y = \alpha^X \bmod q, \qquad \text{for } 1 \leq X \leq q - 1, \tag{1}$$

where α is a fixed primitive element of $GF(q)$ known to both users involved in the D2D communications, then X is referred to as the logarithm of Y to the base α, mod q:

$$X = \log_\alpha Y \bmod q, \qquad \text{for } 1 \leq Y \leq q - 1. \tag{2}$$

While computing Y from X is easy, the calculation of X from Y can be much more difficult and it could require a number of operations in the order of $q^{1/2}$, using the best known algorithm. For this reason, it is necessary to choose a number q consisting of at least 300 digits for the system not to be broken. The security of the technique crucially depends on the difficulty of computing logarithms mod q. When users i and j want to communicate privately, first of all they must agree on the values of q and α. Then, each user generates an independent random number X_i chosen uniformly from the set of integers $\{1, 2, 3, ..., q - 1\}$ and keeps it secret, but sends to the other user

$$Y_i = \alpha^{X_i} \bmod q. \tag{3}$$

The key used for both enciphering and deciphering by the two users is

$$K_{ij} = \alpha^{X_i X_j} \bmod q. \tag{4}$$

User i obtains K_{ij} by obtaining Y_j from user j and letting

$$K_{ij} = Y_j^{X_i} \bmod q = (\alpha^{X_j})^{X_i} \bmod q = \alpha^{X_i X_j} \bmod q. \tag{5}$$

User j obtains K_{ij} in the similar way

$$K_{ij} = Y_i^{X_j} \bmod q. \tag{6}$$

For an untrusted third party it is impossible to generate the same key K_{ij}, since it can not know X_i and X_j in any way because they are kept secret by users [8]. In addition to the DHKE algorithm, the use of message authentication helps to avoid the man-in-the-middle attack, which represents the main vulnerability of the DHKE algorithm. In this way, many attacks to the D2D communication can be avoided. Among these, eavesdropping, impersonation and masquerading, and the already cited man-in-the-middle.

3 Reference Network Architecture

The reference scenario for this paper consists of a generic IoT environment where devices receive contents from the network in a multicast delivery modality. Examples of applicative use-cases that could benefit from such a scenario are: (i) software update of a group of machines owned by a customer/tenant, or (ii) delivery of alerting messages.

MtMS has already defined an architecture and procedures to adapt the standardized MBMS to MTC traffic. In order to improve the efficiency of the entire

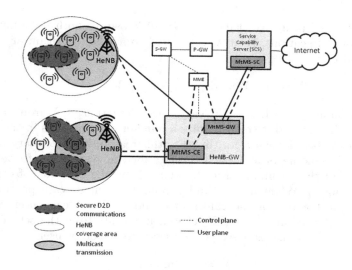

Fig. 1. MtMS-sD2D architecture.

process, devices with the worst channel conditions are excluded from the multicast transmission and are subsequently served via D2D communications by devices which directly received data from the BS. Furthermore, a security protocol is used to protect data transmitted in D2D communications.

Our MtMS-sD2D architecture, depicted in Fig. 1, derives from the MtMS architecture and properly enhances it to support secure D2D communications. It is composed of the following nodes: *home-evolved NodeB (HeNB)*, also known as femto-cell, which provides connectivity to a small-cell of devices, thus guaranteeing latency and energy consumption reductions and improving coverage and reliability compared to the traditional macro-cell; *HeNB gateway (HeNB-GW)*, which aggregates control and data traffic of various HeNBs; *MtMS serving center (MtMS-SC)*, implemented at the service capability server (SCS), which is responsible for initializing the MtMS session, obtaining the multicast content and the information about the receiving devices; *MtMS coordination entity (MtMS-CE)*, which manages the joining procedure, paging the indicated devices; *MtMS gateway (MtMS-GW)*, which receives data from the MtMS-SC and forwards it to the cells with paged devices. MtMS-GW and MtMS-CE are implemented at the HeNB-GW [5]. In the new MtMS-sD2D protocol, the MtMS procedures (i.e., initialization, joining, and content delivery) are modified to support a more efficient and secure transmission of data.

4   Machine-Type Multicast Service with Secure D2D

In the generic IoT environment with MTC data traffic under analysis, three main segments compose the end-to-end path: uplink (UL), core network, and downlink (DL). The *UL* segment includes the random access (RA) procedure

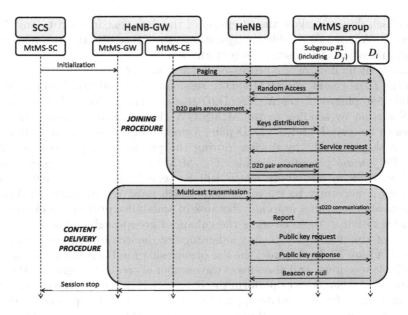

Fig. 2. MtMS-sD2D session.

and the subsequent transmission of sensed data by the involved devices toward the network. Devices requires the *RA procedure* to retrieve the synchronization with the BS. Indeed, in an IoT environment devices can switch to an idle state, during which they turn off the radio interface to save energy. After the RA procedure is accomplished, they can send sensed data. IoT devices can collect data on demand when they are triggered by the network (e.g., in the case of emergency notices) or periodically, as in the case of sensors that monitor environmental pollution. During the RA procedure devices also send to the BS information about their channel conditions (i.e., CQI values). Each device has to send not only information about the condition of the channel that connects it to the BS, but also about the channels (i.e., D2D links) that connect it to its neighbors. Thanks to these information, the BS can evaluate which nodes shall be excluded from the multicast transmission, because of their bad channel conditions, and shall be reached through the establishment of D2D connections. The BS chooses the set of nodes to be served in multicast and those to be served in D2D through an iterative procedure. It analyzes the different possible CQI values in ascending order. For each considered CQI value, the BS determines how many devices, among those in the cell, can receive and decode the data sent through the Conventional Multicast Scheme (CMS) with the Modulation and Coding Scheme (MCS) related to the considered CQI. Devices that fail to receive data, since their CQI level towards the BS is lower than the considered one, must be served in D2D. If the BS can find a transmitter for each D2D receiver, an eligible configuration is created. The iterative procedure ends when the BS analyzes a CQI value which does not allow the reception of the data sent in CMS to any device in the cell. Among all eligible configurations, the BS selects the one that allows the maximization of transmission performance.

Data sent by devices are processed in the *core network*.

In the *DL* segment, the MtMS-sD2D session is accomplished. Figure 2 depicts the different phases of the MtMS-sD2D session. The MtMS-SC initializes the *MtMS session* by sending to the MtMS-GW the multicast content, the list of devices to be served, and the D2D pairs formed on the basis of the CQI values, (in case they are sent by devices during the previous UL procedures). After that, the *joining procedure* begins. The MtMS-CE handles the paging of all multicast devices, also those which will be served via D2D communications. This step is necessary to trigger devices which must receive data. Paging is a very delicate procedure, especially because of scalability problems and overhead. A good solution to these issues is the enhanced group-paging procedure, which consists of simultaneously paging subgroups of devices belonging to the same multicast group [5]. In this case, the size of each subgroup depends on the amount of available resources, and also affects the number of created subgroups. Paging is accomplished when devices perform the RA procedure. In the case of absent UL segment (e.g., software update applications), during this RA procedure devices have to communicate their CQI values. The formed D2D pairs are communicated by the MtMS-CE to the HeNB, which will be in charge of their coordination. Before concluding the joining procedure, HeNB selects a public and a private key for each D2D device, randomly choosing $x_i \in Z_q^*$ (i.e., a set of integers with a prime number q of elements) as the private key and computing $X_i = g^{x_i}$ as the public key, where g is the fixed primitive element of Z_q^* used as generator/base. The couple (x_i, X_i) is sent from the HeNB to each D2D device via a secure control channel. After receiving the keys, the D2D receiver, from here indicated as D_i, sends a service request message to the HeNB. It is composed by

$$ID_i||z||h[(x_i^+ \oplus \text{opad})||h[(x_i^+ \oplus \text{ipad})||ID_i||z]] \tag{7}$$

where:

- ID_i uniquely identifies D_i in the network;
- z is the first public key for generating the secret key k_c that will be used for data encryption and decryption. It is computed as $z = g^c$, where $c \in Z_q^*$ is randomly chosen by D_i;
- $h[(x_i^+ \oplus \text{opad})||h[(x_i^+ \oplus \text{ipad})||ID_i||z]]$ is the $HMAC_{x_i}(ID_i||z)$. Generally, the $HMAC_k(m)$ is used to guarantee the integrity and authentication of the message m. It is based on the use of any cryptographic hash function h applied to a combination of the original message m and the secret key k. In (7), x_i^+ is the key padded out to size, *opad* and *ipad* are specified padding constants. For the simplification of expression, in the remainder of the paper $h[(k^+ \oplus \text{opad})||h[(k^+ \oplus \text{ipad})||m]]$ will be expressed as $h(\bullet, k)$, where $\bullet$ denotes the message attached by the HMAC and k is the secret key hashed together with the message. Note that x_i is only known by the sender D_i and the receiver HeNB. In all future steps, the verification of the HMAC will always

be performed by the recipients of the messages to verify message integrity and authentication, hence from here on this procedure will be omitted.

After receiving the service request message, the HeNB authenticates the requesting device in the normal cellular communication mode, checking if its ID is registered. In the positive case, the HeNB has to inform both D2D devices of their imminent communication. So, it randomly selects $a \in Z_q^*$ and computes $u = g^a$ as the first public key for generating the secret key k_s to use in the exchange of private messages with the selected D2D transmitter (i.e., the relay node). To communicate to D_j that has been chosen as relay of the D2D communication, the HeNB sends to it the following message:

$$ID_j||ID_i||z||u||h(\bullet, x_j). \tag{8}$$

Simultaneously, to acknowledge the reception of the service request message, the HeNB sends to D_i a response message with ID and public key of the selected transmitter:

$$ID_i||ID_j||X_j||h(\bullet, x_i). \tag{9}$$

This concludes the joining procedure. The following step is the *content delivery procedure*. First of all, MtMS-GW must sign data to send to devices with σ_1:

$$\sigma_1 = H_1(M)^{x_0} \tag{10}$$

where H_1 is a hash function, x_0 is the private key of the MtMS-GW, M is the data to be transmitted. After that, it sends data to devices belonging to the first paged subgroup, using a CMS. In particular, MtMS-GW first excludes devices with the lowest CQI values from the multicast transmission and, subsequently, chooses the MCS that all the remaining devices can support. When D_j, which belongs to the served subgroup, receives data from the HeNB, it already knows it has to forward them to the previously notified D2D receiver; so it carries out all the operations aimed at a secure D2D data transmission. First of all, to allow the receiver to generate the secret key k_c, it randomly selects $b \in Z_q^*$ and computes $y = g^b$ as the second public key for k_c. It does not send y directly to D_i, but it sends it to the HeNB, randomly choosing $f \in Z_q^*$, generating the secret key $k_s = u^f = g^{af}$ and using it to encrypt the public key y. Then, D_j must encrypt data, so it generates the communication key $k_c = z^b = g^{cb}$ and uses it to encrypt the data M. After computing $M' = Enc_{k_c}(M)$, D_j signs the message calculating:

$$\sigma_2 = H_1(ID_j||M'||T_s||\sigma_1)^{x_j} \tag{11}$$

where T_s is the timestamp used against the replay attack. Thus, the D2D communication takes place when D_j sends the following message to D_i:

$$ID_i||ID_j||M'||T_s||\sigma_1||\sigma_2. \tag{12}$$

In order to allow the HeNB to generate the secret key k_s used to encrypt the public key y, D_j computes $v = g^f$ as the second public key for k_s, using $f \in Z_q^*$

previously chosen. Finally, it sends to the HeNB a report:

$$ID_i||ID_j||Enc_{k_s}(y)||v||T_s||h(\bullet, x_j). \tag{13}$$

After receiving data, D_i first has to verify the identity of the transmitter. To this aim, it compares the ID_j reported on the message received by D_j with that communicated by the HeNB and, if the two do not match, the packet is dropped, otherwise it proceeds with the next steps. So, it checks the signature of the transmitter σ_2 and, if it is valid, data are considered sent by the entity corresponding to ID_j. Once the identity of the sender is verified, D_i needs to generate the decryption key k_c to obtain the plaintext. To do this, it sends a public key request message to the HeNB:

$$ID_i||ID_j||T_s||h(\bullet, x_i). \tag{14}$$

After receiving this message, the HeNB generates the decryption key k_s in order to decrypt $Enc_{k_s}(y)$, thus it sends the response message to D_i:

$$ID_i||ID_j||y||T_s||T_i||h(\bullet, x_i) \tag{15}$$

where T_i is employed to record the feedback time.

Thanks to the reception of the public key y, D_i can get the communication key by computing $k_c = y^c = g^{bc}$. So, it can decrypt the message M' to obtain the original data M. To verify the origin of data, it also checks the signature σ_1 and, if it is valid, the data are accepted. Otherwise, it is possible that data may have corrupted. In this case, D_i must send to the HeNB a *beacon* as the evidence of the fake message and to track the malicious attacker:

$$\beta = ID_i||ID_j||M'||T_s||\sigma_1||\sigma_2||h(\bullet, x_i). \tag{16}$$

The beacon must be sent within the timestamp T_i', which satisfies that $T_i' < T_i + \Delta T$.

Finally, HeNB must keep track of any malicious behavior by devices. If any beacon arrives during the time interval ΔT, HeNB first checks the validity of σ_1 and if it is invalid, it is judged that the message did not come from the MtMS-GW and may be fabricated by the transmitter. So, HeNB also verifies the validity of σ_2 to ensure that the fake message comes from the entity corresponding to ID_j. A malicious behavior amount (MBA) counter is stored by HeNB for each device which does not transmit data correctly in the D2D communication. Thus, in case of a malicious behavior by D_j, HeNB increments by one its MBA counter. The MBA counter of a node is incremented if, and only if, the HeNB verifies that the node has not correctly transmitted the data, tampering them before sending to the D2D receiver. Thanks to this, it is not possible to attribute a malicious behavior to a device if this has not actually occurred. When the MBA related to one device exceeds a given threshold, then the device is punished by the network; for example, it is considered non-eligible as D2D transmitter in future communications. The value of the maliciousness threshold has to be defined on the basis of the number of D2D transmissions performed, then based on the expected MBA values for users. When it is set to zero, only users with a MBA value of zero can be selected as relays, which means that selecting a malicious user is only possible if the user has never had a malicious behavior so far. As the value of the threshold increases, the algorithm is always less selective, this means that more malicious users are chosen as transmitters, even those which in the past have already behaved maliciously.

A summary of the keys used in the system is reported in Table 1.

Table 1. Keys used in the system.

Secret keys	Public keys	Description
k_c	$z = g^c$	First public key for k_c, sent by D_i to HeNB
	$y = g^b$	Second public key for k_c, sent by D_j to HeNB
k_s	$u = g^a$	First public key for k_s, sent by HeNB to D_j
	$v = g^f$	Second public key for k_s, sent by D_j to HeNB

5   Performance Evaluation

We carried out a simulation campaign by using MATLAB tool to analyze the performance of the MtMS-sD2D architecture.

The considered scenario for the results reported in this paper consists of 1000 devices distributed in the edge of a circular LTE-A cell of 1000 m of radius. A bandwidth of 20 MHz, which corresponds to 100 RBs, is available. A TDD LTE frame type 2 configuration 3 is used. Each slot (or Transmission Time Interval, TTI) in the frame lasts 1 ms, so the entire frame has a duration of 10 ms. The Inband D2D mode is chosen, so uplink slots are reserved to D2D communications. In the downlink slots, a multicast transmission allows to send data to in-coverage devices.

In this performance evaluation, the malicious device is the D2D transmitter that does not correctly terminate data transfer to the receiver. In particular, in any case, data sent by a malicious transmitter are lost and cause waste of resources.

The performance of the proposed MtMS-sD2D protocol is evaluated on the basis of the following metrics:

– *Data lost in D2D communications* because of an unreliable transmitter;
– *Percentage of malicious relays* that have been selected by the network.

A comparison between the secure version of the proposed protocol and the non-secure version is shown.

Figure 3 shows the results in terms of data loss under increasing values of percentage of malicious devices. As can be inferred by the figure, MtMS-sD2D guarantees the lower data loss thanks to the implemented security mechanism. In particular, the achieved improvement is about 30%.

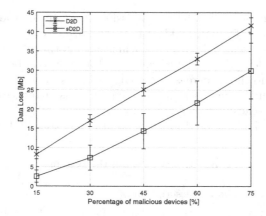

Fig. 3. Data loss under increasing percentage of malicious devices.

Figure 4 shows the percentage of malicious relays when the percentage of malicious nodes grows. The malicious relays are the D2D transmitters that do not correctly transmit data. As previously discussed, the fact that MtMS-sD2D performs a better selection of D2D nodes is also demonstrated by the fact that a smaller number of nodes that effectively perform a malicious action are chosen to be relay of a D2D communication.

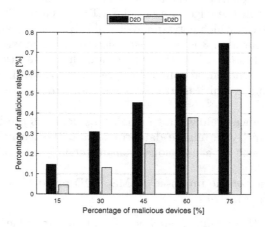

Fig. 4. Percentage of selected malicious relays under increasing percentage of malicious devices.

6   Conclusions

In this paper, we have proposed MtMS-sD2D (Machine-type Multicast Service with secure D2D), an architecture for the delivery of multicast traffic in an IoT scenario that takes advantage from D2D communications made reliable by means of a security mechanism based on the Diffie-Hellman key exchange (DHKE) protocol. Furthermore, we have discussed the designed procedures to be introduced in order to efficiently transmit multicast data toward a set of MTC devices.

Preliminary results showed that the proposed architecture is able to improve system performance by avoiding useless allocation of network resources to malicious nodes. Future work will focus on a further analysis of the performance of the algorithm, also evaluating its impact on the energy consumption required for its implementation on resource-constrained devices.

References

1. Boccardi, F., Heath, R.W., Lozano, A., Marzetta, T.L., Popovski, P.: Five disruptive technology directions for 5G. IEEE Commun. Mag. **52**, 74–80 (2014)
2. Akyildiz, I.F., Nie, S., Lin, S.-C., Chandrasekaran, M.: 5G roadmap: 10 key enabling technologies. Comput. Netw. **106**, 17–48 (2016). Elsevier
3. Asadi, A., Wang, Q., Mancuso, V.: A survey on device-to-device communications in cellular networks. IEEE Commun. Surv. Tutor. **16**, 1801–1819 (2014)
4. Araniti, G., Condoluci, M., Scopelliti, P., Molinaro, A., Iera, A.: Multicasting over emerging 5G networks: challenges and perspectives. IEEE Netw. **31**, 80–89 (2017)
5. Condoluci, M., Araniti, G., Mahmoodi, T., Dohler, M.: Enabling the IoT machine age with 5G: machine-type multicast services for innovative real-time applications. IEEE Access **4**, 5555–5569 (2016)
6. Sicari, S., Rizzardi, A., Grieco, L.A., Coen-Porisini, A.: Security, privacy and trust in Internet of Things: the road ahead. Comput. Netw. **76**, 146–164 (2015). Elsevier
7. Zhang, A., Chen, J., Hu, R.Q., Qian, Y.: SeDS: secure data sharing strategy for D2D communication in LTE-advanced networks. IEEE Trans. Veh. Technol. **65**, 2659–2672 (2016)
8. Diffie, W., Hellman, M.E.: New directions in cryptography. IEEE Trans. Inf. Theory **22**, 644–654 (1976)

Design and Implementation of Integrated ICN and CDN as a Video Streaming Service

Chengkai Yan[1], Quang Ngoc Nguyen[1(✉)] [ID], Ilias Benkacem[2],
Daisuke Okabe[3], Akihiro Nakao[4], Toshitaka Tsuda[1], Cutifa Safitri[5],
Tarik Taleb[2], and Takuro Sato[1]

[1] Department of Communications and Computer Engineering,
Waseda University, Tokyo, Japan
quang.nguyen@aoni.waseda.jp
[2] Department of Communications and Networking, Aalto University,
Espoo, Finland
[3] IoT & Cloud Services Business Division, Hitachi Ltd., Tokyo, Japan
[4] The University of Tokyo, Bunkyo, Tokyo, Japan
[5] MJIIT, Universiti Teknologi Malaysia, Kuala Lumpur, Malaysia

Abstract. In this research, we leverage the emerging concept of network slicing to enable the end-to-end integrated Information-Centric Networking (ICN) and Content Delivery Network (CDN) for 5G networking infrastructure. While CDN is deployed to cache content at the optimal server corresponding to the content and geographical location, this paper focuses on verifying the efficiency of ICN slice for regional content distribution. Specifically, the ICN slice can be established by the regional Orchestrator by following the current NFV/SDN standard. Then, the slice stitching process will be performed to interconnect two slices after their establishments via the Orchestrator. We also implement an OpenStack-based virtual node which supports both IP and ICN protocols and acts as the ICN-Gateway. The joint-testbed evaluations conducted between Japan side (ICN slice) and Europe side (CDN slice) show that the deployment of ICN Gateway and the proposed Node ID-based ICN naming structure can improve network performance and avoid network congestion.

Keywords: Information-Centric Networking (ICN) ·
CDN (Content Delivery Network) · Network slicing · ICN/CDN ·
Video streaming · NFV/SDN

1 Introduction

Nowadays, to match the huge demand for content distribution, we need a new network paradigm shift from IP-based services into information-based services. In this way, we can transfer information in a wide range of services efficiently, especially in the case of High-definition video transmission with high bitrate/speed requirement. In fact, video content has become a major part of the total Internet traffic, and mobile/wireless data traffic is a notable trend for content accesses in the future. According to Cisco's report, IP video traffic occupied 75% of the whole Internet in 2017, and this number will

© IFIP International Federation for Information Processing 2019
Published by Springer Nature Switzerland AG 2019
M. Di Felice et al. (Eds.): WWIC 2019, LNCS 11618, pp. 194–206, 2019.
https://doi.org/10.1007/978-3-030-30523-9_16

increase to 82% by 2022 in which the mobile devices will carry 44% of the total IP data traffic [1]. Thus, ensuring mobile user's VoD (Video on Demand) experience is a key to realize efficient content the distribution model for the Internet.

In this context, ICN (Information-Centric Networking) [2, 3] was proposed as a promising future network approach since 2005. The key features of ICN include in-network caching and using named data instead of IP addresses for forwarding and routing content. However, ICN still has implementation issues because all the content nodes in ICN need to have the memory storage for content caching then make them consume more power compared to the IP routers [4, 5]. Also, the default caching mechanism in ICN produces high cache redundancy by wasting cache space for storing on-path content duplicates as analyzed in our prior work [6, 7].

Currently, many video service providers have selected CDN (Content Delivery Network) as their solution for serving the vast video traffic. The idea of CDN is placing suitable dedicated caches as distributed servers at the edge of various network domains or geographical regions to reduce network load and response time. However, considering the high cost of the cache servers and the video resources, CDN still has the feasibility issue for deployment.

Thus, in this paper, we have proposed to integrate CDN and ICN as a 5G network slice for efficient video streaming service which will be detailed in the next sections.

2 Related Work

In this section, we introduce the major concepts that are related to our proposal.

2.1 Content-Centric Networking (CCN)

Content-Centric Networking (CCN) [2] is a notable ICN platform that enables users to obtain desired content through its name instead of its location as defined in the existing IP-based Internet architecture. CCN is also implemented using ICN routers with caching function rather than IP-routers to realize efficient content dissemination.

In CCN, there are two types of the packet which are Interest and Data packets. Interests consist of a content name, which is requested by the consumer. Data packets carry content data and act as response for content requests, i.e., Interests. The data transmission unit in CCN is chunk, i.e., a content is split into a number of equally sized chunks.

For the content distribution process, firstly, Interests will be sent by the consumer. Then, the Interests will be broadcasted throughout the whole network. This step can be regarded as a searching strategy: Once a user sends an Interest, it will be sent to the nearest node to minimize the transmission time. Besides, users who are in the same area may express the Interests for the same content so that they can get the desired content from the suitable intermediate ICN nodes without the need of downloading it from the content provider (server).

For the data retrieval process, the content name prefix will be searched in the cache memory of the CCN routers, called Content Store (CS). If Interest matches the prefix, data will be returned to the consumer via the corresponding face (network interface).

Otherwise, Interest will continue finding the content in Pending Interest Table (PIT) [2]. If the required content exists, content data is sent back by the reverse path of Interest and a new entry of Interest will be added to PIT. If the content still can not found, that information will also be recorded in PIT. Then, Interest will be forwarded according to Forwarding Information Base (FIB) for the forwarding procedure [2, 8].

Besides the name-based forwarding strategy, another key feature of CCN is in-network caching. Different from TCP/IP design, CCN node has its cache memory so that it can store downloaded contents dynamically. In other words, once the content has been downloaded, it will be cached by the CCN node. Hence, the total content downloading time and E2E (End to End) hop count can be reduced.

2.2   Content Delivery Network (CDN)

Recently, CDN has been widely implemented to serve the content-based services, represented by the well-known CDN operators, e.g., Netflix, Akamai. CDN deploys edge servers which contain contents from the original content producers/servers. In this way, the data traffic of the original server can be split to multiple mirror cache servers, which leads to relieving the burden of the source server. Additionally, based on users' geometric information (such as IP addresses), the DNS (Domain Name System) server can identify which edge server is the nearest one to users. Thus, it can allocate the most appropriate server to the user and the downloading time on the user side can be reduced considerably. Hence, the users' QoE (Quality of Experience) can be improved as well. Also, CDN users from different ISPs (Internet Service Provider) and regions can gain similar bitrate experience [9].

However, CDN still has its disadvantages. Firstly, due to the high cost of deploying CDN mirror edge servers, CDN users are requested to pay an additional fee for the premier services. Next, the content updating process (i.e., pushing new video contents to the edge servers) takes time and may not be suitable for every scenario. In general, CDN is primarily used for VoD (Video on Demand) or downloading services. However, in some specific scenarios, users do not need all the cached contents then some of the valuable cache memory is being wasted. Thirdly, though deploying CDN servers can reduce and separate data traffic from the core server, bottleneck sometimes can still happen.

Specifically, when users' requests become huge in one specific area, the data traffic between users and this area's CDN edge cache servers can cause the network bottleneck. In order to prevent this situation, the service providers and CDN operator should increase the number of available CDN caches, which might lead to a higher cost.

2.3   SDN/NFV (Software-Defined Networking/Network Functions Virtualization)

Due to the increasingly diverse need from the user side, ISPs are currently in need of adaptive services to meet users' various demands. However, different from allocating a single service, customizing multiple types of service via physical network resource configuration is challenging. For example, nowadays, FHD (Full High-Definition) or even UHD (Ultra High-Definition) video streaming service and VoIP (Voice over IP) service are among the most popular applications of network service, but they have different optimized network resource configurations. Particularly, HD/UHD video streaming service requires high bandwidth and throughput while VoIP service requires a stable network environment and low-latency. Moreover, it takes time and a high cost to set up and tune each network service. The introduction of NFV (Network Functions Virtualization) and SDN (Software-Defined Networking) in recent years then aims to satisfy the strong demand of "dynamic network configuration".

NFV uses virtualization technology to split network applications in a simple and adaptive manner. A general NFV architecture usually includes VNFs (Virtualized Network Functions), Hardware resources, Virtualization Layer, NFVI (NFV Infrastructure), NFV Management and Orchestration (NFVM and NFVO). Specifically, NFVI is the key to manage the hardware resources and change the physical hardware into virtualization resources pool so that the computing components can be managed flexibly and conveniently. The VNFs can install and provide service applications. Also, the VNFM and NFVO are responsible for managing and orchestrating the NFV's whole resources and processes [10].

As NFV offers the solution for making physical network resource virtual, SDN is the other technology needed for link virtualization. The most crucial feature of SDN is that it separates the network connection into control-plane and data-plane. By separating the two planes, network control becomes more convenient and flexible since control-plane requires flexibility whereas data-plane requires low-latency. For instance, the processes such as switching routing protocols and generating routing table can be implemented on one control-plane. To complete the separation, a protocol named OpenFlow would be used [11].

2.4 Network Slicing

Network Slicing is a virtualization technology based on NFV/SDN. It enables running multiple logical networks on one common shared-physical network infrastructure to maximize the flexibility and maintainability. Besides, the network resources are split dynamically so that each logical network's parameter such as capacity, bandwidth, and delay can be customized corresponding to the user requests and network status.

Network slicing plays an essential role as a key concept in the upcoming 5G network to realize various high-speed network applications, e.g., IoT (Internet of Things) and 8K streaming services [12]. Particularly, the ISPs could manage and customize each network slice simply and comfortably by defining each network service as one dynamic network slice and separate them logically [13].

In this research, we apply the emerging concepts of ICN, CDN, and SDN/NFV technologies to realize a network slicing design for efficient content delivery over different multiple geographical locations.

3   System Design

In this section, we introduce the concept and mechanism of the proposed CDN/ICN content delivery system.

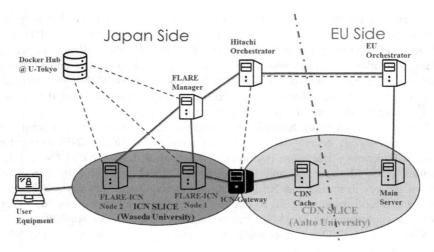

Fig. 1. ICN/CDN system configuration

3.1 The Proposed ICN/CDN System

In this research, we combine CDN with ICN to enable an efficient contents delivery network system with low congestion rate. Besides, to meet the future mobile network's needs, we have also proposed using our system as one 5G service slice in the context of the project "5G! Pagoda", a collaborative Europe-Japan research project for softwarized 5G network evolutions [14].

The benefits of integrating ICN and CDN are three-fold as follows:

Firstly, using CDN and ICN can drastically reduce the congestion ratio of the whole network. Particularly, as aforementioned in Sect. 2, CDN can reduce the data traffic of the core/original server by deploying multiple edge mirror cache servers in various regions. However, when the number of users becomes large enough in one region, the congestion would occur at the edge servers. Therefore, by adding ICN nodes linked to the CDN edge servers, we aim to substantially diminish data traffics of CDN edge cache servers, thanks to the ICN's in-network caching feature [15].

The second benefit is increasing the users' QoE (delay time), especially for contents with high popularity level. By using CDN's cache server for dynamic and optimized content allocations, the download time for the requested content can be reduced considerably [16]. Specifically, this improvement is realized by the efficient retrieval process from the CDN slice to the ICN slice via the appropriate CDN cache and the ICN Gateway.

Additionally, as ICN is a potential future network design at the initial deployment stage and CDN has been a successful content-based business model, by combining CDN and ICN, we can take advantage the merits of both networking models: CDN is used for optimal content allocations at suitable CDN caches nearby the clients while ICN is used for quickly distribute content to users via the ICN nodes with the built-in dynamic in-network caching feature.

3.2 System Overview

To show that our ICN/CDN system can provide an efficient and realistic video delivery model in real-world, we configure the whole system across different continents.

Specifically, the system has been implemented to transfer content objects (videos) published in Finland (Europe EU) to Japan (JP, Asia). In this way, we are expecting to model and realize a promising and practical video streaming system deployment, e.g., Netflix or YouTube videos.

Figure 1 demonstrates our integrated ICN/CDN system configuration. In our design, the system includes two major parts which are CDN slice for contents provider side ("EU Side") and ICN slice for content distribution to users ("Japan Side"). Typically, on the EU region, the original CDN content server deployed at Aalto University, Finland (Aalto server) has been set up to publish video contents. Also, we assume that users will request their desired video contents from the Japan region. Thus, CDN cache mirror server and ICN nodes are deployed on the Japan side.

Since our whole work is to realize the 5G network slicing concept, each network slice is implemented based on SDN/NFV technology. It is also necessary to define a regional Orchestrator to manage every VNF instance dynamically. Typically, the EU Orchestrator is responsible for managing each instance and resource pool on the EU side while Aalto servers represent the CDN publishers/providers.

The ICN slice configuration is shown in Fig. 2 in which ICN nodes are implemented by JP Orchestrator (Hitachi Orchestrator) using CCN platform on the Japan side. Firstly, the video contents are stored in the ICN Gateway (an OpenStack based CDN/ICN edge video cache server on the Japan side). Then, we add ICN Gateway FIB entries to CCN nodes for the efficient forwarding process in ICN. Hence, the video content information from the ICN cache can be shared through the Japan domain via the CCN nodes in ICN slice. To reduce the network load and congestion, we use multiple ICN-enabled edge nodes (with transient caches and substantial lower cache storage compared to CDN caches) to separate the content traffic of the ICN Gateway from the other ICN intermediate nodes.

3.3 End-to-End (E2E) Content Delivery

In this part, we briefly present a complete E2E content delivery procedure of the proposed ICN/CDN system. It contains four major steps which are slice establishment, slice stitching, content request, and content delivery.

Firstly, in the "slice establishment" stage, all the CDN and ICN NFV instances are initiated and allocated virtually. During this stage, both JP and EU' Orchestrators will create and configure each instance with a suitable virtual configuration dynamically.

Then, "slice stitching" stage will be executed. After ICN and CDN instances have been established, JP Orchestrator will inform ICN Coordinator and provide the Coordinator the FIB entries of ICN Gateway so that ICN nodes can determine the suitable routing path. After the ICN nodes add the FIB entries of ICN gateway, the slice stitching process is completed.

Next, the user sends the content request, and the content delivery process will be performed. Upon the slice stitching's completion and the video service is triggered at the CDN slice, the user receives the table of contents which lists all of the available video contents' "exact name" (which will be detailed in Sect. 3.4) with resolution, video name, bitrate and the corresponding CDN cache from CDN coordinator. The user then can choose which video they want to watch. When the user selects the desired video content, the system will generate an ICN Interest to ICN Gateway to check whether this content is already cached in ICN slice or not. If it has been cached, then the target content will be renamed as CCN "exact name" format and sent back to the User Equipment (UE). When the UE receives the exact content name and acknowledge it, the content transmission can start. Otherwise, if the user selects the desired content and the ICN Gateway does not have the content that the user asked, this Interest will be converted as a content request to the suitable CDN server with respective content. The CDN server then pushes the requested content to ICN Gateway. In this way, users can receive the content in the ICN slice when the same content Interests are received again.

3.4   Naming Strategy in ICN

One key feature of ICN is that its information route is based on the content name instead of an IP address. Specifically, each ICN content has its own unique ICN name without the need of name resolution via the DNS (Domain Name Server) system as of the TCP/IP architecture.

However, since in our ICN/CDN video streaming system, both ICN (CCN platform) and IP (CDN) are co-existed, the suitable way to transfer and convert the content name format from IP to CCN is worth to be considered so that UEs in Japan side can receive the desired data efficiently via the Gateway in the ICN slice [17].

Firstly, the initial content name on the CDN side consists of an article name, resolution, bitrate, and video package format. For example, on the Aalto CDN server, a *Demo* video content is named as "*Demo-1920*1080-3000kbps.avi*".

However, in CCN, since we want to let the user know which ICN node is involved in serving a specific content, we decide to implement another naming format by adding a "Node ID". "Node ID" represents the caching node with the requested content name for content distribution in ICN from CDN slice. Thus, in the simplified case, the "Node ID" will be "ICN Gateway". Besides, we add the content source with location before "Node ID" (left-most position) in the content naming structure. As "Finland, EU" (Aalto University) is the content publisher's location in our system design, and the CCN name should be "*/EU/Finland/Aalto-University/ICN-Gateway/Demo-1920*1080-3000kbps.avi*". By using this naming format, the user can be aware of the content transmission so that they can decide whether to receive the content or not. Since the naming format in CCN is Longest-Prefix Match (LPM) for forwarding and routing procedure, we define the proposed CCN name structure as the content "exact name".

3.5   ICN Gateway

As shown in Figs. 1 and 2, between the ICN slice and the CDN slice, we have deployed an additional OpenStack-based node and named it as "ICN-Gateway". The ICN-Gateway enables both CCN and TCP/IP protocol so that the video content from the CDN cache server can be cached inside the CCN's repository. From ICN-Gateway, cached contents would be stored at ICN intermediate nodes then transfer to users for minimizing the latency of subsequent content accesses.

Meanwhile, ICN-Gateway takes responsibility for converting content name from CDN naming format into the proposed CCN's "exact name".

4 System Evaluations

4.1 FLARE-Based ICN Nodes

Regarding the proposed ICN/CDN system implementation, we build the joint test-bed based E2E content delivery at Waseda University in which the virtual content nodes image and configuration setting are installed in deeply programmable nodes, namely FLARE, developed by the University of Tokyo. We select FLARE as it enables an Open Deeply Programmable Switch/Network Node Architecture to verify the merits of the proposal over multi-domain test-bed with multi-core processors toward 5G slicing [18]. FLARE also realizes resource isolation with lightweight control plane and data plane programmability. We then implemented ICN Based Virtualization nodes on FLARE, and the hardware configuration of FLARE is shown in Table 1. Specifically, we use Docker as the container technology to implement ICN nodes' virtualization over FLAREs.

Also, since Hitachi. Ltd. acts as the Orchestrator of the Japan domain (Fig. 1), ICN nodes can be established and managed dynamically so that the ICN slice follows the network slicing standardization [19].

4.2 The Proposed System Configuration

Note that in this research, we focus on the ICN Slice design for content distribution when the content objects are already stored at the ICN Gateway from the CDN Slice, i.e., suppose that Optimal VNFs Placement in CDN Slicing over Multi-domain is already performed. Then, this paper is different from our prior work in the same research theme which presented the overall integrated ICN/CDN system design [16].

For the experiment evaluation, we have set up an ICN slice configuration as shown in Fig. 3. Particularly, at first, an OpenStack based ICN-Gateway caches the test video content. Then, upon receiving the message from Orchestrator (Hitachi Orchestrator), the ICN coordinator can receive the FIB entry of ICN-Gateway. By using this information, FLARE-ICN Node 1 can be set up and make a connection with ICN-Gateway in CCN protocol (slice stitching procedure). Next, two ICN nodes are connected, and finally, on the UE side, UE 1 is connected with ICN Node 1 while UE 2 makes a connection with ICN Node 2 via the CCN protocol. We use this system configuration as the evaluation scenario model to verify the benefit of using CCN nodes with in-network caching feature so that the video contents with high popularity in a geographical domain can be transmitted to the user side efficiently with minimized response time [20].

Table 1. FLARE's detailed configuration.

Parameter	Value
Spec	72 core EZ-Chip Network processor
SFP+	2 ports, up to 128 GB memory/1 TB SSD
GbE	24 ports and 10 GbE
Power	Redundant Power supply

4.3   Test Scenarios

After the slice stitching procedure is completed by the Orchestrator at the Japan side via information exchanges from Gateway at ICN slice, we perform the test scenarios using the above testbed configuration. In particular, we conduct four different test scenarios to verify the efficiency of the proposed ICN/CDN system for content distribution in which the content delivery is conducted twice for each scenario as follows:

- *Scenario 1:* Firstly, the content request is sent from UE1. Then, for the second time, the content request (for the same content) is also sent by UE1.
- *Scenario 2:* First content request is sent from UE2, and a second-time request is from UE1 for the same content.
- *Scenario 3:* The first-time request is from UE1, and then UE2 will send Interest for the same content.
- *Scenario 4:* Both requests are sent by UE2.

It should be noted that the test content file in each Scenario has the same size (either 1 MB or 10 MB). Then, we have evaluated ICN slice performance by measuring downloading time, E2E hops count, throughput, and Round-Trip Time (RTT) [21] which will be detailed in the next subsection.

4.4   The Integrated ICN/CDN System Performance Evaluations and Discussion

The four above network metrics are evaluated as follows:

Downloading Time. Downloading time means spending time since a user sends the first content Interest until the requested file's last chunk is transmitted to the user. Shorter download time refers to a higher transmission rate. As shown in Fig. 4, we have measured downloading time using the 1 MB and 10 MB sized file and in both cases, the second time request's download time is much smaller than the first time. Thus, as long as the content has been cached by ICN nodes once (i.e., the requested content is stored in ICN slice), the buffering time for streaming service on the user side can be reduced considerably. As a result, QoE can be ensured, especially in the case of popular content.

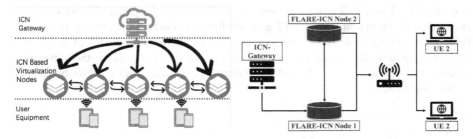

Fig. 2. ICN slice configuration

Fig. 3. FLARE-based testbed configuration

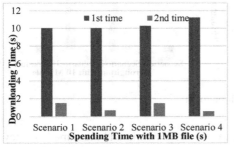

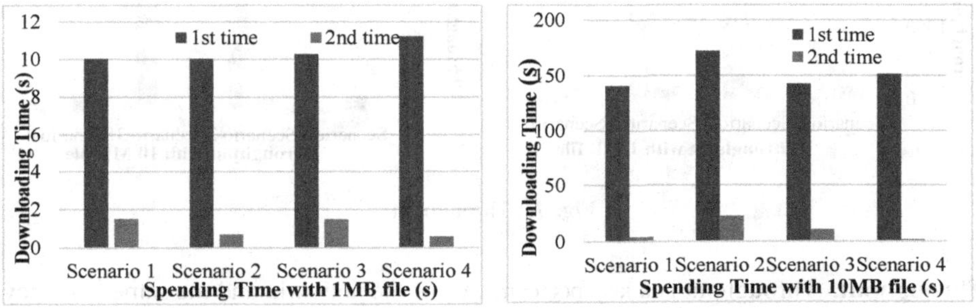

Fig. 4. Download time

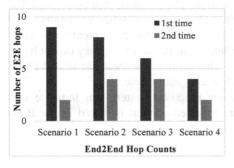

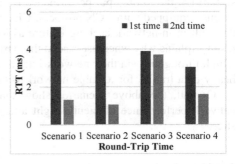

Fig. 5. End-to-end hop counts

Fig. 6. Round-trip time

E2E Hop Counts. Similarly, when measuring the number of hop counts between UEs and the content source, we realize that the second time request's hops are always less than that of the first time (Fig. 5). The reason is that thanks to the in-network caching feature in ICN, for all the four test scenarios, the contents will be cached at the nearest ICN nodes after the first request.

Round-trip Time (RTT). RTT measures the period since a packet is sent until it is responded. As shown in Fig. 6, RTT gets smaller after the first Interest when we test a content file in CCN's default chunk size (4 KB). As the requested content is stored at the nearest nodes (ICN node 1 or ICN node 2) after the first request, the subsequent requests for the same content become smoother, i.e., a reduced RTT shows better QoE on the user side.

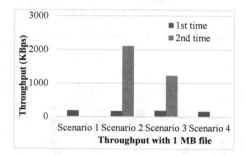 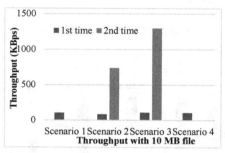

Fig. 7. Throughput

Throughput. Throughput is a key performance of the network, and the same tendency can be realized when measuring throughput in both cases of 1 MB and 10 MB test contents (Fig. 7). Specifically, in scenario 2 and scenario 3, the second time requests always get higher throughput compared to the first time. However, in scenario 1 and scenario 4, the throughput performance is decreased. The reason is that since our UEs are also equipped with CCN protocol, UEs will cache content into their repository with the built-in in-network caching feature as long as they retrieve the content once. This result explains why when users send the same Interest as the first time, they do not have a high throughput via their network interfaces. This deployment then also leads to less heavy data traffics for a stable network with low congestion rate.

Overall, the above scenarios show that our proposed system can improve the network performance efficiently right after a requested content is stored in the ICN slice.

5   Conclusion

In this paper, we have proposed, designed, implemented, and evaluated the combined ICN/CDN architecture as a video streaming service. The joint-testbed evaluations between Japan and Europe show that our approach can reduce the download time effectively, especially when transmitting contents with high popularity. This realizes a potential and feasible network design for efficient video streaming service by leveraging SDN/NFV technologies and combining the benefits of both ICN and CDN for video content distribution.

The concept and design of function chaining design for optimal VNF allocation in network slicing of the integrated ICN/CDN will be the focus of our future work.

Acknowledgment. This research was partly funded by 5G! Pagoda project, which is funded by European Commission's H2020 program under grant agreement No. 723172 and by the SCOPE project of MIC (Ministry of Internal Affairs and Communications) of Japan. This work was also supported by Waseda University Grant for Special Research Projects grant number 2019C-174.

References

1. Cisco Visual Networking Index: Forecast and Trends, 2017–2022
2. Jacobson, V., et al.: Networking named content. In: Proceedings of ACM CoNEXT 2009, December 2009
3. Xylomenos, G., et al.: A survey of information-centric networking research. IEEE Commun. Surv. Tutorials **99**, 1–26 (2013)
4. Nguyen, Q.N., et al.: A context-aware green information-centric networking model for future wireless communications. IEEE Access **6**, 22804–22816 (2018)
5. Nguyen, Q.N., Arifuzzaman, M., Miyamoto, T., Takuro, S.: An optimal information centric networking model for the future green network. In: 2015 IEEE Twelfth International Symposium on Autonomous Decentralized Systems, Taichung, pp. 272–277 (2015)
6. Arifuzzaman, M., Keping, Y., Nguyen, Q.N., Takuro, S.: Locating the content in the locality: ICN caching and routing strategy revisited. In: 2015 European Conference on Networks and Communications (EuCNC), Paris, pp. 423–428 (2015)
7. Nguyen, Q.N., et al.: PPCS: a progressive popularity-aware caching scheme for edge-based cache redundancy avoidance in information-centric networks. Sensors. **19**(3), 694 (2019)
8. Rohmah, Y.N., Sudiharto, D.W., Herutomo, A.: The performance comparison of forwarding mechanism between IPv4 and named data networking (NDN). case study: a node compromised by the prefix hijack. In: 2017 3rd International Conference on Science in Information Technology (ICSITech), Bandung, pp. 302–306 (2017)
9. Zhang, G., Liu, W., Hei, X., Cheng, W.: Unreeling xunlei kankan: understanding hybrid CDN-P2P video-on-demand streaming. IEEE Trans. Multimedia **17**(2), 229–242 (2015)
10. Network Functions Virtualisation (NFV); Management and Orchestration; Report on Architectural Options, ETSI Group Specification NFVIFA 009, July 2017
11. Kreutz, D., et al.: Software-defined networking: a comprehensive survey. Proc. IEEE **103**(1), 14–76 (2015)
12. Taleb, T., et al.: PERMIT: network slicing for personalized 5G mobile telecommunications. IEEE Commun. Mag. **55**(5), 88–93 (2017)
13. Zhang, J., Zhang, X., Wang, W.: Cache-enabled software defined heterogeneous networks for green and flexible 5G networks. IEEE Access **4**, 3591–3604 (2016)
14. 5G! Pagoda Project. https://5g-pagoda.aalto.fi/
15. Wang, X., et al.: Cache in the air: exploiting content caching and delivery techniques for 5G systems. IEEE Commun. Mag. **52**(2), 131–139 (2014)
16. Benkacem, I., Bagaa, M., Taleb, T., Nguyen, Q.N., Tsuda, T., Sato, T.: Integrated ICN and CDN slice as a service. In: IEEE Globecom 2018, December 2018, Abu Dhabi, UAE (2018)
17. Kanai, K., et al.: Proactive content caching for mobile video utilizing transportation systems and evaluation through field experiments. IEEE J. Sel. Areas Commun. **34**(8), 2102–2114 (2016)

18. Nakao, A., et al.: End-to-end network slicing for 5G Mobile networks. J. Inf. Process. **25**, 153–163 (2017)
19. Arumaithurai, M., et al.: Exploiting ICN for flexible management of software-defined networks. In: ACM-ICN 201414 Proceedings of the 1st ACM Conference on Information-Centric Networking, 24–26 September, pp. 107–116, Paris, France (2014)
20. Guan, J., Quan, W., Xu, C., Zhang, H.: The comparison and performance analysis of CCN under mobile environments. In: 2014 IEEE 3rd International Conference on Cloud Computing and Intelligence Systems, Shenzhen, pp. 292–296 (2014)
21. Kerrouche, A., et al.: AC-QoS-FS: ant colony based QoS-aware forwarding strategy for routing in named data networking. In: 2017 IEEE ICC, Paris, pp. 1–6 (2017)

Distributed Applications

Improving Video Delivery with Fourier Analysis of Traffic in Multi-Access Edge Computing

Eryk Schiller$^{(\boxtimes)}$, Remo Röthlisberger, Torsten Braun,
and Mostafa Karimzadeh

Institute for Computer Science, University of Bern, Bern, Switzerland
{schiller,braun,karimzadeh}@inf.unibe.ch, remo.r@gmx.ch

Abstract. This paper presents a new video delivery scheme in mobile networks using Multi-Access Edge Computing (MEC). Our goal is to improve the quality of video streaming experienced by the mobile video consumer. Our approach is based upon Dynamic Adaptive Streaming over HTTP. We present a novel algorithm, which uses information obtained from the Radio Network Information Service of MEC to provide the mobile user with a video quality matching the current radio link quality and channel capacity. We evaluate our approach using a real experiment performed on a Long Term Evolution (LTE) femto cell test-bed. Our algorithm displays enhanced adaptation of video rates in comparison to other state of the art solutions.

Keywords: Long Term Evolution (LTE) ·
Mobile Edge Computing (MEC) ·
Dynamic Adaptive Streaming over HTTP (DASH)

1 Introduction

The European Telecommunications Standards Institute (ETSI) Multi-Access Edge Computing (MEC) [1][1] extends intelligence at the network edge through computing and storage facilities deployed in the close vicinity of the Radio Access Network (RAN). Due to MEC, video will greatly benefit from a low delay of the network edge, RAN-aware video content optimization, and adaptation to wireless network conditions. As ETSI mostly focuses on MEC video transcoding or content optimization for end-users [2], which requires a large number of computing resources at the MEC platform processing the video, other mechanisms are needed for better resource friendly streaming.

Dynamic Adaptive Streaming over HTTP (DASH) [3] opens up new opportunities in terms of MEC content optimization, as in DASH a video is already

---

[1] Notice that in September 2016, ETSI Mobile Edge Computing group changed its name from Mobile Edge Computing to Multi-Access Edge Computing.

© IFIP International Federation for Information Processing 2019
Published by Springer Nature Switzerland AG 2019
M. Di Felice et al. (Eds.): WWIC 2019, LNCS 11618, pp. 209–221, 2019.
https://doi.org/10.1007/978-3-030-30523-9_17

encoded with many representations at the content provider and video transcoding is not required at the MEC platform. The different representations are announced to the video consumer through a Media Presentation Description (MPD) file containing descriptors leading to locations of the video encoded with different qualities and, therefore, requiring distinct data rates for video streaming. Typically, a higher representation requires more throughput than a lower one. The video consumer processes the MPD file and requests the video quality, i.e. representation, according to end-to-end measurements of the channel capacity.

In this work, we provide a MEC-based recommendation system for DASH (c.f., Sect. 3), which personalizes the video representations towards current channel conditions experienced by a User Equipment (UE). We observe the channel of every user by using a MEC Radio Network Information Service (RNIS) (c.f., Sect. 3.2) and compute the per-user radio channel capacity (c.f., Sect. 4) using novel Fourier-based traffic analysis. We then provide a dynamically generated MPD file towards the video consumer containing a limited set of video qualities matching the user channel capacity (c.f., Sect. 3.3). The client periodically fetches its personal MPD file containing suggested representations and regularly requests video segments using the set of representations adjusted by the video server to the experienced momentary channel capacity. Our solution does not change the DASH paradigm. We enrich the video system with personal MPD files. The MPD file is dynamically generated on the MEC-based video server (c.f., Sect. 3.1).

This work is organized in the following way. In Sect. 2, we survey the state of the art in MEC and video delivery. In Sect. 3, we describe the architecture of the system. The algorithm adapting MPD files for users is presented in Sect. 4. The performance evaluation and comparison against regular DASH is elaborated in Sect. 5. Finally, we conclude in Sect. 6.

2   Related Work

2.1   MEC

In ETSI MEC, the mobile ecosystem is enriched with a Multi-Access Edge Cloud (MEC) residing close to evolved Node Bs (eNBs) in LTE/4G or next generation Node Bs (gNBs) in 5G, which allows mobile users to contact MEC applications residing in the close vicinity of the UE [2]. MEC applications can be aware of the state of the air interface (e.g, capacity, congestion, radio signal quality, etc.) through RNIS implemented on top of MEC [2,4]. For example, FlexRAN [5] implements a flexible and programmable Software Defined-Radio Access Network (SD-RAN) platform, which separates the RAN control and data planes through a custom-tailored southbound API. It supports a real-time control channel that enables various degrees of coordination among RAN components.

2.2 DASH

Dynamic Adaptive Streaming over HTTP (DASH or 3GPP-DASH) [3] is a popular standard for video streaming over the Internet allowing for improved user experience in the presence of variable network conditions. Besides the conventional Hyper Text Transfer Protocol (HTTP), DASH consists of two main components, which are the Media Presentation Description (MPD) file and video segments residing on a HTTP server. The MPD file describes the characteristics of the stream. It contains information about the stream availability, segment duration, video representations, and the resource identifiers for each segment. Typical DASH clients first request an MPD file and the first few segments of the video, in order to fill a buffer. When the buffer is filled, the player starts displaying the video to the client and the remaining segments are continuously fetched from the Internet. In conventional DASH Advanced Video Coding (AVC), the representation is selected by the client based on either buffer level or throughput-based algorithms. Buffer-based video streaming considers the buffer fill level to keep/improve the quality of the subsequent segment, if the necessary buffer refill level was experienced while downloading previous segments. Karagkioules et al. [6] surveys different adaptation algorithms. It is worth noting that there exist different kinds of video encodings and this work focuses on video delivery with DASH Advanced Video Coding (AVC). Many projects, especially studying improved caching strategies, work with DASH Scalable Video Coding (SVC) [7]. We work with DASH-AVC, because its implementation is simpler and therefore better adapted for resource-constrained end systems.

2.3 DASH Improved with SDN and MEC

There are several different approaches improving video delivery in networks studied through simulations [8–11]. Cetinkaya et al. [8] uses DASH SVC and Software Defined Networking (SDN) to improve video streaming. The authors suggest routing video flows through the underlying infrastructure taking into consideration the capacity of the backhaul network. Li et al. [9] propose a Mobile Edge Computing (MEC) approach to improve fairness and overall video definition among UEs sharing the same channel. Lai et al. [10] propose a method for improved video delivery in heterogeneous networks with SDN. Fajardo et al. [11] propose a network-assisted HTTP streaming mechanism based on MEC. Their mechanism is able to adapt DASH streams to different channel conditions based on periodical measurements of Channel Quality Indicators (CQIs) and adaptation algorithms matching experienced CQIs to video definitions. Foukas et al. [5] prove a similar approach in a real experiment by using FlexRAN. In their use-case, CQI statistics reported by a UE are gathered at the FlexRAN controller. A DASH-based video streaming server uses information gathered at the controller to match the CQIs to video representations (i.e., bitrates).

2.4 Novelties of This Work

This work is composed of three innovations with respect to (i) the architecture of an NFV-based MEC-assisted system for video delivery c.f., Sect. 3), (ii) Fourier-based radio-channel assessment (c.f., Sect. 4), and (iii) extensive measurements of a real system (c.f., Sect. 5).

We develop a MEC-based approach for video streaming based on real components containing a cloudified Core Network (CN), a MEC cloud, an eNB, and a UE. We demonstrate that a MEC-based video server (i.e., a MEC application) deployed on the MEC cloud can improve DASH-based video delivery for users connected to a wireless network.

Unlike other contributions, in the estimation of channel capacity [5,11], we do not use CQIs to assess the channel capacity. The problem of matching CQIs to channel capacity depends on technology, frequency, environment, vendor, radio scheduling, and hardware. Therefore, it is not feasible to derive exact tables matching CQIs and the desired rate of video delivery in a mobile system. Moreover, the use of CQIs does not apply to congested networks, in which the data rate is limited by the system capacity.

We do not work with absolute values such as channel capacity or representation bitrate. Therefore, our approach is fundamentally different from the typical knapsack problem, in which different representations requiring different bitrates are allocated within fixed channel capacity. In our approach, we observe patterns in channel consumption and wireless metrics. If the load is too high, we recommend the clients to lower their video representations, and when the load is too low, we recommend them to use higher video qualities. Moreover, we evaluate wireless metrics to predict the potential degradation of the channel capacity.

3 Architecture of the Video Delivery

3.1 Functional Architecture

Figure 1 illustrates a MEC compliant network. It consists of RAN, a MEC cloud, and the CN. Since the MEC cloud is installed very close to the RAN, traffic originated by UEs can avoid traversing the CN and directly access MEC Applications (Apps). The MEC Apps benefit from the close vicinity of the eNB and thus experience low latency.

MEC Apps instantiated on a MEC cloud infrastructure through a Virtual Infrastructure Manager (VIM) receive traffic directly from the user plane (e.g., video service) or other MEC related services (e.g., SD-RAN platforms) dealing with radio control and management planes.

3.2 Platform Implementation

A 4G/5G mobile telecommunication platform developed in this work is depicted in Fig. 2. We use OpenAirInterface [12], which implements the Home Subscription Service (HSS), Mobility Management Entity (MME), and Serving/Packet

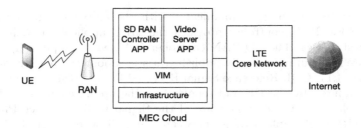

Fig. 1. A simplified depiction of the network architecture.

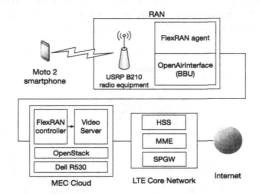

Fig. 2. The implementation of the experimental setup.

Gateway (S/PGW) as a minimal LTE CN and the eNB for RAN. OpenAir-Interface provides the LTE mobile network and radio signal towards UEs. We use the USRP B210 board[2], which provides an LTE Frequency Division Duplex (FDD) transmission in band 7 (2.5 GHz/2.6 GHz) using 5 MHz channels and the Single-Input Single-Output mode. We have a smartphone Moto 2[3] connected to the OpenAirInterface network. As SD-RAN, we use FlexRAN [5]. FlexRAN consists of an agent co-located with the OpenAirInterface Base Band Unit (BBU)[4], and an external SD-RAN controller, which is instantiated on the MEC cloud. Ubuntu-based MEC Apps (i.e., FlexRAN controller and Video Server) are both hosted as VNFs on an OpenStack based cloud with Dell R530 cloud workers (Intel Xeon 2.5 GHz CPU with 80 threads, 192 GB RAM).

3.3   Information Flow in the System

In order to provide the Video Service MEC App with information about the current radio link status (c.f., Fig. 2), we established an information flow between different components. Foukas et al. [5] implemented an SD-RAN controller (i.e.,

---

[2] https://www.ettus.com/product/details/UB210-KIT.

[3] https://www.motorola.com/us/products/moto-z-play-gen-2.

[4] The feature-68-enb-agent branch.

FlexRAN controller) that communicates with the eNB through a FlexRAN agent. The FlexRAN controller provides the MEC application with required radio link statistics. The SD-RAN controller is based on a publish/subscribe architecture and can periodically publish statistics about the per UE radio link quality, e.g., LTE CQI, Reference Signal Received Power (RSRP), etc. CQI values are computed by the UE and reported on the uplink channel to the eNB. They are related to the current state of the Signal to Interference Plus Noise Ratio (SINR). CQI displays values between 0 and 15, where CQI of 15 denotes the best possible quality. RSRP is defined as the linear average over the power contributions (in [W]) of the resource elements (REs) that carry cell-specific reference signals within the considered measurement frequency band [13]. RSRP values reside between -44 dBm and -140 dBm [13].

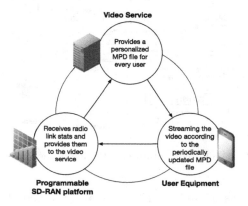

Fig. 3. The information and control flow.

Our video service subscribes with the FlexRAN controller and dynamically updates MPD files based on information provided by the controller. This leads to the information flow as described in Fig. 3. First, a UE starts accessing the video content from the MEC video service triggering traffic between the UE and the eNB. The radio signal quality is reported by the UE through the Radio Resource Control (RRC) to the eNB. eNB enriches the information received from UEs through the RRC channel with per-user traffic and RAN scheduling statistics, and sends this information to the FlexRAN controller using the FlexRAN agent. The FlexRAN controller publishes the information towards the subscribed video service, which in turn adapts (i.e., limits) available video qualities in the MPD file. Finally, the UE periodically downloads the MPD file, which closes the information loop between the system components.

4   Algorithm Selecting Video Representations

4.1   Characteristics of Video Traffic Patterns

We assume that video streaming is the most dominant traffic of the user (i.e., other applications utilize only a small fraction of bandwidth on the mobile device) and also, that there is only one video stream running per user. It is not a strong assumption, while multiple video streaming is rare and users typically use one application on a UE at a time. Therefore, we assume minimal background traffic from other sources (i.e., instant messengers, email, etc.).

In our initial measurements, using a setup discussed in Sect. 3.2, we observe a specific periodical pattern, which is typical for video delivery with DASH AVC using buffer-based adaptation algorithms confirmed by other sources [5,6,14]. The traffic requested by the client appears as a periodical rectangle function (i.e., a channel is periodically occupied and idle with a certain frequency). This is caused by a periodical re-fill of the buffer. When the buffer level decreases below a certain threshold, a new segment is requested by the client. The periodicity of traffic peaks (i.e., rectangles) in the experienced goodput is approximately equal to the segment duration (e.g., 2 s) as the client consumes the video content in real time (a 2 second segment is consumed within 2 s).

Figures 4a and 5b and related traffic plots reported by Augustin et al. [15] show that the DASH video pattern can be clearly distinguished from full-capacity downlink/uplink transmissions, which cause an approximately constant traffic pattern limited by the channel capacity. We confirm the difference between the video stream pattern and full-capacity traffic in the time and frequency domain. Please notice a traffic peak at 0.5 Hz in Fig. 5b, which relates to the segment size $t_s = 2$ s.

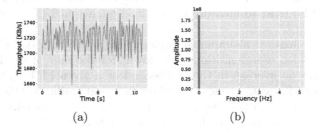

(a)   (b)

Fig. 4. Downloading a file using `wget`, results in constant throughput (a) and a FFT (b) with a spike at 0 Hz.

Our idea is to use the Fast Fourier Transform (FFT) to discover traffic patterns on the downlink. If the link is saturated, it displays constant throughput behavior displayed in Fig. 4a. When we observe the saturation pattern on the link, we unload it by forcing the client to use lower video representations. Otherwise, if the link displays a regular video traffic with a significant peak correlated

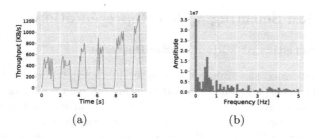

(a)   (b)

Fig. 5. Streaming a video reveals the DASH pattern in throughput (a) and a FFT (b) with a spike at 0 Hz and 0.5 Hz, corresponding to the segment size of two seconds.

to the segmentation frequency, e.g., segments of 2 s cause peaks at 0.5 Hz, we can either keep the current definitions or force the client to use higher video representations. For more information about the use of Fourier Transforms, please consult [16] (c.f., p. 257).

We operate with sampling frequencies of around 10 Hz. There is no oversampling, as the periodicity of discrete packet-based transmission will be discovered with sampling rates of around 1000 Hz. For example, if a UE is exchanging packets of size 1500 B = 12000 bits with a throughput of 12 Mbps, data packets will be received at a frequency of 1000 Hz. Very high sampling rates of around 1000 Hz should be therefore avoided because of the risk of oversampling (i.e., moving spikes from 0.5 Hz to 1000 Hz).

4.2 Implementation

We specify a DASH *server side adaptation* mechanism, which also includes information about the quality of the wireless channel. Multiple Key Performance Indicators (KPIs) exist to measure the channel quality in LTE. In our case, we use RSRP [13].

Algorithm 1 presents a simplified implemented procedure. It limits available qualities (i.e., video representation scale-down) for the user, if the RSRP drastically decreases on average in the last second or a given FFT frequency ratio between video traffic at frequency $\frac{1}{t_s}$ and the constant traffic at 0 Hz is too small i.e., lower than min_Δ, indicating that the radio link is overloaded. On the other hand, it increases the video quality (i.e., video representation scale-up), if the given frequency ratio is above a certain threshold max_Δ.

The representations in the MPD file refer to the video qualities in ascending order, i.e., the lowest quality is provided by representation #1. In the scale-up, the server decides to replace the lowest representation with the next higher available quality. In scale-down, the highest representation is replaced with the next lower one available (c.f., Fig. 6).

Algorithm 1. Simplified adaptation algorithm, based on radio link utilization and received radio signal power.

```
 1: procedure MAIN LOOP(T, i)        ▷ Duration T of video and interval i of sampling
 2:     t ← 0                                        ▷ Variable running from 0 to T/i
 3:     x ← segment duration
 4:     delay ← time period (e.g., 1 sec)
 5:     max_Γ ← max tolerated RSRP drop (e.g., 5)
 6:     min_Δ ← min margin (e.g., 0.04)
 7:     max_Δ ← max margin (e.g., 0.4)
 8:     ▷ As long as the video is playing
 9:     while t <= T/i do
10:         S_t = RNIS.getStats()
11:         if S_t.rsrp − S_{t − delay/i}.rsrp > max_Γ then
12:             Video rep. scale down; (c.f. Fig. 6a)
                                        ▷ Run a FFT over the last sampled data
13:         fft = runFFT(S_{t − x/i ... t}.throughput)
14:         if fft[1/x]/fft[0] >= max_Δ then
15:             Video rep. scale up; (c.f., Fig. 6b)
16:         if fft[1/x]/fft[0] <= min_Δ then
17:             Video rep. scale down; (c.f., Fig. 6a)
18:         t = t + 1
19:         sleep(1)
```

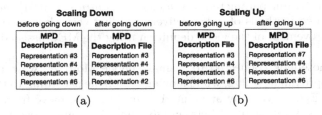

Fig. 6. The scaling down (c.f., Fig. 6a) and scaling up (c.f., Fig. 6b) procedures.

5   Evaluation of Video Delivery

The evaluation of the scheme is provided on a real LTE femto-cell testbed. Essentially, the physical layer, the noise, and competing video streams are taken into account in our measurements providing precise real-world measurements of our scheme.

5.1   Preparations of the Video Stream

In the experiment, we use the GPAC project toolset[5], namely MP4Box, to encode and segment the video. MP4Client streams the video at the client side. In order to

---

[5] GPAC, multimedia open source project: https://gpac.wp.imt.fr/.

provide a DASH stream that could saturate the OpenAirInterface [12] wireless link (max. capacity of around 8 Mbps), we require a video with a high bit rate. Thus, we use a UHD 4K video. We encoded the video using MP4Box in 10 different bit rates, resulting in 10 different video representations requiring network capacity between 50 kbps up to 8 Mbps. The videos are divided into segments of $t_s = 2\,$s, which is appropriately short for on demand video delivery in changing conditions of mobile networks.

5.2   Video Delivery Experiments

We use an OpenAirInterface-based [12] LTE setup (c.f., Sect. 3.2). We operate in a femto-cell scenario, where a user is moving inside a building (e.g., office space, train station, etc.). The eNB and video service are handling one UE.

In our experiment, we cover an office and a hallway with LTE signal and use a mobility pattern between different points of different radio signal qualities as shown in Fig. 7. We use the buffer-based adaptation technique (as implemented in the MP4Client). We compare our MEC-assisted approach, i.e., a video server receiving radio statistics from the SD-RAN controller (c.f., Sect. 3.1) and periodically updating the MPD file according to our algorithm specified in Sect. 4 against a native DASH solution (a video service providing static MPD files). Please notice that an MPD file is requested by the client once for the entire video stream or periodically every t_s for the regular and MEC-enabled DASH respectively. The algorithm parameters are $max_\Gamma = 5$, $min_\Delta = 0.04$, $max_\Delta = 0.4$. We compare two methods of video delivery residing very close to the user. We show the improvement of the video definition using the MEC-assisted server side adaptation.

Using a notebook connected to a smart phone Moto 2^6, we run the video stream for approximately 90 s, while moving the phone according to the mobility pattern (c.f., Fig. 7). We stay at point A from 0 to 15 s, move from A to point B during 5 s, stay at point B between 20 s and 35 s, and move from B to C during 6 s. Then, we stay at C between 41 s and 60 s, and go back to B again during 6 s, and stay there between 66 s and 90 s. On the way between A to C, and C to B, we experience decreasing and increasing signal levels respectively.

5.3   Results for One UE: Buffer-Based Adaptation

There are many different client-side adaptation mechanisms. However, in this work, we compare our MEC enabled video streaming technique with state-of-the-art, buffer-based mechanisms implemented in the GPAC client. Due to variable radio conditions, the comparison is based on a statistical basis repeating the same experiment 10 times. The measurements of requested representation qualities against segment number and client buffer fill levels against time in 10 experiments vary significantly.

---

[6] https://www.motorola.com/us/products/moto-z-play-gen-2.

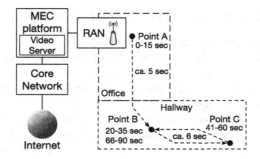

Fig. 7. Moving pattern in the office and hallway.

Analysis over 10 measurements for each of the adaptation mechanisms, i.e., regular DASH vs. our MEC-assisted DASH, provides an appropriate statistical estimation of the experienced buffer level and video quality at the UE. Figure 8a and b show the difference between the slower buffer-based adaptation and the faster MEC-assisted adaptation. Our algorithm provides a higher initial representation, c.f., Fig. 8a from segment #10 onwards, but then suffers from a quick drop in the buffer, as we move away from the eNB, c.f., Fig. 8b at around 20 s, when moving from point B to C. Due to the margin, the buffer stays at an appropriate level and we can keep the higher quality of the video. At point C (c.f., Fig. 7), which manifests the worst radio conditions, we need to decrease the video representation (segment #28). The buffer relaxes and performs better than regular DASH. Notice that in regular DASH, we experience a similar, but stronger drop in the buffer level and this affects the video quality in a negative way (c.f., Fig. 8a red line, at around segment #33-#40). With MEC-assisted DASH, we improved the video quality in the good signal conditions (between 10 and 20 s) up to 40%, while keeping the buffer level at an approximately 35% lower, but stable level.

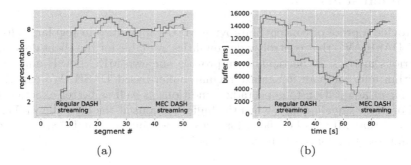

(a)   (b)

Fig. 8. (a) Requested video representation against segment no# averaged over 10 experiments for regular and MEC-assisted DASH. (b) Buffer level against time averaged over 10 experiments for regular and MEC-assisted DASH. (Color figure online)

5.4   Results for Two UEs: Throughput-Based Adaptation

We attach two laptops, i.e., machine #1 and machine #2. Every laptop is equipped with a Huawei E3276 dongle[7]. The laptops have fixed positions (i.e., RSRP displays −78 dB and −82 dB for machine #1 and machine #2 respectively). They simultaneously and concurrently stream the same video stream from the video server through the LTE network (c.f., Sect. 3.2). In comparison to rate based regular DASH, our algorithm (i.e., mainly the Fourier channel assessment as the RSRP values remain stable throughout the experiment) provides slightly decreased representation qualities (c.f., Fig. 9a, machine #2), however, operates with a much more reasonable buffer fill level (c.f., Fig. 9b). This is beneficial in mobile scenarios, in which the connecting quality can quickly vary, so the buffer shall not be maintained at low levels. This proves that our algorithm also behaves appropriately in multi-user scenarios.

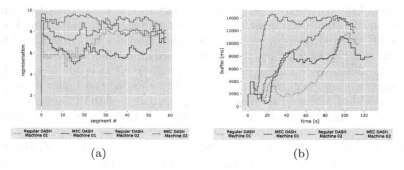

(a)   (b)

Fig. 9. (a) Average representations on machines #1 and #2. (b) Average buffer fill level on machines #1 and #2.

6   Conclusions

We provide a proof of concept improving MEC capabilities in regular, "off-the-shelf" DASH AVC that controls video qualities available for the client depending on various metrics. In particular, we provide our own MEC DASH adaptation algorithm and compare it against regular buffer-based DASH. We experience much faster adaptation to good radio conditions as well as better experience in terms of worse signal quality, when the buffer remains at the higher level. We are convinced that MEC is beneficial for video streaming so that DASH can profit from improved performance in spite of mobility.

---

[7] https://consumer.huawei.com/en/mobile-broadband/e3276/.

References

1. Giust, F., et al.: MEC Deployments in 4G and Evolution Towards 5G. ETSI White Paper No. 24 (2018)
2. Patel, M., et al.: Mobile-Edge Computing - Introductory Technical White Paper. ETSI White Paper (2014)
3. 3rd Generation Partnership Project (3GPP): Transparent end-to-end Packet-switched Streaming Service (PSS); Progressive Download and Dynamic Adaptive Streaming over HTTP (3GP-DASH). Technical report, 3GPP (2015)
4. Chang, C.Y., Alexandris, K., Nikaein, N., Katsalis, K., Spyropoulos, T.: MEC architectural implications for LTE/LTE-a networks. In: Proceedings of the Workshop on Mobility in the Evolving Internet Architecture MobiArch 2016, pp. 13–18. ACM, New York (2016)
5. Foukas, X., Nikaein, N., Kassem, M.M., Marina, M.K., Kontovasilis, K.: FlexRAN: a flexible and programmable platform for software-defined radio access networks. In: Proceedings of the 12th International on Conference on Emerging Networking Experiments and Technologies CoNEXT 2016, pp. 427–441. ACM, New York (2016)
6. Karagkioules, T., Concolato, C., Tsilimantos, D., Valentin, S.: A comparative case study of http adaptive streaming algorithms in mobile networks. In: Proceedings of the 27th Workshop on Network and Operating Systems Support for Digital Audio and Video NOSSDAV 2017, pp. 1–6. ACM, New York (2017)
7. Müller, C., Renzi, D., Lederer, S., Battista, S., Timmerer, C.: Using scalable video coding for dynamic adaptive streaming over http in mobile environments. In: 2012 Proceedings of the 20th European Signal Processing Conference (EUSIPCO), pp. 2208–2212, August 2012
8. Cetinkaya, C., Ozveren, Y., Sayit, M.: An SDN-assisted system design for improving performance of SVC-dash. In: 2015 Federated Conference on Computer Science and Information Systems (FedCSIS), pp. 819–826, September 2015
9. Li, Y., Frangoudis, P.A., Hadjadj-Aoul, Y., Bertin, P.: A mobile edge computing-assisted video delivery architecture for wireless heterogeneous networks. In: 2017 IEEE Symposium on Computers and Communications (ISCC), pp. 534–539, July 2017
10. Lai, C., Hwang, R., Chao, H., Hassan, M.M., Alamri, A.: A buffer-aware http live streaming approach for SDN-enabled 5G wireless networks. IEEE Netw. **29**(1), 49–55 (2015)
11. Fajardo, J.O., Taboada, I., Liberal, F.: Improving content delivery efficiency through multi-layer mobile edge adaptation. IEEE Netw. **29**(6), 40–46 (2015)
12. Nikaein, N., et al.: Demo: OpenAirInterface: an open LTE network in a PC. In: Proceedings of the 20th Annual International Conference on Mobile Computing and Networking MobiCom 2014, pp. 305–308. ACM, New York (2014)
13. 3GPP: Evolved Universal Terrestrial Radio Access (E-UTRA); Physical layer; Measurements. Technical Specification (TS) 36.214, 3rd Generation Partnership Project (3GPP) (03 2017), version 14.2.0
14. Han, B., Qian, F., Ji, L., Gopalakrishnan, V.: MP-DASH: adaptive video streaming over preference-aware multipath. In: Proceedings of the 12th International on Conference on Emerging Networking Experiments and Technologies CoNEXT 2016, pp. 129–143. ACM, New York (2016)
15. Augustin, B., Mellouk, A.: On traffic patterns of http applications. In: 2011 IEEE Global Telecommunications Conference - GLOBECOM 2011, pp. 1–6, December 2011
16. Smith, S.W., et al.: The scientist and engineer's guide to digital signal processing (1997)

Analysis of Distributed Real-Time Control Systems with Shared Network Infrastructures

Paul J. Kuehn[(✉)] and Imran Nawab

Institute of Communication Networks and Computer Engineering, University of Stuttgart, Pfaffenwaldring 47, 70569 Stuttgart, Germany
paul.j.kuehn@ikr.uni-stuttgart.de,
imrannawab74@gmail.com

Abstract. Distributed control applications are considered where the control functions are implemented by software of a centralized controller and where system state information and control commands are communicated through a shared communication infrastructure. Through the shared communication infrastructure the control functionalities of the individual control loops may influence each other and can have an affect on Service Level Objectives (SLO) to be guaranteed for each individual control application. In this contribution a novel approach is suggested for an enhanced CSMA/CD local area network infrastructure where the application control layer is directly put on an enhanced Media Access Control (MAC) layer of the communication infrastructure to minimize control delays. A comprehensive model is derived for the resulting network with all competing applications and protocol functions for safe communications. The performance of the MAC layer request is analyzed exactly by a stochastic phase T_C representing its aggregated behavior. The delay performance of the individual control applications is analyzed by means of a queuing model of type GI/G/1 where GI represents the total control request arrival process and G a virtual service time T_C from which the aggregated network delay parameters are derived. The distributed network control system (NCS) model with the shared infrastructure is analyzed exactly by methods of Control Theory by computational algorithms and MATLAB Simulink tool support.

Keywords: Distributed control systems · Local area network · Shared communication infrastructure · Performance evaluation

1 Introduction

Distributed applications require a reliable and real-time efficient network support. For economic reasons network resources cannot be reserved for each application and have to be shared by many other applications. Typical examples are distributed sensor-controller communications known as "Networked Control Systems" (NCS), applied in integrated manufacturing processes, traffic control systems, or Cyber-Physical Systems. Besides the unavoidable network delays transmission errors may occur through noise interferences or information losses caused by buffer limitations. These effects require a strong communication protocol support to guarantee Service Level Objectives (SLO).

© IFIP International Federation for Information Processing 2019
Published by Springer Nature Switzerland AG 2019
M. Di Felice et al. (Eds.): WWIC 2019, LNCS 11618, pp. 222–232, 2019.
https://doi.org/10.1007/978-3-030-30523-9_18

The performance of distributed control applications is further affected by all other applications which share the common communication infrastructure. For the development of such distributed real-time control systems methods are required by which the influence of all interfering sources can be estimated in order to predict their effects on each considered application and their individual SLO requirements.

Research has already been directed to subjects of specific distributed application systems as, e.g., sensor networks, city, smart energy, or air traffic control systems, robot and integrated production control systems, or for disaster control operations, c.f. [1–13]. In most of these cases dedicated networks have been applied which are designed or configured for the specific application SLOs as Local Area Networks (LAN/WLAN) with priority options for real-time support. Typically, control and network analyses are treated independently; this paper attempts at an integrated multi-layer analysis approach by aggregating the complete network infrastructure into a stochastic equivalent phase which is inserted in the specific application control layer. In a first paper [14] we have studied a single Networked Control System where the whole functionality of the underlying network is aggregated into a functional module operated on the Link Layer (2b) with acknowledgment signaling and Timeout control for each frame.

In the remaining part of this paper we inspect in Sect. 2 several principal alternatives for shared communication networks, specifically with respect to that layer on which the Application Layer is based upon. In particular, we define a local area network as shared infrastructure for all control applications, i.e., an infrastructure where the control application is placed upon an enhanced common Media Access Control (MAC) Layer (2a) to increase reliability and real-time performance of the control systems. In Sect. 3 a comprehensive model is developed for the performance evaluation of the shared infrastructure (MAC Layer) which is represented by an extended task graph. Its performance is analyzed exactly resulting in an aggregated virtual service time which represents the whole MAC layer including all control communications. In Sect. 4 single-server queuing models are suggested which represent the whole NCS with all control loops from which the aggregated performance of the control systems will be derived based on the shared infrastructure. Results are presented and discussed in Sect. 5, conclusions are drawn in Sect. 6.

2 Architectural Alternatives for NCSs

Communication networks, their interfaces and protocols are standardized for reasons of interoperability, e.g., by the general ISO model for Open System Interconnection (OSI) or by the dominating IETF RFCs for the Internet and its well-known principal layers, c.f. Fig. 1. Our distributed control functionalities are belonging to Layer 7 which can, in principle, be placed on top of any of the above layers as, e.g., a pure hardware solution directly across wires of the PHY Layer 1 for signal transmissions as in classical electrical control systems, the MAC Layer 2a of shared LANs for frame exchanges, the Link Layer 2b for safe exchange of frames as in our paper [14, 15], the Network Layer 3 for an unreliable end-to-end exchange of packets (but with enhanced transport options), or the Transport Layer 4 for a safe exchange of byte streams end-to-end. The functional support increases in the upward direction but the end-to-end delays

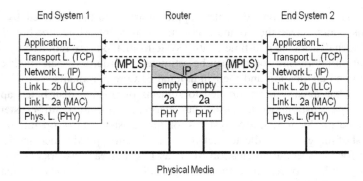

Fig. 1. Reference model for open system interconnection

increase accordingly. For our control application Layers 3 and 4 are less attractive or have to be complemented with respect to reliability and real-time performance. In this paper we restrict our aims to applications within a local area, such as for manufacturing plants, inventory and logistics management, traffic control or IoT applications. We prefer therefore to put the Application Layer directly upon the MAC Layer. This MAC layer has, however, to be enhanced with functions of the LLC with respect to error control and with respect to performance efficiency.

3 Enhanced MAC Layer Architecture for Shared Infrastructures

3.1 Modeling of the Enhanced MAC Layer

Conventionally, media access control takes care of an efficient access to the common transmission medium among independently acting "stations" through functions as channel activity sensing, contention resolution, access right signaling by Token circulation, or reservation requests. To integrate error control and request/response functionalities in the MAC layer we can make use of the following further optional possibilities: (1) Acknowledgment signaling after frame reception, (2) Different Inter-Frame Spacing for service class distinctions, (3) Slot-based contention resolution for channel access, (4) Carrier Sensing for collision detection (CD) during transmission, and (5) Channel Reservation for Request/Response cycles. Properties (1) and (2) were suggested by the main author already in 1983 [16] for service differentiation and real-time channel access enhancements in LANs; these functions have been adopted later in connection with the development of the WLAN standards for the IEEE 802.11 series of protocols. Property (3) is known from early MAC protocols as the periodic CSMA p-persistent channel access based on attempts within a slot time Δt [17]. In WLANs a station synchronization takes place by an ACK signal after a successful frame transmission. Property (5) can be used for channel reservation for a whole request/response control cycle. The problem of "Hidden Stations" in WLANs and its handling through the RTS/CTS-based channel reservation through the Network Allocation Vector (NAV, c.f. [23]) can be applied in our approach; for real-time control applications within plants the centralized controller stations should be located within a mutually reachable area; in that case the RTS/CTS cycle method could be neglected. Based on the properties (1)–(4) we suggest the following model of the enhanced MAC Layer of the shared communication infrastructure, c.f. Fig. 2. The "Shared Medium" in Fig. 2 can be a wired or wireless channel which can be accessed by the stations. One or several controllers are the recipients of the frames sent from stations (not shown explicitly in Fig. 2).

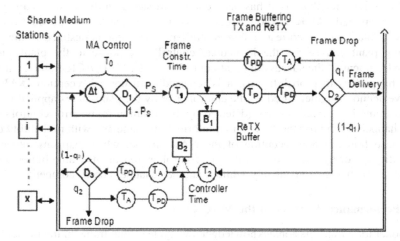

Fig. 2. Enhanced MAC layer performance model for multiple networked control systems with shared local area network communication infrastructure

The "Shared Medium" can be a wired or a wireless channel accessed by the stations. One or several controllers are the recipients of frames being sent by the stations (they are not shown explicitly in Fig. 2).

Abbreviations in Fig. 2 and for the analysis are self-explaining, where x indicates the number of stations, D are probabilistic decisions, T indicates random time variables, P and q probabilities; index numbers refer to different applications of the variables. Δt is the slot time for channel access and has to be larger than the largest round-trip time.

Two operating modes will be distinguished for the channel access and reservation: **Mode 1** for Event-based control and **Mode 2** for Time-based control. In Mode 1 sensor signals for a full request/response cycle are generated only when certain defined sensor threshold values are exceeded, e.g., a speed, water, or temperature level or fire/gas concentration alarms. Arrival processes are typically clustered rare events. Mode 2 addresses periodic channel reservations for a full request/response cycle sensor-controller-actuator. The arrival process type is D (deterministic), i.e., constant inter-arrival times.

The operation of control activities across the shared infrastructure is based on the access competition for the common channel infrastructure among all plant stations. When a plant station has won the access competition, all other stations have no access right to the channel until the ongoing plant-controller control cycle has been successfully completed. The plant station and the responding controller station have exclusive access to the channel. Two buffers B_1 and B_2 are used for intermediate buffering of the plant-state frame and the controller-response frame, respectively, for repeated frame transmission in case of a transmission error, c.f. dashed links in Fig. 2. After each successful cycle both buffer contents are cleared by which mutual interferences between competing stations are excluded. To avoid illegal channel tapping of information a strict encryption coding is required. When a plant has gained access to the common channel, the access right remains with that station and with the controller until the activity for that event has been completed successfully. Two signaling messages are applied: **ACK** acknowledges a complete request/response control cycle between a plant and its corresponding controller. This frame is destined to the corresponding plant and carries the immediate controller response to the plant and the acknowledgment of the successful plant-controller cycle. If the ACK-frame is in error, which happens with probability q_2, it is repeated until correct reception. **NAK** is a negative acknowledgment used by the controller or by the plant and is applied in cases when a frame is received in error (detected by the common frame error control check) which happens with probability q_1 for an information frame and with probability q_2 for a response frame. Upon reception of the NAK- frame, which happens either with probability q_1 (or q_2) the receiver (plant or controller) repeats its frame buffered in B_1 (or B_2), respectively, immediately without another channel access competition.

3.2   Performance Analysis of the MAC Layer

The model for a transmission/acknowledgement cycle of one frame in the model Fig. 2 is a special case of a Directed Acyclic Graph (DAG) and can be analyzed exactly. The exact mathematical analysis of general DAGs (which includes also logical synchronization conditions) has been suggested by the main author in [18] and has been applied, among others, to the exact analysis of NCSs for the LLC 2 protocol models "Send-and-Wait" (SW) and "Selective Repeat" (SR) with Timeout recovery [15] where parallel activities had to be considered to avoid a life-lock of the protocol function in case of a frame loss. The performance analysis will be explained through a step-wise aggregation of independent stochastic phases T_i for $i \in \{0,1,2,P,PD,A\}$ by the task Graph Reduction method introduced in [15]. This allows for the exact analysis of the control model within which the whole aggregated time for channel access and communication is represented by an equivalent stochastic phase $T_C(x)$.

As outlined in Sect. 3.1 the channel access is based on the principle of the p-persistent CSMA/CD protocol with x stations, c.f. [17]. The channel access resolution is based on slotted periods of length Δt. We will assume that each station takes part in the channel access competition by deciding to send its frame with a randomly chosen probability p in the next slot. If several stations send during this slot, a collision occurs which is detected by the CD-function and all involved stations abort sending. The same procedure is repeated in the successive slots until that case when only one station has attempted the channel access during this slot: This station has won the competition and proceeds with construction of the frame. The channel access time T_0 is indicated in Fig. 2 and defines the aggregated duration for an arbitrary channel access as multiples of the slot time Δt, where $T_0 = (j + 1)\Delta t$, $j = 1,2,..$ The slot time has to be sized to $\Delta t \geq 2\tau$; τ denotes the propagation delay time for signals between the two most distantly located stations which guarantees that a safe decision can be made after each slot. The total channel access time $T_0 = (j + 1)\cdot\Delta t$ is constituted from j multiples of Δt times for the contention resolution plus one Δt accounting for the slot during which the channel competition has been won. Explicit formulas are obtained for: the probability P_S for a successful frame transmission, the 1st and 2nd ordinary moments of the random contention interval J, the LS-transform $\Phi_0(s)$, the mean $E[T_0]$ and coefficient of variance c_0 of T_0 and the optimized probability p for the random channel access probability p.

T_C indicates the random time of a successful completion of the whole time measured from the successful channel access to a completed Sensor-Controller-Actuator cycle. It has been exactly analyzed by the mathematical task-graph reduction method [18] resulting in the LT $\Phi_C(s)$, the mean $E[T_C]$ and the coefficient of variation c_c of T_C. From these quantities we can approximate the cumulative distribution function (CDF) of T_C by phase-type distributions of hypo- or hyper-exponential type ($0 \leq c_c < \infty$).

Note: The complete mathematical analysis and their explicit results cannot be presented here for reasons of limited space and will be part of a forthcoming paper (but can be provided on request from the main author). We will only outline the principal course of derivation of the key performance metrics for the Channel Access Time T_0 and the Duration of a successful control cycle time T_C. Same holds true for the analysis of the application layer control models: the derived results for T_C are used as a "virtual service time" within a queuing model of the Application Layer.

4 Application Layer Performance

4.1 Application Layer Queuing Models

4.1.1 Open-Loop NCS Applications

The application Layer is placed directly above the shared communication infrastructure of the extended MAC layer. It will be modeled by means of queuing systems of the type GI/G/1, where GI (General Independent) indicates a stochastic point process of control request arrivals, G (General) represents the aggregated MAC layer service phase T_C for one complete request/response cycle with its channel access, frame transmission, and acknowledgment time components. Figure 3 illustrates the total system model. For an "Open-Loop NCS", i.e., for a one-way communication between a station and a controller or vice-versa. The competitive effects of the shared media for all control circuits is reflected in the resulting delay for processing of each control request.

Queuing theory is a highly developed discipline with more than 100 years of research and experience and a rich selection of analytic results. For a number of specific arrival/service process types exact results exist, e.g., for M/G/1, GI/M/1 model types, where M stands for Markovian and G for General process types with typically FIFO (first-in, first-out) queuing disciplines. For LIFO (last-in, first-out) and RANDOM disciplines first and second order moments of the waiting times are also known [21]

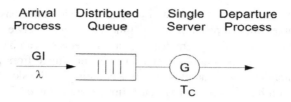

Fig. 3. Aggregated queuing model for a NCS with shared communication infrastructure with FIFO, LIFO, and RANDOM order of service

from which we can approximate the delay distributions through the Weibull-distribution function [19]. Once a correct model has been defined, many cases can be solved by use of tabled results on standard queuing system types [19, 20]. We therefore want to encourage to make use of both tabled results or simulations (when there are no analytic results available) based on adequate system models.

4.1.2   Closed-Loop NCS Applications

Closed-Loop applications originate typically from **automatic control systems**, c.f. the basic model in Fig. 4. The closed-loop model consists of a Plant which can be adjusted by a signal of the Actuator A through the Controller C. The output signal Y ("state of the Plant") is fed back to the Controller C where it is compared with a Reference Signal R as control objective; the difference E between R and Y forms the input to the Controller C. The Controller determines a reaction signal which is communicated to the Actuator to affect that Y will be driven towards the reference value R. This basic control loop of the Control System becomes a Networked Control System (NCS) when Controller and Plant reside at different locations. As a typical application example, the controller function is implemented by software operated at a centralized computer system. The network adds to the total delay in both directions and is especially critical in applications with strict real-time SLO requirements, especially when there are further delays through the shared use of the communication network.

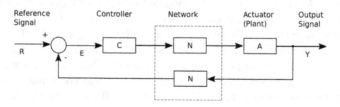

Fig. 4. Structure of a Networked Control System (NCS)

The model of Fig. 4 has been analyzed before [14] with a **dedicated network infrastructure** where the "Network" is a two-way logical link control (LLC) connection (Layer 2b) operated under control of the "Send-and-Wait" or under the "Selective Repeat" protocol with Timeout recovery in case of frame loss or excessive frame delay between A and C and between C and A separately. In this contribution we extend the model to a NCS with a **shared network infrastructure**, i.e., a local area network operated on layers 1 (Physical Layer) and 2a (Media Access Control Layer) by a wired or a wireless network. To analyze the extended model two items have to be solved:

(1) to replace the Network block N by our Enhanced MAC-Layer of Sect. 3.1
(2) to analyze the resulting control system of Fig. 4.

The analysis of the control systems can be performed in different ways. Classical Analog Control Theory or Discrete Time State Theory.

The classical **analog control theory** for linear systems is based on analytical functions for the analog time signals and their Laplace transforms and by definition of standard controller functions as the PID Controller (P: proportional, I integral, D: differential). The resulting solution for y(t) as a response to a standard reference signal r (t) represented by the delta function $\delta(t)$ for an "impulse response" or by the unit step function u(t) for a "unit-step response" analyzed in the Laplace-domain resulting in Y (s) = LT{y(t)}. More complex systems are non-linear which are more difficult to analyze. The **discrete time state control theory** is based on detailed system state variables and their description by systems of state equations and using, e.g., the MATLAB Simulink tool or a computational solution of matrix equation systems. We have applied these method in [14].

5 Selected Numerical Results and Discussion

5.1 MAC Layer Performance

An example for the extended MAC Layer LAN will be studied to demonstrate the real-time optimized performance of the CSMA/CD p-persistent MAC protocol for different numbers of stations attached to the LAN. The parameters are as follows:

Slot time	$\Delta t = 10 \ \mu s$
Frame transmission time (constant)	$T_A = T_P = 100 \ \mu s$
Propagation delay time (constant)	$T_{PD} = 5 \ \mu s$
Frame Construction/Controller Time	$T_1 = T_2 = 50 \ \mu s$
Number of Stations	$x = 1, .., 100$
Channel Transmission Rate	$r = 100$ Mbit/s

The aggregated arrival process of requests of all stations is assumed to follow a Poisson process, i.e., the inter-arrival times are negative-exponentially distributed (Type M). This assumption is justified especially when many independent arrival processes are superimposed, even when the individual stations send requests at regular instant distances and when stations are not synchronized among each other. The accuracy increases with increasing number of stations. The resulting queuing model is of the type M/G/1 with either a FIFO queuing discipline in the ideal case or RANDOM in a more realistic case. In the RANDOM case the coefficient of variation of delayed requests is significantly larger, which affects SLA-guarantees of delay quantiles. The key results are given in Table 1. The dimensions for $E[T_C]$ and t_W are given in

Table 1. Performance results of the MAC layer

x	$E[T_c]$	c_C	ρ	t_W	c_{DF}	c_{DR}
1	0.366	0.264	0.007	0.246	0.65	0.70
2	0.386	0.270	0.015	0.262	0.67	0.71
5	0.391	0.310	0.034	0.267	0.68	0.72
10	0.392	0.270	0.078	0.276	0.69	0.77
50	0.393	0.270	0.393	0.62	0.82	1.03
100	0.393	0.270	0.787	1.182	0.94	1.45

multiples of 1 ms. The results for c_{DF} and c_{DR} are given for the queue disciplines FIFO (left column part) and RANDOM (right column part). The results indicate the following properties:

(1) The duration of the control cycles $E[T_C]$ depends only minimally on the number of stations as a result of the optimized parameter p of the CSMA/CD p-persistent access protocol. The coefficient of variation is low and quite stable over the whole range of the number of attached stations. The coefficient of variation is low and quite stable over the whole range of the number of attached stations.

(2) The mean waiting time of delayed access requests t_W remains stable for low and medium loads and approaches infinity asymptotically when the system capacity is approached. The coefficient of variation c_{DF} of delayed requests results primarily from repeated frame transmissions in case of transmission errors and is hypo-exponential; c_{DR} becomes, however, hyper-exponential for higher loads.

(3) The parameters can be used for system resource sizing when certain SLOs have to be met: (3.1) Meeting SLA with respect to the **mean waiting time** of an arriving request t_W which has to be delayed: The number of attached stations or the request rate by each station can be fixed up to a prescribed upper threshold t_{WTh} of the mean delay t_W of an arriving and delayed request independently of the applied queue discipline. (3.2) Meeting SLA with respect to the real-time critical **delay quantile** q such that a delayed request will not have to wait longer than a threshold time t_{Th} with probability

$$q = P\{T_W \leq t_{Th} | T_W > 0\}.$$

This SLO depends on the queue discipline and is harder to meet for RANDOM than in case of FIFO service, c.f. the increased coefficient of variation of delay c_{CR}.

Example: We construct the complementary CDF $W^C(t)/W$ for delayed requests using the first and second order parameters t_W and c_D from Table 1 by the Weibull DF tabled in [19] for various parameters of c_D. A SLO of p = 0.001 for a delay threshold $t_{Th} = 5E[T_C]$ is reached for $\rho = 0.078$ for the FIFO queue discipline. The same SLO is reached for the RANDOM queue discipline only at $15E[T_C]$ due to the much higher coefficient of variation. As a consequence the allowable load or allowable number of stations has to be reduced accordingly to meet the SLO objective.

5.2   Discussion and Summary

1. The explicitly worked out performance results are easy to apply even for users without specific expertise in applied queuing theory. The use of the Simulink toolset is very helpful for both, the analytic evaluation of control systems or for the system analysis by stochastic simulations, but reveals deficiencies concerning coverage of network and protocol properties.
2. Hard real-time performance requirements are not well supported by current local area networks and the Internet. The current developments towards the future 5G mobile network are an aim for future IoT applications. Advanced WLAN concepts within the IEEE 802.11 standards for Distributed Control Functions (DCF), Point Control Functions (PCF), and Hybrid Control Functions (HFC) are still not sufficient to meet hard real-time control requirements. The concept of an enhanced MAC-layer protocol based on the optimized CSMA/CD p-persistent protocol allows to adapt the local area network to distributed networked control applications, in particular for indoor integrated production plants for the ms-range of IoT systems. The concept can easily be extended to multi-class applications to meet different real-time classes through different inter-frame spacing as already suggested and studied in [16]. The current approach of an enhanced MAC layer is in principle also applicable for future 5G network slicing concepts.

Summary: Distributed IoT applications require efficient network support, especially for real-time critical problems. Shared network use is attractive for economic reasons. Current LANs are designed for the integration of quite different type of services but don't allow for an efficient real-time control. In this contribution a novel concept for networked control systems is suggested which is in particular able to meet hard SLO requirements. The concept is based on an enhanced and optimized MAC layer for the CSMA/CD p-persistent media access protocol. The whole NCS is modeled for a safe and efficient communication support where the network functions are aggregated by a stochastic variable T_C which is part of the application control loop. The method has been applied to a sample LAN and to distributed NCSs. Details of the performance analysis and NCS examples did not fit into the limited space and will be published separately; they can be provided from the main author on request.

References

1. Seuret, A., Hetel, L., Daafous, J., Johanssen, K.H. (Eds.): Delays and Networked Control Systems. Advances in Delays and Dynamics, vol. 6. Springer, Cham (2016). https://doi.org/10.1007/978-3-319-32372-5
2. Gupta, R.A., Chow, M.-Y.: Networked control system: overview and research trends. IEEE Trans. Ind. Electron. **57**(7), 2527–2535 (2010)
3. Zampieri, S.: Trends in networked control systems. In: Proceedings of 17th World Congress IFAC, Seoul, Korea, 6–11 July 2008
4. Liu, K., Friedman, E., Johansson, K.H.: Discrete-Time Networked Control under Scheduling Protocols, Chapter 9 of [1], pp. 151–165

5. Tipsuwan, Y., Chow, M.-Y.: Control methodologies in networked control systems. Control Eng. Pract. **11**(10), 1099–1111 (2003)
6. Liu, G.P., Mu, X., Rees, A., Chai, S.C.: Design and stability analysis of networked control systems with random communication time delay using the modified MPC. Int. J. Control **79**(4), 288–297 (2006)
7. Zhang, L., Hristu-Varsakelis, D.: Communication and control co-design for networked control systems. Automatica **42**(6), 953–958 (2006)
8. Li, H., Sun, Z., Chow, M.-Y., Chen, B.: State feedback controller design of networked control systems with time delay and packet dropout. In: Proceedings of 17th World Congress IFAC, Seoul, 6–11 July 2008
9. Blind, R., Allgöwer, F.: On the stabilizability of continuous-time systems over a packet based communication system with loss and delay. In: Proceedings of 18th World Congress IFAC, Cape Town, South Africa, pp. 6466–6471, 24–29 August 2014
10. Nilsson, J.: Real-Time Control Systems with Delays, Ph.D. Dissertation, Lund Institute of Technology, Lund, Sweden (1998)
11. Dong, J., Kim, W.-J.: Markov-chain-based output feedback control for stabilization of networked control systems with random time delays and packet losses. Int. J. Control, Autom. Syst. **10**, 1013–1022 (2012)
12. Vilgelm, M., Ayan, O., Zoppi, S., Kellerer, W.: Control-aware uplink resource allocation for cyber-physical systems in wireless networks. In: European Wireless Conference, Dresden, Germany, VDE (2017)
13. Vilgelm, M., Mamduhi, M.H., Kellerer, W., Hirche, S.: Adaptive decentralized MAC for event-triggered networked control systems. In: 19th ACM International Conference on Hybrid Systems: Computation and Control (HSCC), Vienna, Austria, 12–14 April 2017
14. Kuehn, P.J., Scholz, S., Cao, S., Li, F.: Performance modeling of networked control systems. In: 9th International Congress on Ultra Modern Telecommunications and Control Systems (ICUMT). IEEE Xplore, Munich, Germany, 6–8 November 2017
15. Kuehn, P.J.: Real-time performance modeling of link layer protocols for multi-layer protocol aggregation. In: 21st Conference on Innovation in Clouds, Internet and Networks (ICIN). IEEE Xplore, Paris, France, 19–22 February 2018
16. Kiesel, W., Kuehn, P.J.: A new CSMA-CD protocol for local are networks with dynamic priorities and low collision probability. IEEE J. SAC **1**(5), 869–876 (1983)
17. Leon-Garcia, A., Widjaja, I.: Communication Networks - Fundamental Concepts and Key Architectures. Series in Computer Science, Chapter 6. McGraw-Hill (2004)
18. Kuehn, P.J.: Performance and energy efficiency of parallel processing in data center environments. In: Klingert, S., Chinnici, M., Rey Porto, M. (eds.) E2DC 2014. LNCS, vol. 8945, pp. 17–33. Springer, Cham (2015). https://doi.org/10.1007/978-3-319-15786-3_2
19. Kuehn, P.: Tables on Delay Systems (1976). http://www.ikr.uni-stuttgart.de/Content/ Publications
20. Selen, L.P., Tijms, H.C., van Hoorn, M.H.: Tables for Multi-Server Queues. Elsevier, Amsterdam (1985). ISBN 0-444-87722-3
21. Takacs, L.: Delay distributions for one line with poisson input, genetal holding times and various orders of service. BSTJ, 487–503 (1963)
22. Nawab, I., Kuehn, P.J.: Performance Analysis of Networked Control Systems with Shared Communication Infrastructures, M-Thesis, Institute of Communication Networks and Computer Engineering, University of Stuttgart (2018)
23. Bianchi, G.: Performance analysis of the IEEE 802.11 distributed coordination function. IEEE J, SAC **18**(3), 535–554 (2000)

The Effect of Hardware/Software Features on the Performance of an Open–Source Network Emulator

Domenico Capriglione[1] , Gianni Cerro[2] , Luigi Ferrigno[2] ,
and Gianfranco Miele[2]

[1] University of Salerno, Fisciano, Italy
dcapriglione@unisa.it
[2] University of Cassino and Southern Lazio, Cassino, Italy
{gianni.cerro,luigi.ferrigno,g.miele}@unicas.it

Abstract. The authors investigate a network emulator performance versus the variability of hardware/software features of the hosting machine. In particular, the evaluation of static and dynamic delays is carried out considering several testing conditions. In detail, as concerns emulator configurations, the influence of packet rates on imposed delays values and distributions are analyzed; as for hardware and software, different values for RAM, CPU cores and operating system are tested. Results, reported as mean values and standard deviation, show two main trends: the resource availability has an important impact on the emulation stability and on the measurement repeatability; secondly, higher differences in performance levels for low imposed delay values, which is the most interesting zone in a few milliseconds latency world. The paper aims to show that the capability to emulate network impairments is generally influenced by hardware/software capabilities and it must be considered when using network emulation for specific test purposes.

Keywords: Computer networks · Network emulation ·
QoS measurements · System virtualization

1 Introduction

Modern testing schemes, in most engineering fields, are especially focused on simulations, model planning, test execution in a software–based environment and extrapolation of theories and laws on the basis of the obtained results. This is particularly true in telecommunication and computer science [16]. Protocol and novel communication technology tests usually rest on simulators [14], and emulators [9] having the purpose to replicate the real environment where commercial releases should find their place. In this field, an important role is played by network emulation [7,13,18]. It has the goal to emulate all possible impairments a telecommunication network can experience in real cases, such as delays,

© IFIP International Federation for Information Processing 2019
Published by Springer Nature Switzerland AG 2019
M. Di Felice et al. (Eds.): WWIC 2019, LNCS 11618, pp. 233–245, 2019.
https://doi.org/10.1007/978-3-030-30523-9_19

jitters, packet losses, packet duplication, just to cite a few. Emulators can be hardware [15] or software [1,3]. Usually hardware emulators are costly but they present certified level of performance, while software emulators and, particularly, open source software emulators are free, flexible but their reliability is left as an open issue to be investigated.

Starting from previous experience of the authors in such field [2,5], this paper describes the investigation of the effect of hardware/software available resources on the performance of a widely–known open source network emulator, namely Net–Em [10,11], that is part of the Linux traffic control facilities and allows to emulate several impairments in a network link. To achieve such goal, there are two main possibilities: having several physical machines with different hardware or applying a virtualization process and changing resource availability via software. In this paper, the second choice has been selected. Virtualizing the system leads to other sources of uncertainty and several papers address the issue [8,12,17]. In our case, those contributions have been deliberately neglected, since the aim of the work is to evaluate the effect of having limited–hardware/heavy–software resources on the obtained performance. All results are presented in relative values, taking as nominal performance the one experienced with the maximum available resources. The output of this work represents a step forward in the way to assign a metrological value to a software network emulator that, through a self-calibration procedure, could provide the final user with a quantitative evaluation of its own expected capabilities in reproducing the required impairments.

The organization of the paper is the following: Sect. 2 is going to describe the adopted methodology along with the planned test conditions; Sect. 3 is intended to present obtained results both in terms of mean value and standard deviations. Section 4 discusses about the meaning of the obtained results in terms of general statements the paper wants to convey and it also provides possible improvements and developments of the experimental set–up.

2   Materials and Methods

In this section, we provide a detailed description of the adopted test set–up. It consists of the adopted network emulator, namely Net–Em, the virtualization schema, how the measurements are performed and which test conditions represent the most interesting scenarios to be investigated.

2.1   The Adopted Network Emulator

Net–Em (abbreviation for Network Emulator) can be seen as a tool inside traffic control (TC) routines by Linux Systems [10,11]. For a given network, composed of several links, its functionalities allow to add impairments such delays, delay variations (jitter), packet losses and other limitations to one or more links of the networks. In this paper, only delay is considered as parameter of investigation.

As delay setting regards, Net–Em requires three input parameters: the mean value (μ), the standard deviation (σ) and the correlation coefficient (ρ). If not differently specified, it generates a uniform distribution using as parameters μ and σ and considering ρ to correlate currently generated delay with the previous one (associated to the previous packet). Furthermore, thanks to *iproute2* tool collection, other random distributions can be associated to delay generation, such as normal, Pareto and Pareto normal functions.

2.2   The Virtualized System

The realized test set–up is composed of three virtual machines residing on the same PC. Figure 1 provides a sketch of the realized system. It is based on VirtualBox, that is a virtualization product provided by Oracle, able to work on all main operating systems and it is available for free as Open Source Software under GPL terms. Main functionalities are summarized by Oracle in their white paper [6].

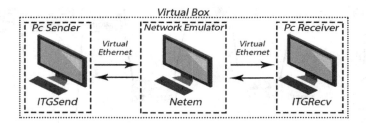

Fig. 1. A sketch of the virtualized system

Inside VirtualBox container, to create a network topology, three different virtual machines have been installed with the following tasks:

- PC Sender: this machine is responsible to send data, with different features in terms of traffic duration, packet rates and contents.
- Network Emulator: it is the core of the system. It receives data from the sender and forwards them to the PC Receiver. According to imposed test conditions, the forwarding process is consequently perturbed.
- PC Receiver: this machine is responsible to receive data and store them for further processing.

As reported in Fig. 1 (see *ITGSend* and *ITGRecv*), a suitable software is adopted to generate and retrieve traffic data [4].

An important tool of this suite is *ITGDec*, that can be used off–line to analyze traffic features, as packet delays, packet-losses etc.

To be able to use Net–Em, all virtual machines are equipped with Linux Operating Systems: Ubuntu 17.10 on PC Sender and PC Receiver, while different versions on Network Emulator in order to assess the influence of software, as well.

In terms of hardware equipment, both PC sender and receiver are given with 2 GB RAM and dual–core processors.

2.3   The Measurement Procedure

The authors have developed a measurement procedure proposed in [5]. This procedure is adopted in current paper as well, to verify performance levels of the proposed set–up and emulator.

In particular, measurement procedure is reported in Fig. 2, where the timeline of the test operations is depicted.

It consists of three main steps:

- initialization;
- machine time synchronization;
- Traffic flow activation and data storage.

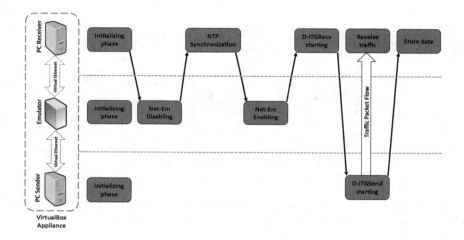

Fig. 2. The adopted measurement procedure

In detail, during initializing phase, traffic profiles, emulator settings and receiver logging function are adjusted. In the second step, machine time synchronization is carried out. In particular, to avoid any influence, the emulator machine works only as a relay machine able to forward traffic from PC Sender to PC Receiver without adding any impairment condition. In this case, adopting Network Time Protocol (NTP), we aligned Sender to Receiver absolute time. In this way, delay estimation is coherently computed, adopting as sending instant the time-stamp included by the Sender in each packet header.

The third step consists of enabling the emulator, setting suitable parameters, such as delay value and distribution and link of interest for impairment application. After setting–up testing conditions, receiver and sender are respectively activated and traffic flow is started. Packets pass through the emulator, which corrupts the link to the receiver. They are finally received by PC receiver and there stored to be off–line processed.

2.4   Performed Test Conditions

The evaluation of performance is subjected to the imposition of several test conditions.

In particular, we can divide test conditions in two categories:

- imposing delay conditions to the emulator;
- changing hardware/software features of the network emulator hosting machine.

As regards imposed delay conditions, we set:

- static delays: $[0, 5, 20]$ ms;
- dynamic Gaussian delays: mean value $\mu = 20$ ms and standard deviations $\sigma = [1, 2, 5]$ ms.

As regards hardware/software features, we set:

- CPU cores: $1, 2, 4$;
- RAM memory: $[500, 2048, 4096]$ MB;
- Operating System: Ubuntu Desktop, Ubuntu Server.

Furthermore, we tested each delay value under several network stressing conditions, i.e. by imposing different packet rates to the data flow. In detail, adopted packet rates are: [200 500 1000 2000 5000 10000] pkt/s. The data flow duration is fixed to 15 s.

For each operating condition (combination of Net–Em and hardware features), 20 tests are performed to estimate repeatability of the obtained measurements.

3   Results

Measurement campaign results are reported in terms of mean value and standard deviation. Their representation is organized in:

- effect of CPU core number variation on static (Figs. 3 and 4) and dynamic delays;
- effect of RAM variation on static (Figs. 5 and 6) and dynamic delays (Table 1);
- effect of Operating System variation on static (Figs. 7 and 8) and dynamic delays (Table 2).

3.1   Static Delay Evaluation

CPU Effect. As first test group, static delays have been imposed to Net–Em. Three different values are considered: 0 ms, 5 ms and 20 ms and results are evaluated by testing the emulator under different CPU core numbers. In particular we consider 1, 2 and 4 cores. To be cautionary, 4 GB RAM have been used and Ubuntu Server Environment has been adopted as operating system version.

Most critical situations are those referred to lowest imposed delays, namely 0 ms and 5 ms. In 0 ms case, the emulator is working only as a relay machine, without adding any delay on the path. The experienced delay is always greater than zero, due to the virtual link intrinsic delay. Such value is decreasing with packet rates and it does not exhibit a clear trend behavior with respect to core variation. The only clear difference is in terms of standard deviations: in detail, 2 core situation, reported in orange in Fig. 3, exhibits the most repeatable behavior for any specific test condition (this phenomenon is reported with the green vertical bar in the same figure). Generally, 4–core–configuration outperforms single core case, both in terms of lower average value and standard deviation. Therefore, for 0 ms case, the best configuration is 2–core and the worst one is single core.

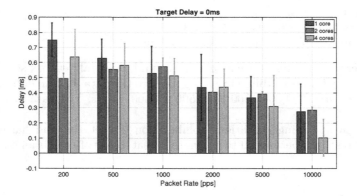

Fig. 3. Static Delay results with target value equal to 0 ms. Effect of CPU core number variation.

In 5 ms case (see Fig. 4), delay mean values have a lower variability. In particular, there is a light overestimation for all packet rate conditions, and core number influence is less evident. Still, 2–core–case has a very stable behavior and a very low standard deviation. Even if not reported for a sake of brevity, when imposed delay is equal to 20ms, slight differences among different hardware features are negligible, and results are in–line with target performance, except at 200 packet rates, where single core case has a lower repeatability.

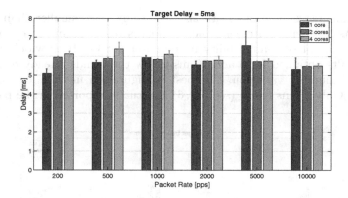

Fig. 4. Static Delay results with target value equal to 5 ms. Effect of CPU core number variation.

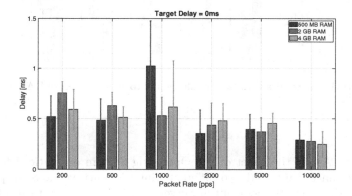

Fig. 5. Static Delay results with target value equal to 0 ms. Effect of RAM size variation.

RAM Effect. To evaluate the central memory effect on the performance of the network delay emulation, we tested three different and typical RAM sizes: 500 MB, 2048 MB, 4096 MB. As core evaluation on static delays has proved the suitability of using 2–core case, that is the CPU configuration adopted for RAM tests. Also in this case we use 0 ms, 5 ms and 20 ms as target delay values. When we consider 0 ms case, i.e. Fig. 5, values are generally higher than the ones obtained when core influence is evaluated. In particular, very high standard deviations have been obtained, especially for 500 MB case. In this figure, result trends can be divided into two cases: before 1000 pkt/s and after 2000 pkt/s. In the first part, 2 GB case appears as the best configuration in terms of repeatability, while in the second part 4 GB results exhibit a lower standard deviation.

This is an expected behavior, since when packet rates are higher, the number of packets and the data flow size increase and wider memory availability can help in managing emulation. Data size is, in any case, smaller than available memory. As a general statement, measurements result in any case compatible, where the concept of compatibility in measurement has been widely explained in [5]. Results obtained for 5 and 20 ms follow the trends already explained in case of core number variation. The best configuration in these cases results 4 GB RAM. Only 20 ms figure (see Fig. 6) is actually reported in the paper.

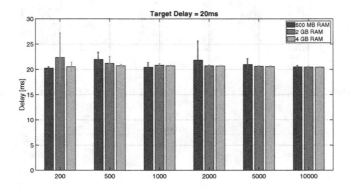

Fig. 6. Static Delay results with target value equal to 20 ms. Effect of RAM size number variation.

OS Effect. As for the effect of the Operating System on static delay emulation performance, we tested two different Linux Ubuntu versions, in particular Ubuntu Desktop 18.10 and Ubuntu Server 18.10. The idea is to use the same version of the operating system, in order to understand if the Graphical user interface and the processes connected to it could have an effect on the delay

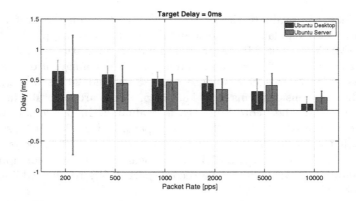

Fig. 7. Static Delay results with target value equal to 0 ms. Effect of Operating System variation.

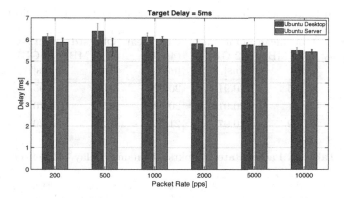

Fig. 8. Static Delay results with target value equal to 5 ms. Effect of Operating System variation.

emulation. Ubuntu Server is, indeed, a command–line operating system. Also in this case, we tested three static delays and results prove a generalized increase of the measured delay when Ubuntu Desktop is adopted. This phenomenon can be observed at lower packet rates for 0 ms delay (see Fig. 7), while it is always true when imposed delay values are set to 5 ms and 20 ms. Standard deviations have comparable values in all cases, except for a particular case at 200 pkt/s for 0 ms delay. In this case, Ubuntu Server case exhibits a really unstable behavior. For sake of brevity, only 0 ms and 5 ms delay cases are reported in Figs. 7 and 8.

3.2   Dynamic Delay Evaluation

The evaluation of Dynamic Delay emulation performance requires several levels of verification. Firstly, we tested only Gaussian Distribution. Therefore, when measurements are carried out, results must be evaluated in terms of average value, standard deviation and correspondence between the imposed probability density function (pdf) and obtained empirical pdf. In this subsection, we show results that are relative to all cited parameters.

In order to be concise, we present results in form of tables. In detail, for each influence factor (processor, memory, system), two tables report results obtained in two packet rate conditions: low traffic (200 pkt/s) and high traffic (5000 pkt/s). Since results in terms of mean and standard deviation values are very similar, we do not report all tables for sake of brevity. In particular, RAM and OS effects are reported only.

Reported tables prove how standard deviation values are often lower than the expected ones, except one case: Table 2, in 1 ms line, where all configurations (Desktop, Server) exhibits a higher value. This phenomenon can be referred to the limited capability of the emulator to reproduce distribution. Still, hardware resources are not responsible for these synthetic data, since they are all comparable.

Table 1. Packet Rate 200 pkts - Dynamic Delay - RAM effect

Imp. values (μ, σ) [ms, ms]	Obt. mean (512 MB) [ms]	Obt. mean (2 GB) [ms]	Obt. mean (4 GB) [ms]	Obt. std (512 MB) [ms]	Obt. std (2 GB) [ms]	Obt. std (4 GB) [ms]
(20,1)	21.05	20.91	20.99	0.99	0.95	1.00
(20,2)	21.07	20.91	20.98	1.71	1.70	1.70
(20,5)	21.09	20.97	21.01	4.22	4.20	4.24

Table 2. Packet Rate 200 pkts - Dynamic Delay - OS effect

Imp. values (μ, σ) [ms, ms]	Obt. mean (Desktop) [ms]	Obt. mean (Server) [ms]	Obt. std (Desktop) [ms]	Obt. std (Server) [ms]
(20,1)	21.02	22.60	1.03	1.20
(20,2)	21.03	22.57	1.72	1.88
(20,5)	21.05	22.48	4.25	4.34

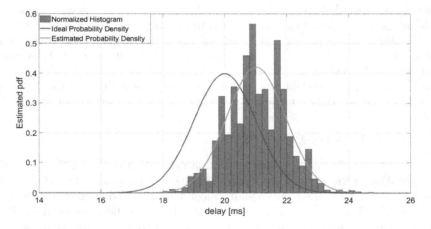

Fig. 9. Comparison of probability distributions: 500 MB RAM – 1 core CPU – Ubuntu Desktop OS (Color figure online)

Furthermore, in order to show adherence between observed and expected probability distributions, Figs. 9 and 10 are reported. Each figure is characterized by three information graphics:

- a red line: the ideal probability density function, as imposed in Net–Em settings;
- a yellow line: the derived probability density function, applying Gaussian analytic law to obtained mean and standard deviation;
- a normalized histogram: real data distribution.

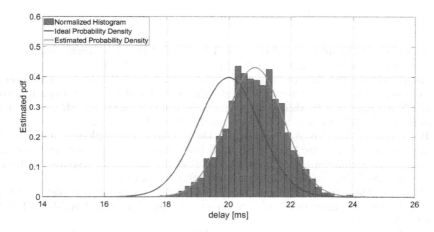

Fig. 10. Comparison of probability distributions: 2 GB RAM – 2 core CPU – Ubuntu Desktop OS (Color figure online)

What really makes the difference when comparing results obtained with different hardware resources are the actual probability density functions (briefly reported as distribution in the text, with some ambiguity). Indeed, when 500 MB RAM and 1 core are used, the obtained empirical distribution is quite far from being Gaussian, as the histogram bins do not appear to follow the yellow distribution line. When resources increase (see Fig. 10), experimental distribution approaches the expected one.

In both cases, the red line, i.e. the ideal distribution, is not well achieved by the data. This can be a problem related to the emulator itself, since it is not dependent on the adopted hardware resources.

4   Discussion

In this paper, an analysis of the impact of variable hardware resources on the performance of a common adopted network emulator is reported. As stated in the introduction, we did not mean to evaluate the emulator capabilities but their stability when different resources are available. We can affirm two main results: in static delay case, a sensitive impact can be observed in case of very low imposed delay (in our case, 0 ms) and with high imposed packet rates. When delay constraints are relaxed (5 ms or 20 ms), hardware resources become less important; in dynamic case, the emulator is capable to pretty adhere to synthetic values of a probability distribution, but hardware limitations appear as preeminent when the probability density function is analyzed. These results make the emulation possible also on low power machines, if some strict constraints can be relaxed and required high performance devices when precise and very low delays are desired. Further analyses will take care of other quantities, such as packet loss emulation, in variable resources scenarios.

References

1. Ahrenholz, J., Danilov, C., Henderson, T.R., Kim, J.H.: Core: a real-time network emulator. In: 2008 IEEE MILCOM, pp. 1–7, November 2008
2. Angrisani, L., Capriglione, D., Cerro, G., Ferrigno, L., Miele, G.: Experimental analysis of software network emulators in packet delay emulation. In: 2017 IEEE International Workshop on Measurement and Networking (M&N), pp. 1–6, September 2017. https://doi.org/10.1109/IWMN.2017.8078382
3. Beshay, J.D., Francini, A., Prakash, R.: On the fidelity of single-machine network emulation in Linux. In: 2015 IEEE 23rd International Symposium on Modeling, Analysis, and Simulation of Computer and Telecommunication Systems, pp. 19–22, October 2015. https://doi.org/10.1109/MASCOTS.2015.18
4. Botta, A., Dainotti, A., Pescapè, A.: A tool for the generation of realistic network workload for emerging networking scenarios. Comput. Networks **56**(15), 3531–3547 (2012)
5. Capriglione, D., Cerro, G., Ferrigno, L., Miele, G.: How to quantify *trust* in your network emulator? In: Chowdhury, K.R., Di Felice, M., Matta, I., Sheng, B. (eds.) WWIC 2018. LNCS, vol. 10866, pp. 171–182. Springer, Cham (2018). https://doi.org/10.1007/978-3-030-02931-9_14
6. Coter, S., King, G.: Oracle VM 3: Building a Demo Environment using Oracle VM VirtualBox. Technical report, Oracle Corporation (04 2016)
7. Deng, B., Wang, X., Jiang, M., Liu, Y.: An emulation architecture for the integration of virtual and physical networks. In: 2017 8th IEEE ICSESS, pp. 399–405, November 2017
8. Edwards Sr, T.S.: Systems and methods for improving virtual machine performance, US Patent 8,332,571, December 2012
9. Ferenc, G.Z., Dinic, M.D., Markovic, A.I., Jovanovic, P.D.: UHI boot protocol implementation in android emulator for MIPS architecture. In: 2017 25th Telecommunication Forum (TELFOR), pp. 1–4, November 2017
10. Hemminger, S., et al.: Network emulation with NetEM. In: Linux Conf Au, pp. 18–23 (2005)
11. Jurgelionis, A., et al.: An empirical study of NetEm network emulation functionalities. In: 2011 Proceedings of ICCCN, pp. 1–6, July 2011
12. Kousiouris, G., Cucinotta, T., Varvarigou, T.: The effects of scheduling, workload type and consolidation scenarios on virtual machine performance and their prediction through optimized artificial neural networks. J. Syst. Softw. **84**(8), 1270–1291 (2011)
13. Kretsis, A., Corazza, L., Christodoulopoulos, K., Kokkinos, P., Varvarigos, E.: An emulation environment for SDN enabled flexible IP/optical networks. In: 2016 18th ICTON, pp. 1–4, July 2016
14. Masruroh, S.U., Fiade, A., Iman, M.F., Amelia: Performance evaluation of routing protocol RIPv2, OSPF, EIGRP with BGP. In: 2017 International Conference on Innovative and Creative Information Technology (ICITech), pp. 1–7, November 2017
15. Nakauchi, K., Kobayashi, K.: Studying congestion control with explicit router feedback using hardware-based network emulator. In: Proceedings of PFLDNET 2005, Lyon, France (2005)
16. Sarkar, N.I., Halim, S.A.: A review of simulation of telecommunication networks: simulators, classification, comparison, methodologies, and recommendations. J. Sel. Areas Telecommun. (JSAT), 10–17 (2011)

17. Tickoo, O., Iyer, R., Illikkal, R., Newell, D.: Modeling virtual machine performance: challenges and approaches. ACM SIGMETRICS Perform. Eval. Rev. **37**(3), 55–60 (2010)
18. Zheng, P., Ni, L.M.: EMPOWER: a cluster architecture supporting network emulation. IEEE Trans. Parallel Distrib. Syst. **15**(7), 617–629 (2004). https://doi.org/10.1109/TPDS.2004.21

Energy and Quality Aware Multi-UAV Flight Path Design Through Q-Learning Algorithms

Hend Zouaoui[1], Simone Faricelli[1], Francesca Cuomo[1(✉)] ⓘ,
Stefania Colonnese[1] ⓘ, and Luca Chiaraviglio[2,3] ⓘ

[1] University of Rome La Sapienza, Rome, Italy
{zouaoui.1800809,faricelli.1647406}@studenti.uniroma1.it,
{francesca.cuomo,stefania.colonnese}@uniroma1.it
[2] University of Rome Tor Vergata, Rome, Italy
luca.chiaraviglio@uniroma2.it
[3] Consorzio Nazionale Interuniversitario per le Telecomunicazioni (CNIT),
Rome, Italy

Abstract. We address the problem of devising an optimized energy aware flight plan for multiple Unmanned Aerial Vehicles (UAVs) mounted Base Stations (BS) within heterogeneous networks. The chosen approach makes use of Q-learning algorithms, through the definition of a reward related to relevant quality and battery consumption metrics, providing also service overlapping avoidance between UAVs, that is two or more UAVs serving the same cluster area. Numerical simulations and different training show the effectiveness of the devised flight paths in improving the general quality of the heterogeneous network users.

Keywords: Q-learning · UAV · Heterogeneous networks

1 Introduction

In mobile networks, the Quality of Experience (QoE) depends on the bandwidth request of users over space and time. Relying on fixed Base Stations (BSs) to satisfy the users bandwidth request may not comply with the fluctuating nature of that request [1]. In some particular cases, e.g. events when a large number of users is concentrated in the same area, or disasters affecting the network, the QoE drops dramatically. Employing UAVs as mobile network elements provides a possible solution to mitigate this effect [2].

In this work, we address the problem of planning the path of UAVs mounting eNodeB (eNB) functionality to provide support to the fixed BS and offer a constant good quality to users in an area where the request fluctuates in a cyclic fashion every 24 h. The use of UAVs as BSs has been advocated and discussed in several recent papers (see e.g., [3–5]). Different approaches can be adopted for computing the optimal deployment of the UAVs such as optimization or planning algorithms, for instance MILP in [10], and attractive approaches leveraging

© IFIP International Federation for Information Processing 2019
Published by Springer Nature Switzerland AG 2019
M. Di Felice et al. (Eds.): WWIC 2019, LNCS 11618, pp. 246–257, 2019.
https://doi.org/10.1007/978-3-030-30523-9_20

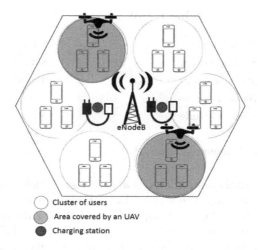

Cluster of users
Area covered by an UAV
Charging station

Fig. 1. Example scenario: one eNB, 6 clusters, 2 UAVs and 2 CSs

machine learning techniques [6]. More in detail, the problem of planning the path of the UAVs has been previously addressed in [7], by employing the well established Q-learning algorithm [8]. However, the work in [7] is tailored to a single UAV, which poses limits to the applicability in a complex scenario composed of multiple UAVs. Moreover, the method in [7] does not take into account the need to recharge the UAV battery and the case in which many UAVs are collaborating. To overcome these important issues, in this paper we target the problem of planning the path of a set of UAVs carrying BSs, by taking into account: (i) the energy consumed by each UAV, and consequently the battery recharge and (ii) the deployment of many UAVs in the same area. We then employ a Q-learning based approach to solve the aforementioned problem in a realistic scenario. Our results demonstrate the effectiveness of the proposed approach.

The rest of the paper is organized as follows. Section 2 presents the considered scenario where clusters of nodes are identified. The Q-learning design is described in Sect. 3 where both the models and the approach are described. The relevant performance analysis is in Sect. 4 while Sect. 5 concludes the paper.

2   Considered Scenario

We consider a scenario (as shown in Fig. 1) in which several HetNet users are under the coverage of a fixed eNB. We then assume that the total area covered by the fixed eNB is divided into a set of non-overlapping clusters. Each user is then assigned to a cluster, based on its spatial location inside the area [12]. Each cluster is then characterized by a bit rate request, which is computed as the average bit rate of the users in the cluster. Without loss of generality, we also assume that the coverage of each UAV is overlapping the area of the cluster it is serving.

Table 1. UAV parameters

Parameters	Value
Max speed ($v_{\max}$)	8.3 m/s
Max acceleration ($a_{\max}$)	4 m/s^2
Battery autonomy	30 min
Flight altitude	50 m
Weight	6 kg
eNB mounted radius (UAV footprint)	500 m

Clearly, the transmission undergoes a path loss, which depends on the distance between the user and the serving BS (either the fixed eNB or the UAV). Depending on the channel conditions, each user will be subject to a given channel quality, which is characterized by a specific Spectral Efficiency, typically expressed in terms of Channel Quality Indicator (CQI). Clearly, the channel quality has a large impact on the achievable throughput, and hence on several user application (like video streaming as in [13]).

In this scenario, a UAV supposedly flies at an altitude higher than the buildings height and covers a circular area on the ground. On the other hand, UAVs have to deal with a limited battery, which has to be mandatory recharged before running out of energy. A number N_{CS} of Charging Stations (CSs), equal to the number of UAVs, are placed on a given distance from the central eNB. The UAVs can access the CSs and autonomously charge their battery.

The flight path optimization is carried out offline in a centralized way. The offline approach, also adopted in [11], (i) allows to prioritize service on area where the expected reward is higher, (ii) relieves the UAVs of inter-UAV communication, and (iii) assures that UAVs do not overlap in serving the same areas. This is realized by deterministically preventing overlap during the learning stage, whereas in online distributed optimization this can be tackled by decentralized strategies, like the bio-inspired one presented in [9].

3   Q-Learning Design

3.1   UAV Characterization

The UAV model used in the simulation analysis has the features shown in Table 1. We use those features to parameterize the simulation so that both the time needed to perform each action and the energy consumed are realistic. We assume that the UAVs are all similar, and that they move between clusters barycenters and CSs through a straight line. While a UAV is moving or charging or waiting at a CS, it does not serve any user (i.e., it does not allocated any bandwidth).

3.2   Users Clustering

The central eNB is covering an area of radius R, this area can be divided in clusters of radius r that depends on the mounted eNB footprint. Among these clusters, the central one benefits of the best CQI and does not need to be covered by a UAV. If we do consider all the remaining clusters, the size of the Q-learning problem (represented by a Q-matrix as discussed below) maybe very big and in that case the computations would be very long, we also do know that in real life, some clusters have a high or low bandwidth request depending on the geographical area, for example: green spaces, schools, houses, industrial buildings, warehouses etc.

Therefore, to optimize the computations, we can consider a number N_C of clusters $\mathcal{C}$ identified by their position (x, y) in space and defined as follow:

$$\mathcal{C} = \{ c^{(i)} = (x^{(i)}, y^{(i)}), \ i = 1...N_C \}$$

Each cluster is also characterized by a Spectral Efficiency value $\mathcal{SE}\ [bps/Hz]$, which is maximal near the eNB station (4 bps/Hz) in our case, and drops exponentially with the distance from it. The number of clusters is supposed to be larger than the number of UAVs N_{UAV}, where each UAV can cover one cluster at a time and a cluster cannot be covered by more than one UAV.

3.3   Energy Aware Q-Learning Algorithm

We describe here the energy aware learning algorithm, exploiting the widely known Q-learning approach formerly introduced in [8] and ever since applied in a huge variety of frameworks, particularly in [7] where it is applied for one UAV path planning. In a nutshell, the Q-learning problem space consists of an agent, a set $\mathcal{S}$ of states which the agent can achieve, and a set of actions per state $\mathcal{A}$. The algorithm computes a reward for each state-action couple. At each iteration, referred to as one epoch, the algorithm explores a chain of consecutive states and updates the objective function Q stored in a matrix. Within the e-th epoch, each one composed by N_k steps corresponding to a fixed number of time-slots in our case, the computation explores a sequence of states as follows: from each state $s_k \in \mathcal{S}$ the agent can choose an action $a_k \in \mathcal{A}$ that will lead the agent to a next state $s_{k+1} \in \mathcal{S}$, k being the index of the state within the e-th epoch state sequence. Executing an action a_k in a specific state s_k provides the agent with a reward. The learning algorithm maximizes its cumulative reward according to an ε-greedy policy. This means that at each state, with probability ε it chooses a random action and with probability $1 - \varepsilon$ it selects the action that gives a maximum reward [7]. The value ε is initialized at 1 and is updated at each epoch to slowly decrease, this makes the algorithm try many random actions at the beginning and maximize the reward at the end of the training.

In the proposed energy and quality aware learning algorithm, the agent is one of the UAVs, and the states and actions are defined as follows: $s = s(P, B, T)$ where:

- P is the center position of a cluster or of a CS, $P \in \{Cl_1..Cl_{N_C}, CS_1..CS_{N_{CS}}\}$
- B is the battery level which is an integer varying from 1 to N_B, $B \in \{1..10\}$
- T is the k-th training step, which is also the actual timeslot, varying from a value of 1 to N_k.

The actions $a \in \{GoCl_1..GoCl_{N_C}, GoCS_1..GoCS_{N_{CS}}, Cover, Charge, Stay\}$, are:

- go to a cluster or to a CS;
- remain at the actual cluster and cover;
- remain at the actual CS and charge;
- idle at the actual CS without charging and wait.

The *Stay* action is usually performed when the reached CS is already taken by another UAV. It is important to note that not all actions are accessible from all states.

The Q-matrix where the state-action rewards are stored is of size $N_{States} \times N_{Actions} \times N_{UAV}$, where:

$$N_{States} = (N_C + N_{CS}) \times N_B \times N_k \qquad N_{Actions} = N_C + N_{CS} + 3$$

When at a state s an action a is performed, we obtain a state $s' = (P', B', T')$

Where P' is the new position if the action performed was Go and remains unchanged for the other actions. And B' is the new battery level that decreases if the action was GoP' or *cover*, increases if the action was *charge* and remains unchanged if the action was *stay*. And $T' = T + 1$.

We initialize the Q-matrix by setting a $-\infty$ reward for the forbidden actions at each state. The rules to define the forbidden actions are stated below:

- At a cluster's center, it is forbidden to charge or to stay (idle mode, not covering).
- In a CS, it is forbidden to cover.
- When the battery is full, it is forbidden to charge.
- From any location, it is forbidden to go to a cluster from which the battery level won't allow to reach a CS in the next time-slot.
- When the battery is low, it is forbidden to cover a cluster.

The Q-matrix is filled during the learning, at each step k of an epoch e, the function $Q(s_k, a_k)$ is computed using the following formula:

$$Q^{(e)}(s_k, a_k) \leftarrow (1 - \alpha_k).Q^{(e-1)}(s_k, a_k) + \alpha_k.[R_k + \gamma \max_{a_{k+1}} Q^{(e-1)}(s_{k+1}, a_{k+1})] \quad (1)$$

Where $\alpha_k \in [0, 1]$ is the learning rate, $\gamma \in [0, 1]$ is the discount factor that trades off the importance of earlier versus current reward [7]. The elementary reward R_k below denoted $R_{TOT}^{(t)}$ has two components, one related to the bandwidth and one to the battery consumption. It is defined as the gain in bandwidth per time-slot subtracted by the battery consumption observed during the transition from state s_k to the new state s_{k+1} performing the action a_k:

$$R_{TOT}^{(t)} = \alpha \times R_{BW}^{(t)} + \beta \times R_E^{(t)} \quad (2)$$

α and β are coefficients used to give a weight to each component.

The bandwidth related component is calculated as follow:

$$R_{BW}^{(t)} = \sum_{i=1}^{N_C} \left[\delta_i \times B_{UAV} \times \frac{\mathcal{SE}_{UAV}}{bitrate_i} + (1 - \delta_i) \times \frac{B_{BS}}{N_c - \sum_{i=1}^{N_c} \delta_i} \times \frac{\mathcal{SE}_{BSi}}{bitrate_i} \right]$$
$$- \sum_{i=1}^{N_C} \left[\frac{B_{BS}}{N_C} \times \frac{\mathcal{SE}_{BSi}}{bitrate_i} \right] \tag{3}$$

where $\delta_i = 1$ if the UAV is covering cluster i, 0 otherwise, B_{UAV} and B_{BS} are the bandwidth (expressed in Hz) available for the UAV and the base station respectively equal to 5 and 20 MHz. The $bitrate_i$ is the data rate request of cluster i at time-slot t. The $\mathcal{SE}_{UAV}$ is the spectral efficiency with respect to the UAV (assumed as 4 bps/Hz), while $\mathcal{SE}_{BSi}$ is the spectral efficiency with respect to the base station which is the highest at the center of the area and decreases exponentially with the distance, namely it is 2.3222 for clusters 2–7, 1.0333 for clusters 8–13 and 0.6139 for clusters 14–19.

Given the total bandwidth resources B_{UAV} and B_{BS}, the reward term $R_{BW}^{(t)}$ accounts for the excess data rate offered by the network (with or without UAV) with respect to the average data rate requested by each users' clusters.

The battery related component is based on the model established in [14], and depends on the action a as below:

$$R_E^{(t)} = \begin{cases} -(E_L + E_V + E_D) & \text{if } a = Go \\ -(E_L + E_{BS}) & \text{if } a = Cover \\ 1000 & \text{if } a = Charge \\ 0 & \text{if } a = Stay \end{cases} \tag{4}$$

Where E_L, E_V, E_D and E_{BS} are respectively the level flight energy, vertical flight energy, blade drag profile energy and the users serving energy computed as in [14], with the following parameters: weight of the UAV plus the BS, gravitational acceleration, air density, area of the UAV's rotor disk, profile drag coefficient and the BS power consumption.

In order to perform multi-UAVs path planning, we first train a single UAV for a large number of epochs, filling a part of the Q-matrix for all the possible (State, Action) combinations. The remaining parts of the Q-matrix, relative to the other UAVs are then initialised with the obtained values, as the reward for a (*state, action*) combination does not depend on the specific UAV performing it: hence $Q(s, a, d) \leftarrow Q(s, a, 1)$. The optimal path for the first UAV is given by taking the action with the maximum reward at each state. These actions are set as forbidden for all the following UAVs, to avoid having two UAVs colliding in the center of a cluster. The following UAVs are trained one by one for a smaller number of epochs, always setting the optimal path undertaken by a UAV as forbidden for the following ones.

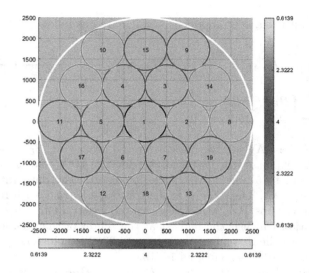

Fig. 2. Active clusters and spectral efficiency in space

Table 2. Scenario's parameters

Parameters	Value
eNB radius R	2.5 [km]
Cluster radius	0.5 [km]
Total amount of clusters	19
Active clusters	8
Number of UAVs and CSs	4
CSs distance from eNB	1.5 [km]
Total time considered	24 h
Time-slot duration	10 min

4 Performance Analysis

To evaluate the performance of the proposed approach we implemented a custom simulator in Matlab and evaluate the algorithm in a scenario where 4 UAVs move in an area around an eNB radius of 2.5 km. To this aim we set the parameters as in Table 2.

The 8 active clusters are selected randomly between the total 19 clusters, the maximum spectral efficiency is 4. The CSs are placed at a 1.5 km distance around the center, on the axis X and Y. The resulting simulation scenario is represented in Fig. 2.

To simulate the UAV's behaviour, we make the following assumptions:

– the battery levels are integer values between 1 and 10;

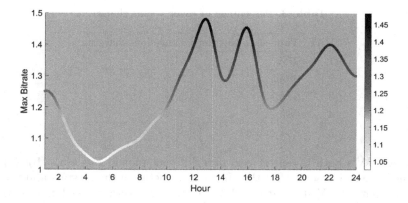

Fig. 3. Data rate over time

- one battery unit per time-slot is consumed when performing covering;
- taking into account the total flight time, we calculate the battery consumption for the movement (that may be 1, 2 or 3 units depending on the travelled distance);
- one battery unit is gained per time-slot when charging;
- one time-slot is enough for a UAV to reach any destination[1].

We consider 24 h long epochs, divided in 288 time-slots of 5 min. The requested data rate of the 8 considered clusters changes value at every time-slot, but is repeated every 24 h. For the data rate request we generate random values (between 1 and 1.5 Mbps) for 4 clusters and simulate a realistic request for the remaining 4. To achieve that, an entire day of max bit rate request is assumed, computing an interpolation of 24 points, setting a certain value of the bit rate for each hour. It has been assumed a high request during office hours (9–12, 14–16), a medium request during the afternoon and a low request during sleeping hours. From the obtained curve, showed in Fig. 3, we map the values of the data rate for each time-slot.

With these parameters, our Q-matrix is of size $12 \times 10 \times 288 \times 15 \times 4 = 2,073,600$. To let our agents learn, or to train them, we run the previously described Q-learning algorithm for 30000 epochs for the first UAV and 2000 epochs for the 3 others, after some trials, we fine-tune the elementary reward coefficients α at 0.995 and β at 0.005. The learning rate α_k is set at $\frac{1}{1+Number_{NodeVisits}}$, with $Number_{NodeVisits}$ the times the cell corresponding to that particular $(state, action)$ couple has been visited and updated during the training. Our agents have as an objective to maximize their respective rewards by improving the QoE of the users, to manage their batteries, and to avoid service overlapping of the clusters. The results show that the agents do improve the QoE, and satisfy the service overlapping conditions, all while managing their battery.

---

[1] With one time-slot (5 min) we can reach any destination, but with different consumption of battery levels depending on the travelled distance.

Table 3. Percentage of cover versus charge

UAV	Time-slots covering	Time-slots charging
1	27%	33%
2	30%	35%
3	28%	35%
4	28%	36%

Each UAV's path is represented in a different plot in Fig. 4(a), (b), (c) and (d) where we can observe that the UAVs move between the clusters and the CSs and also that a UAV stays at a certain cluster for several time-slots to cover.

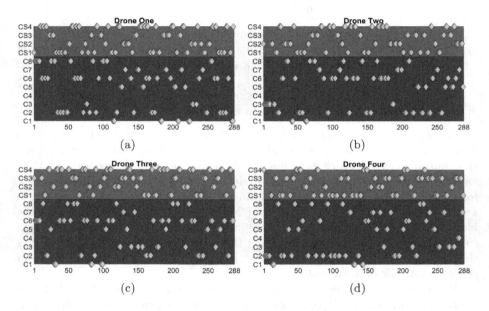

Fig. 4. Positions of the 4 UAVs over time

The percentage of time-slots spent covering and charging with respect to the total time-slots for each UAV are presented in Table 3. Knowing that the energy consumed while covering for 1 time-slot is 1 battery level, the same as the energy gained when charging for 1 time-slot, it is expected that the percentage of time-slots charging is a bit greater than the percentage of time-slots covering, as the energy obtained while charging is spent while moving and covering. If we had used a larger battery level representation, in rounded up percentage for example, and applied the same energy model as used to calculate the reward, the energy gained during 1 time-slot charging would allow to cover for 9 time-slots, but this means multiplying the Q-matrix size by 10.

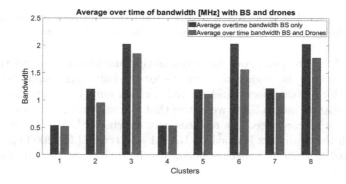

Fig. 5. Average improvements of bandwidths

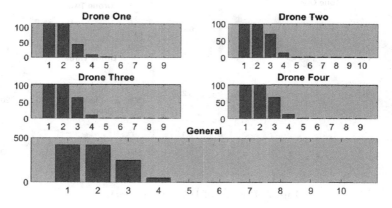

Fig. 6. Battery levels

Concretely the improvement of the bandwidth (MHz) is shown in Fig. 5 which shows the average data rate request (Mbps) divided by the spectral efficiency (bps/Hz) for all the clusters with and without the use of the UAVs. The vertical axis represents the average bandwidth and the horizontal axis represents the different clusters. The blue bars represent the value of the bandwidth without the use of the UAVs, the orange bars represent the bandwidth with the use of the UAVs. Overall, the allocated bandwidth is improved for all the clusters, more specifically the clusters with the highest original bandwidth request witness a consequent improvement. Cluster 4 in particular, which is the closest to the BS and has the highest $\mathcal{SE}$ has no improvements with the UAVs.

The management of the battery can be evaluated by observing Fig. 6 which represents the number of times a battery level was reached. Normally the battery should be used almost fully before being recharged fully, and all the levels should be reached an almost equal number of times. In the case the agent learns to optimize the charging/covering actions, it may manage the battery differently, this adaptation makes the battery levels unequally distributed. In our case, the most frequent levels are 1, 2 and 3, this could be improved by increasing the reward coefficient β for the action *charge* or by assigning a higher reward for full charging.

The total reward per epoch increases during the learning for all the UAVs. Figure 7 represents the reward over epochs for the four UAVs separately. UAV 1 was trained for 30,000 epochs and started with an empty Q-matrix, the reward starts at -16 and reaches 5000, we notice that it is still increasing and requires a longer training to converge. The rewards over epochs for UAVs 2,3 and 4, which started with the Q-matrix learned by UAV 1 and trained for 2000 epochs, their initial reward is 2000 and reaches 6000, also here the reward is increasing but not converging yet.

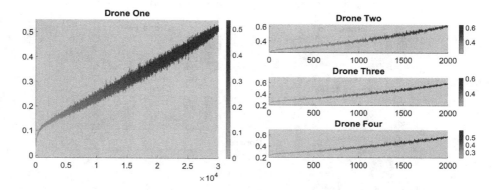

Fig. 7. Reward of UAVs over epochs

5   Conclusion and Future Work

We have presented an energy and quality aware flight planning strategy based on a Q-learning approach. The proposed solution is able to tackle a scenario where multi-UAVs are deployed. Moreover, we explicitly take into account the limited UAV battery. More in detail, we have defined separate states, actions and rewards for each UAV. In addition, we have imposed the service overlapping avoidance by setting a priority order. This has reduced the size of both the states and the actions domains, thus leading to satisfying results. Several training steps with different parameters were performed before reaching these results. However, we point out that there is always room for improvement, by e.g., increasing the number of epochs, fine-tuning the reward function parameters, or through a different state representation with a larger domain for the battery level.

Acknowledgement. This work has received funding from the University of Rome Tor Vergata BRIGHT project (Mission Sustainability Call).

References

1. Sackl, A., Casas, P., Schatz, R., Janowski, L., Irmer, R.: Quantifying the impact of network bandwidth fluctuations and outages on web QoE. In: Seventh International Workshop on Quality of Multimedia Experience (QoMEX), Pylos-Nestoras, pp. 1–6 (2015)
2. Lyu, J., Zeng, Y., Zhang, R.: UAV-aided offloading for cellular hotspot. IEEE Trans. Wireless Commun. 17(6), 3988–4001 (2018)
3. Zeng, Y., Lyu, J., Zhang, R.: Cellular-connected UAV: potential, challenges and promising technologies. IEEE Wireless Commun. 26(1), 120–127 (2019)
4. Mozaffari, M., Saad, W., Bennis, M., Nam, Y.-H., Debbah, M.: A tutorial on UAVs for wireless networks: applications, challenges, and open problems. IEEE Commun. Surv. Tutorials (2019, in press)
5. Zeng, Y., Zhang, R., Lim, T.J.: Wireless communications with unmanned aerial vehicles: opportunities and challenges. IEEE Commun. Mag. 54(5), 36–42 (2016)
6. Zhang, Q., Mozaffari, M., Saad, W., Bennis, M., Debbah, M.: Machine learning for predictive on-demand deployment of UAVs for wireless communications. In: IEEE Global Communications Conference (GLOBECOM), Abu Dhabi, United Arab Emirates, pp. 1–6 (2018)
7. Colonnese, S., Carlesimo, A., Brigato, L., Cuomo, F.: QoE-aware UAV flight path design for mobile video streaming in HetNet. In: 2018 IEEE 10th Sensor Array and Multichannel Signal Processing Workshop (SAM) (2018)
8. Watkins, C.: Learning from delayed rewards. Ph.D. thesis, May 1989
9. Trotta, A., Di Felice, M., Montori, F., Chowdhury, K.R., Bononi, L.: Joint coverage, connectivity, and charging strategies for distributed UAV networks. IEEE Trans. Rob. 34(4), 883–900 (2018)
10. Song, B.D., Kim, J., Kim, J., Park, H., Morrison, J.R., Shim, D.H.: Persistent UAV service: an improved scheduling formulation and prototypes of system components. J. Intell. Robot. Syst. 74(1), 221–232 (2014)
11. Scherer, J., Rinner, B.: Persistent multiUAV surveillance with energy and communication constraints. In: Proceedings IEEE International Conference on Automation Science and Engineering, Fort Worth, TX, USA, pp. 1225–1230 (2016)
12. Afshang, M., Dhillon, H.S.: Poisson cluster process based analysis of HetNets with correlated user and base station locations. IEEE Trans. Wireless Commun. 17(4), 2417–2431 (2018)
13. Colonnese, S., Cuomo, F., Chiaraviglio, L., Salvatore, V., Melodia, T., Rubin, I.: Clever: a cooperative and cross-layer approach to video streaming in HetNets. IEEE Trans. Mob. Comput. 17(7), 1497–1510 (2018)
14. Chiaraviglio, L., Amorosi, L., Malandrino, F., Chiasserini, C.F., Dell'Olmo, P., Casetti, C.: Optimal throughput management in UAV-based networks during disasters. In: 1st Mission-Oriented Wireless Sensor, UAV and Robot Networking Workshop (INFOCOM 2019 WKSHPS - MiSARN 2019), April 2019

Author Index

Printed in the United States
By Bookmasters

Printed in the United States
By Bookmasters